Literature, Religion, and Postsecular Studies
LORI BRANCH, SERIES EDITOR

FEMALE PIETY
and the Invention of
AMERICAN PURITANISM

BRYCE TRAISTER

THE OHIO STATE UNIVERSITY PRESS | COLUMBUS

Copyright © 2016 by The Ohio State University.
All rights reserved.

Library of Congress Cataloging-in-Publication

Traister, Bryce, author.
Female piety and the invention of American Puritanism/Bryce Traister.
pages cm.—(Literature, religion, and postsecular studies)
Includes bibliographical references and index.
ISBN 978-0-8142-1298-1 (cloth : alk. paper)
1. Puritans—New England—17th century.
2. Puritans—Religious life—New England.
3. Puritan women—New England—17th century.
4. New England—History—17th century.
5. New England—Religious life and customs.
6. Hutchinson, Anne, 1591–1643.
7. Rowlandson, Mary White, approximately 1635–1711.
I. Title.
II. Series: Literature, religion, and postsecular studies.
BX9354.3.T73 2015
285'.90974—dc23
2015031772

Cover design by Mary Ann Smith
Text design by click! Publishing Services
Type set in Goudy
Printed by Thomson-Shore Inc.

Cover image: Scanned reproduction of a wood engraving from *Scribner's Popular History of the United States* (New York: Scribner's, 1897), 555.

CONTENTS

Acknowledgments   vii

INTRODUCTION
The Invention of American Puritanism
1

CHAPTER 1
The Woman Who Gave Birth to America
29

CHAPTER 2
The Quakers' New England Bodies
69

CHAPTER 3
Mary Rowlandson and the Invention of the Secular
115

CHAPTER 4
Salem Witchcraft's Defense of Faith
166

AFTERWORD
Remembering American Puritanism
203

Bibliography   209
Index   223

ACKNOWLEDGMENTS

Jenny Franchot did not live even to see this book begin, but her intellectual spirit is the driving force behind it. Thanks, Jenny.

There was a time not too long ago when it looked like this book would never be more than an infrequently accessed folder on a desktop. It was at all times, during those difficult years, a frequently accessed source of self-pity. So I would like to thank the friends of Bill W. for seven years of teaching me about humility, accountability, and the importance of helping others. The late Tim Liddiard extended a hand when I really needed it.

The Social Sciences and Humanities Council of Canada provided generous funding that enabled me to undertake research at the Boston Public Library, the Huntington Library, the Friends House Library, London, and the British Library. The Centre for American Studies at the University of Western Ontario also provided generous support that enabled me to attend conferences, and to spend intellectually and spiritually stimulating time, again at the Friends House Library in London, in the late winter of 2010, and then again at the British Library in March of 2014. Thanks especially to Christine Wall and Donald Abelson at the Centre.

Sarah Rivett and Stephanie Kirk invited me to attend the conference "Religious Transformations in the Early Americas" at Washington University in Saint Louis in the spring of 2009, where I delivered some material from this manuscript. I would like to thank them and all of the attendees of that event for their encouragement, which gave me some much needed confidence to finish a first draft of this. At that conference and at others, Jonathan Beecher Field, Lisa Gordis, and Laura Stevens have been particularly valued friends to me and this work. Elizabeth Dillon, Sandra Gustafson, David Shields, Dana Nelson, Meredith Neuman, and Ivy Schweitzer have also patiently listened to me over the years as I puzzled through these ideas.

At The Ohio State University Press, Nan Goodman was a self-revealed and rigorously generous reader of this manuscript. Lori Branch, the series imprint editor, read this project at a crucial moment in its production. Lindsay Martin of OSUP came into the process and saw it through to production. Tara Cyphers and Kristen Ebert provided exquisite copyediting and production; it has been a real pleasure working with such an engaged and professional community at Ohio State.

Closer to my academic home at Western University, Tom Carmichael, Lily Cho, Manina Jones, Thy Phu, Marty Kreiswirth, Kinny Kreiswirth, Stephen Adams, Patrick Deane, the late Paul Gaudet, Russell Poole, Christie Milliken, Mike Zryd, Matthew Rowlinson, Christine Roulston, Emma Donoghue, Sasha Torres, and, especially, Brian Wall have all provided encouragement and sustenance of one form or another over the years. Jan Plug, Kathleen Okruhlik, Donna Pennee, Michael Milde, and Janice Deakin have as administrators each supported me in all kinds of ways. Tim DeJong and Taylor Kraayenbrink each provided terrific research assistance; I am lucky to work in an English department populated by so many stellar students. Beth McIntosh, Vivian Foglton, Teresa MacDonald, Leanne Trask, and, especially, Anne McFarland have been wonderfully supportive staff in the English and Writing Studies Department at Western University, a community I had the great privilege of serving as chair during the later years of this book's production.

I was lucky to learn from some extremely gifted teachers and thinkers while a student at Berkeley, in particular Dori Hale, Donald McQuade, Sam Otter, Nancy Ruttenburg, and Mitch Breitwieser, each of whom taught me how to be an Americanist. Cathy Gallagher, Ann Banfield, the late Julian Boyd, and, again, Jenny Franchot were all responsible for teaching me how to think independently. They are not responsible for any of the errors contained herein.

A portion of this book appeared in the 2007 issue of *Early American Literature*. Thanks to the journal for permission to reprint it here, and to David Shields for his editorial support at the time.

I would like to thank two extraordinary nonacademic people whose friendship I am honored to claim: Dawn McGoey and Jon McGoey. In addition to years of friendship to me and my family, Dawn and Jon gave me a miraculous gift—a week of uninterrupted peace and beauty at their family cottage in Ontario's Muskoka country, at which I completed the first draft of the manuscript. Then there's the McGoey basement, site and probable cause of all those terrible third-period Leafs meltdowns, a place where "yep!" often means "nope!" and yet a bad hockey game is still a good time.

I am blessed with a mother, Martyn Belmont, who knew when to stop asking when this book would be finished, but who has always been a bedrock source of support and encouragement for me. My daughter, Hannah Conway, and son, Matthew Traister, remind without telling me, and on an almost daily basis, what really matters (video games, really bad television, and much laughter: "such as, and . . .").

And: Alison Conway—this one is for you. Now and always, my love.

INTRODUCTION

The Invention of American Puritanism

THIS BOOK ARGUES that over the course of the seventeenth-century colonial settlement period in New England, extraordinary religious women, as well as a piety extraordinarily feminized, came to anchor New England Puritan culture. This "female piety" came to occupy a dual and paradoxical position within the modernizing culture of Puritan New England. On the one hand, it served as a primary location of vital religious experience and a point around which the institutions of Puritanism contentiously gathered. On the other, feminine piety advanced a fundamentally anti-institutional position that resisted any easy inscription into ecclesiastical authority and the nonreligious institutions in which it found expression. The seventeenth-century New England–based Protestantism considered in the following pages helped produce an incipient secular liberalism by means of religious and feminine elocutionary power, even as this modernizing regime came to place female piety, if not religion more broadly, on the privatized margins of its emergent public sphere.[1] For it was never atheism haunting New England's house; rather, a persistent spiritual extremism, voiced largely albeit not exclusively by women, served as both foundation of and threat to Puritanism's elaboration as the defining political

---

1. Elizabeth Dillon, *The Gender of Freedom: Fictions of Liberalism and the Literary Public Sphere* (Stanford, CA: Stanford University Press, 2004), argues that female privacy serves as the "backbone" of public sphere liberalism (11–49).

and cultural force of seventeenth-century settlement in what is now the northeast United States. If radical female spirituality contributed to the cultural and historical construction of American Puritanism, then our re-engagement with that past will help us better conceptualize the continued role of religious experience and the responses it generates in the contemporary political and cultural life of the United States.

Today the term "American Puritanism" recalls the nation's impossible past. It may still be the story we teach in schools, but it is no longer one we accept categorically. The erosion of the "Puritan origins story" that has taken place in the last generation or so of American studies is part of a broader critique and destabilization of narratives of national identity formerly derived from the Puritan historiographical imaginary. American studies today is a scholarship of restless reorientation that begins as a gesture of disavowal. This isn't to say that we deny the historical existence of Puritans in New England, or their belief in an omnipotent God, or their ideas about religious destiny, and so forth. Rather, we currently deny that story a place of primacy in how we read the contemporary nation's past, to say nothing of how we consider that past in relation to the present day. In the last several versions of "New American Studies" polemic and position-taking, American Puritanism has been little more than a footnote or a lonely essay.[2] It is worth saying at the outset that the hostility to the Puritans-origins myth is in no small part driven by a broader and more fundamental scholarly commitment to secularism as the preferred alternative to the religious ordering of things gathered under the sign of "American Puritanism."[3]

---

2. For an example of the broad critique of "Puritan Studies," see Carolyn Porter, "What We Know We Don't Know: Remapping American Studies," *American Literary History* 6, no. 3 (1994): 467–526. Porter observes: "Americanists have been discovering that you cannot simply accept multiculturalism (grudgingly or enthusiastically), adding a few representative texts to your survey course and proceeding as before with the old stories about the Puritans, the romance, the frontier, or what have you" (469). That said, twenty years later, scholars still feel an urgent need to get out from under Puritanism, as for example Donald Pease's suggestion that early practitioners of American studies "selected the Puritans' Exodus as the origin story for the tradition of American exceptionalism" that would become "the theological matrix of . . . the cold war state" and, eventually, the contemporary "security state." See Pease, *The New American Exceptionalism* (Minneapolis: University of Minnesota Press, 2009), 76, 79. None of the major collections of broad-stroke "New American Studies" essay anthologies contain much scholarship on the colonial Puritan period, and all of them position themselves in direct opposition to "Puritan origins" scholarship, e.g., *Cultures of United States Imperialism*, ed. Amy Kaplan and Donald Pease (Durham, NC: Duke University Press, 1993); and *American Studies: An Anthology*, ed. Janice Radway and Kevin Gaines (Oxford: Blackwell, 2009).

3. Jenny Franchot, "Invisible Domain: Religion and American Literary Study," *American Literature* 67, no. 4 (1995): 833–42.

For some we have too much American Puritanism, and for others not nearly enough. One reason we have trouble today making sense of our contemporary relation to American Puritanism is to be found in the complicated historiography that has grown up around the episodes this book studies. Beyond the enclosures of academic discussion of such matters, "American Puritanism" presents a confused and confusing object for contemporary reflection and debate. In popular parlance, "Puritanism" can refer to anachronistic prudery, the moral viewpoint of simpletons, and an antimodern disposition toward all things contemporary or even enjoyable.[4] It has become code for the contemporary "witch-hunt," for the idea of authoritarian institutions interfering with individual autonomy, and for conflicts over sexuality and sexual politics in the modern age.[5] Where it isn't denying pleasurable pursuits and individual self-expression, the term has provided politicians of all stripes with a reliable grammar of national purpose, future greatness, and hope. The contested life of American Puritanism that this book considers could be said to reappear in the contemporary languages of religious victimization *and* belligerence voiced both by those claiming to be "discriminated" against on account of their creedal affiliations, and by those claiming the same treatment because they don't have them, or somehow offend those who do. American Puritanism, to put it another way, has issued a double-tongued martyrology that permits all Americans, ironically enough, to participate in a culture of victimization that was almost serially performed in seventeenth-century Puritan New England.[6] Somehow, "American Puritanism" manages, Whitman-like, to "contain multitudes" and, in doing so, purports to force contradiction into coherence, diversity into singularity, and polyvocality into

---

4. The famous modern-day critique, of course, belongs to H. L. Mencken, who defined Puritanism as "the haunting fear that someone, somewhere, may be happy." He also defined it as "the huggermugger morality of timorous, whining, unintelligent and unimaginative men—envy turned into law, cowardice sanctified, stupidity made noble, Puritanism." Mencken, *A Book of Prefaces* (New York: Knopf, 1917), 22.

5. See, for example, Matthew Hutson, "Still Puritan After All These Years," *New York Times*, August 3, 2012; John Rosenberg, "Political Correctness Is the New Puritanism," *Minding the Campus*, August 15, 2010; and Paul Harris, "Passion vs. Puritanism as America Is Gripped by a War Over Sexuality," *Guardian/Observer*, March 20, 2012.

6. One obvious contemporary location of this phenomenon is in the debate over same-sex marriage taking place in the United States in the first few decades of the twenty-first century. The "anti-gay-marriage" argument has appeared in a broadly ecumenical language of "belief" being violated by those arguing in favor of the state recognizing same-sex marital relationships. Conversely, many supporters of the movement have claimed they are being discriminated against by these very religious perspectives.

univocality. Stated this way, one might go so far as to say that American Puritanism is just another word for "American liberalism."[7]

Although derived from religious structures of feeling and history, these languages of national purpose and renewal have enjoyed a remarkably pervasive and persuasive afterlife in the secular.[8] Indeed, it is one of this book's central contentions that the term "American Puritanism" is itself an invention of the secular, by which I mean that it really only makes sense to view the nation's religious origins story from a distance fundamentally enabled by the belief in religion's disappearance from contemporary regimes of knowledge. The career of American Puritanism, if we can put it that way, has therefore developed within the context of what we now call the "secularization thesis" of Western modernity, a set of arguments which has, until quite recently, maintained the view that sometime around or about the early eighteenth century, and for a lot of reasons, religion just gave out.[9] We shall turn in a moment to secularization and its current state of discontent, but for now suffice to propose that the "American Puritanism" we use both to identify and to dismiss the religious origins story of U.S. national identity has to some extent been symptomatic of an *intact* secularization thesis. Indeed, arguably the three most influential readings of American Puritanism—Perry Miller's "declension" thesis of the later seventeenth century, Sacvan Bercovitch's "Puritan Origins" argument, and Ann Douglas's *The Feminization of American Culture*—all assume the totality of robust religion's decline and collapse as the very condition for even thinking about the history, concepts, and culture contained within and by the term "American Puritanism."[10] This book suggests that the way in which our scholarship has framed and organized the cultural field of American Puritanism is itself a symptom of secular thinking, and that by repositioning one of the prominent archives of that field—here under-

---

7. This is the fundamental argument of Sacvan Bercovitch's seminal *The Puritan Origins of the American Self* (1975; repr., New Haven, CT: Yale University Press, 2011).

8. The important sociological reading here remains Robert Bellah, *The Broken Covenant: American Civil Religion in Time of Trial*, 2nd ed. (1975; repr., Chicago: University of Chicago Press, 1992).

9. This view represents a composite of the now classical sociological perspectives of Emile Durkheim, Max Weber, and Karl Marx.

10. Perry Miller, *Errand into the Wilderness* (1956; repr., Cambridge, MA: Harvard University Press, 1978); Sacvan Bercovitch, *Puritan Origins*; and Ann Douglas, *The Feminization of American Culture* (New York: Knopf, 1977). Bercovitch's follow-up, *The American Jeremiad* (Madison: University of Wisconsin Press, 1978), extends his consensus argument into the domain of nineteenth-century literary rhetoric.

stood as the archive of female piety—we can bring the scholarly conversation about American Puritanism into dialogue with broader questions of gender, secularism, and modernity in the contemporary academy.

Recent interventions into the secularization thesis of classical sociology have resulted in a new consensus: that secularization never happened. At least it did not happen as the thoroughgoing metaphysical and epistemological totality it has long been held to be. Talal Asad, to cite one important voice in the turn away from radical secularity, invites us to rethink this broader historical secularization narrative by "understanding how the sacred . . . can become the object not only of religious thought but of secular practice too" (37). Charles Taylor proposes and at great length criticizes a concept of secularity being the result of "a move from a society where belief in God is unchallenged and indeed, unproblematic, to one in which it is understood to be one option among others, and frequently not the easiest to embrace" (3). In succinctly elegant language, Judith Butler notes that "secularization may be a fugitive way for religion to survive" (72). Taylor, Asad, and Butler—and by this point a legion of scholars writing in the last decade across the range of humanities and social science approaches to religion—have advanced arguments that successfully challenge the established order of secularism.[11] Thanks in part to these interventions into the secularization thesis of the modern West, we are in a position to consider religion's continuing "presence" in avowedly secular orders of globalization—including the political, the economic, the linguistic, and the broadly cultural. And we are also now in a position to challenge the view that religion was, at some point in our past, the totalizing condition that it needed to have been in order to front the old secularization narrative

---

11. In some ways, a good deal of the early-twenty-first-century discussion of secularism began with Carl Schmitt's now well-known statement "all significant concepts of the modern theory of the state are secularized theological concepts." See Schmitt, *Political Theology: Four Chapters on the Concept of Sovereignty*, trans. G. Schwab (Chicago: University of Chicago Press, 2005). The sociological, historical, and literary studies critique of secularization is extensive, and most agree, although for different reasons and to very different effect, that secularization was neither as complete nor as concerted an effort as previously held. There are by now countless other such examples. Gauri Viswanathan usefully criticizes the declension thesis of the European secularization narrative that divides a religious then from a secular now, arguing instead that secularization promoted some forms of "authentic" religion at the expense of others. See Viswanathan, "Secularism and Heterodoxy," in *Comparative Secularisms in a Global Age*, ed. Linell Cady and Elizabeth Hurd (London: Palgrave, 2010), 229–30. For direct engagement with Taylor in particular and with the "new secular studies" more broadly, consult the essays collected in *Varieties of Secularism in a Secular Age*, ed. Michael Warner, Jonathan VanAntwerpen, and Craig Calhoun (Cambridge, MA: Harvard University Press, 2010).

in the first place. As Graham Ward puts it: "In the traditional worldview the *saeculum* had no autonomous existence. In a liturgical cosmos no one and nothing remains separate from divine providence."[12] Lucien Febvre similarly suggests that prior to Western secularism, "Christianity was the very air one breathed ... the atmosphere in which a man lived out his entire life—not just his intellectual life, but his private life in a multitude of activities, his public life in a variety of occupations."[13] If we no longer believe that secularization was the totalizing self-emancipation of modernity from religion, then we also no longer need to believe that religion was a maximum security prison-house of the past preventing our escape into the enlightenment and the pleasures of modernity.

This book reinterprets American Puritanism from the perspective provided by this newly complicated understanding of secularism, and considers the role of female piety in seventeenth-century New England as an important element in the revision to the broader secularization story. In American studies, the critique of the Puritans-origins myth has depended on the "old" secularization thesis as its enabling premise. Curiously, the reigning view of "American Puritanism" in the last thirty or so years of American studies has aligned with the modernist view of religion either being no longer important, or being overemphasized at the expense of other more important considerations. In any case, contemporary Americanist and modernist can say together: neither Puritans nor Religion have a hold on *us*. We are no longer the Puritans whose cultural and historical presence we regard as belonging to some other time, to some other knowledge regime, or to some other cultural zeitgeist. "For secular culture," as Franchot observes, religion has become "the Other, the loss by which, ironically, we have come to know ourselves: we are not belief. We are that which we have lost. Belief's transformation into pastness is, in fundamental respects, the narrative of Western culture's birth into the modern."[14] Intellectual, literary, and cultural history, to say nothing of popular parlance, all use the term "Puritanism" to capture this historical and ideological sense of America's "pastness" and Otherness. We might even say that Puritanism is America's Other, in all of its uncanny familiarity, a legacy

---

12. Graham Ward, *True Religion* (London: Blackwell, 2003), 21.
13. Lucien Febvre, *The Problem of Unbelief in the Sixteenth Century: The Religion of Rabelais*, trans. Beatrice Gottlieb (Cambridge, MA: Harvard University Press, 1985), 336.
14. Jenny Franchot, "Unseemly Commemoration: Religion, Fragment, and the Icon," *American Literary History* 9, no. 3 (1997): 503.

some Americans are as eager to claim as others are to reject. If we are no longer to cleave to a secularity understood in this way, then what possibilities emerge for a reconsideration of American Puritanism as something other than a suspicious historiographical convenience?[15]

One possibility will involve viewing seventeenth-century New England Puritan culture as actively contributing to, rather than desperately resisting, the production of a complex secular America. The persistence of religion in the United States, and more particularly Christianity, remains one of the nation's remarkable—even exceptional—features among fully industrialized nations, and the totalizing secularity thesis has never adequately explained this phenomenon. If colonial Protestant religion is truly part of the nation's past, then why does nearly every significant political and cultural debate in the United States today make reference to religion? In fact, contemporary political life in America reflects a fundamental division between choosing "religious" *or* "secular" answers to the nation's most pressing political issues, be it reproductive choice, prayer in schools, the exercise of public speech, or even the choosing of medical insurance. The radical "either/or" mentality of contemporary political and cultural conflict reproduces the "either/or" perspective of the old secularization argument. But we now have opportunity to rethink these questions as part of the broader revision to our thinking about secularism. The archive of seventeenth-century New England, when read in this way, very much supports the "postsecular" perspective of contemporary religious and cultural studies, which generally seeks to invalidate the old secularization narrative by talking about how religion persists within the secular, and how secular concepts find expression within formations of the sacred as well.[16] This more interactive and relational understanding of religious and secular formations in America's early colonial history will give us better purchase on how to engage and intervene in these debates as they continually emerge in contemporary U.S. cultural politics.[17]

---

15. For an excellent summary of specifically early American studies and its relation to renewed debates about religion and secular modernity, see Sarah Rivett, "Early American Religion in a Postsecular Age," *PMLA* 128, no. 4 (2013): 989–96.

16. "Postsecular" is a term used to indicate religious studies critique after the demise of the secularization thesis. For discussion of this term as it applies in particular to early American scholarship, see Michael Kaufmann, "Post-secular Puritans: Recent Retrials of Anne Hutchinson," *Early American Literature* 45, no. 1 (2010): 31–59.

17. Cf. Tracy Fessenden, *Culture and Redemption: Religion, the Secular, and American Literature* (Princeton, NJ: Princeton University Press, 2007): "Such a rethinking of the complex,

So what is that archive, and how can we revisit it? For scholars of early American colonial culture and history, this book's archive will be a familiar one: the Antinomian Controversy of the 1630s; the "Quaker Invasion" of the 1650s and early 1660s; Mary Rowlandson's *Sovereignty and Goodness of God* (1682); and the culture of Salem witchcraft at the end of the century. There are a number of connective threads that link these episodes together. First, all of them involve conflict between formations of religious orthodoxy and expressions of dissent. This is significant for us because the relation between authority and its critique, whether religiously construed or not, provides a basic syntax for virtually every influential "theory of American culture" ever written, including those by Perry Miller (the New England Mind and its decline); F. O. Mathiessen (Europe and America); Leslie Fiedler (culture and escape); Sacvan Bercovitch (consensus as dissensus); Ann Douglas (patriarchal religion and its feminization); Donald Pease (hegemonic America and its suppressed other); Amy Kaplan (American empire and its colonial subjects), and so on.[18] Although with varying degrees of emphasis, these seventeenth-century episodes of religious conflict have appeared and continue to appear in the critique and historiography of the United States. What is more, they have provided a historical basis for later generations of culture-makers, public historians, and soothsayers of all kinds to tell their own stories about the United States and its relation to colonial Puritan religious history.

Second, this study considers these episodes as constituting an important archive of American Puritanism because several generations of committed scholarship have found them to be so. Tautology or not, the American Puritanism this book excavates would simply have no historical content without due consideration of the conflicts, people, events, and arguments that gave rise to that composite in the first place. It is, notwithstanding this point, worth remarking that the manufacture of "American Puritanism" was not limited exclusively to these much-studied episodes. In the later years of the seventeenth century, for example, the funeral and scaffold sermons became an increasingly popular genre of religious

---

recombinatory, often volatile exchanges between religions and between religious and secular domains ha[s] in fact characterized our history . . . [and] point[s] also to the possibility of a newly energized and contestatory pluralism" (217).

18. This is, obviously, only a partial and selective list. For a still extremely valuable survey of these tendencies, see Russell Reising, *The Unusable Past: Theory and the Study of American Literature* (New York: Methuen, 1986).

expression. Anne Bradstreet attracted some notice with her poetry, while Edward Taylor, who quietly wrote rather a lot of it himself, did not; they are both partial contributors to the "American Puritanism" recalled in the term. Sermonic culture, both spoken and printed, was absolutely part of the circulation of religion and constitutive of everyday experiences in Puritan New England, as the scholarship of Sandra Gustafson, Lisa Gordis, and Meredith Neuman has found.[19] The Protestant tradition of spiritual autobiography, practiced by ministers and laypersons across the century, also found expression in the church discipline of New England Congregationalism, which required its prospective members to relate their conversion experience prior to attaining full membership and access to the Lord's Supper.[20] These and still other texts and events, including of course ongoing conflict with indigenous peoples and other European empires, are part of the fabric of "American Puritanism," albeit not parts with which this book is significantly concerned.[21]

Third, all of these episodes crucially involve, engage, and to varying degrees constitute at least a nascent idea of an early modern public in seventeenth-century New England. That sense of the "public," as the work of Elizabeth Dillon and Jonathan Beecher Field has in particular found, was utterly dependent on and found expression through religious belief: its expression, narration, evangelism, and even rejection. It would be difficult to overestimate the significance of this revision of the idea of the public,

---

19. Sandra Gustafson, *Eloquence Is Power: Oratory and Performance in Early America* (Chapel Hill: University of North Carolina Press for the Omohundro Institute of Early America, 2000); Lisa Gordis, *Opening Scripture: Bible Reading and Interpretive Authority in Puritan New England* (Chicago: University of Chicago Press, 2003); and Meredith Marie Neuman, *Jeremiah's Scribes: Creating Sermon Literature in Puritan New England* (Philadelphia: University of Pennsylvania Press, 2013).

20. For discussion of Puritan admission rituals, see Emory Elliott, *Power and the Pulpit in Puritan New England* (Princeton, NJ: Princeton University Press, 1975); and Charles Lloyd Cohen, *God's Caress: The Psychology of Puritan Religious Experience* (New York: Oxford University Press, 1986).

21. For recent treatments of the relationship between New England Puritanism and indigenous populations, see Laura Stevens, *The Poor Indians: British Missionaries, Native Americans, and Colonial Sensibility* (Philadelphia: University of Pennsylvania Press, 2004); and Matt Cohen, *The Networked Wilderness: Communicating in Early New England* (Minneapolis: University of Minnesota Press, 2009). On empire conflict, see Ralph Bauer, *The Cultural Geography of Colonial American Literatures: Empire, Travel, Modernity* (New York: Cambridge University Press, 2003); and Gordon Sayre, *"Les Sauvages Americains": Representations of Native Americans in French and English Colonial Literature* (Chapel Hill: University of North Carolina Press, 1997) and *The Indian Chief as Tragic Hero: Native Resistance and the Literatures of America, from Moctezuma to Tecumseh* (Chapel Hill: University of North Carolina Press, 2005).

for it crucially grounds and makes possible a critique of an American-located secularization thesis, which holds that the "public sphere" was entirely the result and the location of Enlightened secular agency.[22] This book's archive subtends a seventeenth-century story, a great deal of which took place visibly, publicly, and indeed, very noisily at times. Public trials, scaffold scenes, wilderness "removes," and jailhouse examinations constitute many of the scenes the following pages closely consider. We often tell the story of the Puritan mind in relation to solitude, introspection, and the quiet places of contemplative piety, but it just as importantly came into being in and as part of the public circulation of religious experience, strife, expression, and, often enough, silence. Privacy and publicity were mutually constitutive terms whose structural relationship was being worked out over the course of the seventeenth-to-eighteenth-century colonial experience, and this study analyzes the specifically religious contributions to that sociopolitical relationship.

The special relationship between a quiet, introspective Puritan piety, and its eruption into the world as speech, remonstrance, polemic, and disquietude brings us to a fourth and, for this book, the most important reason for studying these episodes together: they each, significantly, involve women and what this study calls "female piety." Radical religious women and feminine spiritual performances define and bring into visibility all of these well-known colonial events. Aspects of religious performance either performed by women or feminized in their performance have long been viewed as a problem for New England religious authority and for the historiography of seventeenth-century Puritanism more broadly. This book closely analyzes the interactive and gendered relation between religious performance and institutional authority as the fundamental content of the historical construct we call "American Puritanism": a discourse of American religious and cultural history from which concepts of an American national secular emerged.[23]

---

22. Jonathan Beecher Field, *Errands into the Metropolis: New England Dissidents in Revolutionary London* (Hanover, NH: University Press of New England, 2009). Both Dillon, *The Gender of Freedom*, and Field are responding to the work of Michael Warner, *The Letters of the Republic: Publication and the Public Sphere in Eighteenth-Century America* (Cambridge, MA: Harvard University Press, 1990).

23. For the foundational discussion of the female contribution to New England Puritanism, see Amanda Porterfield, *Female Piety in Puritan New England: The Emergence of Religious Humanism* (New York: Oxford University Press, 1992). My argument proposes that the "feminization" of piety was less a gradual, diachronic story of progress (or decline) into "humanism" than it was

Radical female piety and its reception by lay and clerical authority lodged gender relations within the text of American Puritanism. Secularist historiography in both the United States and Europe has similarly located both religion and its often unacknowledged feminine performances on the margins of narratives of modernity premised on the "disappearance" of religion, the emergence of Enlightenment philosophy, and the rise of democratic (and secular) revolutionary states in the eighteenth-century West. In the United States context, the "rise" and "decline" of seventeenth-century American Puritanism anchors a foundational story of the nation's emergence. This book argues that female piety was a crucial component of Puritanism's seventeenth-century success and failure. The performances of female piety we consider in the following pages thus gesture in two different directions. As radicalized, mystical, extemporaneous, and ascetic linguistic and bodily sets of religious activity, female piety recalled and performed older, even ancient, spiritual practices notable for their intense commitment to a deeply religious worldview. At the same time, indeed sometimes in the very same activity, seventeenth-century female piety articulated and helped to imagine categories of personhood, cultural politics (including feminism), psychological realism, and even natural rights discourse we characteristically associate with "modernity," "secularism," and "Enlightenment." By reading the feminine back into Puritanism, we will also be reading religion forward into secularism.

It is worth asking at the outset what was particularly "feminine" about the piety we consider in the following pages. To begin answering that question we shall briefly consider the spiritual portraits of what Jonathan Edwards called "Two Notable Converts" who appear toward the end of his "A Faithful Narrative of the Surprising Work of God" (1737), one of his most significant attempts to manage what has come to be known as the "Great Awakening." Edwards wrote the text to publicize and thereby prolong "a remarkable religious concern at a little village . . . extraordinarily carried on amongst us in the winter" of 1734. His other purpose was to defend the theological legitimacy of these and other converts from the "scoff and ridicule" of their many critics, who decried the visible pieties of Edwards's greatly awakened subjects as being little more than enthusiastic delusion. Not so, Edwards argues over the course of the "Faithful

---

a serial eruption of feminine spirituality whose first instance was more or less coterminous with the founding of Boston.

Narrative" and elsewhere in those years. Even before being stirred by God, these spiritual protagonists were as altogether sober, rational, and measured as any saint in the salvific history of New England. For Edwards, the spiritual lives of these women enable a language of rational and religious Enlightenment.[24]

Edwards's first notable convert, "an adult person" named Abigail Hutchinson (*FN* 191), images one of the more graphic visions of female spiritual experience and physical suffering to be found in the colonial New England archive. Under Edwards's narrative ministrations, Hutchinson's spiritual eminence becomes directly tied to her extreme physical suffering and eventual death. Over the course of this postmortem portrait of her "extraordinary discoveries of the glory of God and Christ" (*FN* 194), Edwards goes into nauseatingly detailed description of her suffering, vomiting, choking, and, finally, death, quite possibly by the starvation brought on by a tumor's closing of her esophagus: "having pined away with famine and thirst, so that her flesh seemed to be dried upon her bones" (*FN* 198). Physiology and theology sustain each other, as the tumor seated in her throat grows at the same rate as does the grace Christ has kindled in her soul. "She had a raging appetite for food, but yet when she saw that she could not swallow it, she seemed to be as perfectly content without it, as if she had no appetite to it" (*FN* 197). Abigail Hutchinson's attempts to articulate her spiritual experiences lead to more suffering and spiritual agony. Indeed, it is the tumor's choking off of speech that magnifies her spiritual achievement and compels her, in the end, to turn inward. Abigail's ravaged body indicates the wondrous vitality of her suffering piety, a formula that links bodily infirmity to pious intensity, feminine submission to spiritual power. She becomes, as had other women in the New England Protestant tradition before her, representationally extraordinary precisely through the credible testimony of her choked silence. Her wrecked body, moreover, becomes the exemplary text on which the minister imprints his own soteriological ambition. In doing so, Edwards claims and appropriates her spiritual ambition as that of eighteenth-century New England Protestantism as Edwards wants us to see it.

---

24. Jonathan Edwards, "A Faithful Narrative of the Surprising Work of God," in *The Great Awakening: The Works of Jonathan Edwards*, vol. 4, ed. C. C. Goen (New Haven, CT: Yale University Press, 1972), 191, 152, 159, 144, 191. Further references are cited parenthetically with the abbreviation *FN*.

Involuntary bodily fits and infirmity, along with "natural" contemplative inwardness, ecstatic trance and speech, and attitudes ranging from indifference to hostility toward ecclesiastical and liturgical authority together constitute a record of radical female piety in seventeenth- and eighteenth-century New England. Of course, this isn't to say that colonial men did not also commit themselves at times to such intense forms of spiritual seeking. But it is to suggest that the received history of New England Puritanism has been written without considering the extent to which these female performances of radical spirit make the best case, as they do here for Edwards, for spiritual credibility in a time of significant skepticism about religious matters. More broadly speaking, female piety both marked and transgressed the boundary between religious and postreligious regimes of knowing. To the extent the portrait of Abigail Hutchinson recalls an earlier seventeenth-century archive of feminine religious vitality, it simultaneously makes the case for religion as an important component of modern life.

Edwards's other representative convert, the precocious four-year-old Phebe Bartlet, is notable not least for her extreme youth. Brought into a discourse of salvation by overhearing her brother discussing his own spiritual struggles (FN 199), Phebe becomes an evangel by experience rather than by learning. As with others participating in the midcentury Connecticut River valley revivals, the spirit comes to her and, in so doing, signals both the fullness and the lack of her redemption; Edwards relates how "she once of her own accord spake of her unsuccessfulness, in that she could not find God," only to disclose how, a few moments later, "she suddenly ceased crying, and began to smile, and presently said, with a smiling countenance, 'Mother, the kingdom of heaven is come to me!'" (FN 200). It is the spiritual privacy of Phebe Bartlet that Edwards seeks to publicize as the true power of his revival:

> She was observed very constantly to retire several times in a day, as was concluded, for secret prayer; and grew more and more engaged in religion, and was more frequent in her closet; till at last she was wont to visit it five or six times in a day: and was so engaged in it, that nothing would at any time divert her from her stated closet exercises. (FN 199)

Although spiritual persuasion is secured by the suffering female body in the case of Abigail Hutchinson, in the portrait of Phebe Bartlet, Edwards highlights her moral innocence and withdrawal from the corrupting influences of the world. Bartlet could not be dissembling her religious fitness given her extreme youth, her utter lack of worldliness, and, to be sure, her gender. In a world now open to its investigation by the new scientific empiricism, Edwards's young woman chooses a gesture of self-cloistering so as to engage more fully in authentic religion. Bartlet's antiworldly asceticism was nothing if not the very image of female deportment enjoined in the advice manuals of the day. The vocabulary Edwards attaches to Bartlet's spiritual experiences is one that had in the Anglo-American world been appearing in both religious and nonreligious discussions of female conduct and self-governance for some time.[25]

While some of Edwards's most influential revival narratives stake their claim for religious authenticity on the experiences of women—including, perhaps most famously, the portrait he sketched of Sarah Pierpont, his future wife—what this book calls "female piety" was not a religious set of practices reserved for women alone. Readers of Edwards's own *Personal Narrative* will note the similarity between Bartlet's repeated self-removals and emotional ritualism with those the younger minister describes as crucial to his own redemptive history.[26] Indeed, the religious behaviors frequently described by New Light evangelical leaders like Edwards, the Methodist George Whitefield, and Presbyterian minister Gilbert Tennent were themselves described within discourses of the feminine. In his journal, published to coincide with his New England speaking tour, Whitefield describes a spiritual regime very similar to Phebe Bartlet's, including repeated secret prayer or "Retirement to his Glory," and an equally frequent spiritual emotionality, as his "Soul was frequently dissolved into Tears."[27] George Whitefield's preaching style was framed within a gendered discourse of spirit as well. To the extent that descriptors like emotionality, antiworldliness, and innocence characterized the discursive regime

---

25. For two such discussions of female conduct in eighteenth-century England, see Amanda Vickery, *The Gentleman's Daughter: Women's Lives in Georgian England* (New Haven, CT: Yale University Press, 1998); and Nancy Armstrong, *Desire and Domestic Fiction: A Political History of the Novel* (Oxford: Oxford University Press, 1987). For the American colonial context, see Laurel Thatcher Ulrich, *Good Wives: Image and Reality in the Lives of Women in Northern New England, 1659–1750* (1980; repr., New York: Knopf, 2010).

26. Jonathan Edwards, *The Works of Jonathan Edwards: Letters and Personal Writings* vol. 16 (New Haven, CT: Yale University Press, 1998), 790–804.

27. George Whitefield, *A Continuation of the Journal of the Reverend Mr. George Whitefield* (Philadelphia, 1740), 34–35.

of eighteenth-century New England's revival culture, we might observe provisionally that the piety of eighteenth-century revivalism was a feminine performance.[28] One such performance appeared as an extract in the *Gentleman's Magazine* published in a July 1741 edition of the *New York Weekly Journal*, which reported that

> many silly Women have gone out every Morning, and left their poor Children in Bed till their Return, which sometimes is till nine o'Clock in the Morning, without any Regard to the grand Inconveniences to which there are exposed by such Neglect, contrary to the Laws of Nature ... Their Doctrines, whatever they are, God knows, have this fatal Tendency, to make their Hearers distracted.[29]

Critics and supporters alike (including Whitefield himself) associated his excessive spiritual agency with female interlocutive interest, and so the "feminization" of George Whitefield might better be described as another publication of Phebe Bartlet.

Female piety thus served as the occasion for a "voice of reason" to speak. The rhetorical aggression of the *Gentleman's Magazine* extended to theological polemic as well, as for example Harvard minister Charles Chauncy's 1742 *Enthusiasm Described and Caution'd Against*. In that text, Chauncy recalls how, "when a lad," he was an "eye-witness to such violent agitations and foamings in a boisterous female speaker as I could not but behold in surprise and wonder." Witness to such "convulsions and distortions" and "quaking and trembling," Chauncy recalls the history of New England's seventeenth-century Quakers and assigns a diagnosis to the malady so remembered: all such enthusiasm reduces to "a bad temperament of blood and spirit; 'tis properly a disease, a sort of madness."[30]

---

28. For other approaches to issues of gender in eighteenth-century revivalism, see Sandra Gustafson, *Eloquence Is Power*, 14–74; Phyllis Mack, *Visionary Women: Ecstatic Prophecy in Seventeenth-Century England* (Berkeley: University of California Press, 1992), 24–44; and Susan Juster, *Disorderly Women: Sexual Politics and Evangelicalism in Revolutionary New England* (Ithaca, NY: Cornell University Press, 1994), 14–45.

29. *New York Weekly Journal*, no. 429, February 15, 1742. There is an extensive archive of anti-Whitefield and antirevival newspaper and journal reportage published in the 1740s. For a discussion of the publication history of the Great Awakening, see Frank Lambert, *Inventing the Great Awakening* (Princeton, NJ: Princeton University Press, 1999), 9–13.

30. Charles Chauncy, *Enthusiasm Described and Caution'd Against* (Boston: J. Draper, 1742), 4.

The spectacle of religion excites a diagnostic language of rational and retrospective assessment that translates extravagant female spirituality into medical condition, thereby recasting a performance of radical female piety as an outbreak of female illness. Chauncy's polemic doesn't merely question the legitimacy of Edwards's female converts. It rewrites their history from what one might call a modern, preclinical, and secularist perspective that abjects independent femininity and expressive piety. Framing radical piety within such a perspective is thus not simply a key feature of a new cultural rationalism. It is a gesture which, conceptually speaking, anchors that emerging secularism in the deep waters of spiritual history. In this sense, we might propose that both Edwards and Chauncy are doing the same thing: they are framing extraordinary female spirit into a picture of modern religious life. In their respective narratives of eighteenth-century revival and its discontent, both Edwards and Chauncy are furthering and containing a seventeenth-century narrative of radical and often embattled female piety as the story of America's Puritan past. This book shows how a history of seventeenth-century female spiritual experience in New England could produce both Edwards *and* Chauncy—that is to say, both extraordinary power and its skeptical containment—as that history's coda.

Female Piety and the Invention of American Puritanism proposes that, considered as an historical and ideological construct, "American Puritanism" attempts to contain and regulate the meaning of the nation's colonial religious past in much the same way that clerical and institutional authorities in seventeenth-century New England attempted to manage and direct the religious radicalism of their time.[31] "Our" modern perspective on American Puritanism is less the result of Puritanism's disappearance than it is a consequence of its creation as a complex sign of loss and repudiation. To view the matter through a slightly different lens, in the seventeenth century, institutional authority takes a view of radical female spirit that a discourse of the secular nation would come to take of its own religious past, a perspective that depended on taking religion as its object just as much as that view worked to marginalize it. Seventeenth-century Puritan religious disputes actively contributed to the emergence of a consensus

---

31. Gustafson makes a similar argument in relation to the eighteenth-century evangelism of Jonathan Edwards. See Gustafson, *Eloquence Is Power*, 61–74; for a discussion of gender and religious individualism, see Michael Kaufmann, *Institutional Individualism: Conversion, Exile, and Nostalgia in Puritan New England* (Hanover, NH: Wesleyan University Press, 1998), 1–37.

that backhandedly defined "American Puritanism" as part of the "secular" nation's past, even as the nominalizing gesture of "American Puritanism" identifies religion as a key feature of the nation's historiographical script. American Puritanism, as this book develops the term, is as much the product of American secularism as American secularism is the product of American Puritanism. This study makes visible the feminine content of that relationship, and argues that gendered economies of religious encounter profoundly inform the manufacture of American Puritanism. From the prophetic radicalism of Hutchinson and the Quakers, to the private spiritual economy of Rowlandson and the "distractions" of the Salem accusers, feminine piety repeatedly established a noncoincidence with social and clerical orthodoxy, and yet in that condition of inspired dissent provided opportunity for colonial orthodox and institutional authority to reassert itself. This complex and shifting relationship between feminine religious inspiration and its assiduous management by and through the assertions of clerical and civic intervention help explain the national fantasia of religion being viewed as both altogether significant and fundamentally irrelevant to contemporary cultural politics in the United States. The reception of female piety by cultural authority—more broadly, religious belief and its liberal critique—historically anticipates the emergence of an American culture still debating many of its most pressing political and social issues in reference to religion's place within avowedly secular cultural and political regimes. Puritan New England's internal debates, organized as they were around female piety and institutional arrangement, produced a cultural hermeneutic that continues to inform America's understanding of its past.

Americanist critique has often looked to figures like Anne Hutchinson, the early Quakers, Mary Rowlandson, and the victims of Salem as religiously instantiated precursors to "secular" ideas like independence, toleration, and even legitimate revolution. These are central, indeed privileged concepts within American secular thinking, and yet the premodern historical figures we credit for presciently advancing such notions were no less "Puritan" in their religious commitments than the hoary old Puritans we today popularly hold responsible for the suppression of these ideas, or for the persecution of those who pursued them. The religious beliefs and pietistic performances of these seventeenth-century seekers, mystics, and contemplatives—both women and men—crucially advanced colonial America's march into secularism and nationhood. Understanding American Puritanism as both historical narrative and historiographical construction will give us some purchase on the broader concept in play here: that American secularism is itself both narrative and construct, and that New England's Puritan culture in the seventeenth century crucially contributed to its consolidation.[32] In taking seriously the claim, here voiced by Colleen McDannell, that "the Puritan model is a historiographical construct, not a historical observation," this book proposes that radical female piety furthered even as it performatively delayed the advent of colonial secularism, and it did so by repeatedly, and often forcefully, articulating itself in ways that both invited and resisted colonial religious and civil authority's attempts to suppress, corral, translate, or simply ignore it.[33] Rather than propose that female piety in the seventeenth century becomes female "privacy" in the eighteenth—a claim that parallels the old secularization thesis—we are going to be exploring some of the ways in which ideas about religion, gender, and their interaction contributed to and so complicate that story today. While Anne Hutchinson's dissent proleptically contributed to the emergence of Puritan and eventually "American" orders of civil and church polity, her mystical self-reliance simultaneously undermined its fitness within the emerging regime of Enlightened modernity. Hutchinson's faith, to put it differently, was both ancient and modern, both backward glancing and prophetically ambitious, as was the self-cancelling "convincements" of the Quakers; the self-enclosing public biblicism of Mary Rowlandson; and the self-promoting confessional agency of the Salem accused and accuser. We shall over the course of this book be attending to some of the ways in which radical female piety persists within and as secular concepts of modern identity and personhood.

Female piety and its reception within the highly controlled discursive space of New England religious culture offer concepts of nation, politics,

---

32. In saying so, I do not wish to be misunderstood as advocating for colonial New England or the Puritanism we associate with it as being the only possible religious history of the nation. Recent work in comparative religious and cultural studies has opened new vistas for considering alternate histories of North American colonization, empire, and nation-building. See, for example, Joanna Brooks, "From Edwards to Baldwin: Heterodoxy, Discontinuity, and New Narratives of American Religious-Literary History," *American Literary History* 22, no. 2 (2010): 439–53; Sarah Rivett and Stephanie Kirk, "Religious Transformations in the Early Modern Americas," *Early American Literature* 45, no. 1 (2010): 61–91; Elizabeth Maddock Dillon, "Religion and Geo-politics in the New World," *Early American Literature* 45, no. 1 (2010): 193–202; and Jared Hickman, "Globalization and the Gods, or the Political Theology of 'Race,'" *Early American Literature* 45, no. 1 (2010): 145–82.

33. Colleen McDannell, *Material Christianity: Religion and Popular Culture in America* (New Haven, CT: Yale University Press, 1995), 6.

natural rights, and justice we today understand to be "secular" inventions. By returning to the religious culture of seventeenth-century New England, this book develops an account of religion's contribution rather than opposition to an American Enlightenment.[34] To be sure, however we view these concepts today—whether as religiously or postreligiously conceived—there is little doubt that American national mythology has consolidated the secularization thesis into a primary narrative of American national self-invention, particularly as told in the revolutionary and early-republican periods of United States historiography. In telling a different version of this story, *Female Piety and the Invention of American Puritanism* hopes to promote further discussion of how its primary subject matter both contributed to the consolidation of a specifically American and exceptionalist paradigm of the nation and destabilized the nationalist tendencies of those origins stories by sponsoring broader humanist discourses within a globalizing ethics of rights, sovereignty, and natural justice. These concepts are crucial to some of the most ambitious ethical projects of the modern West, and the emergence of postsecular critique makes it possible to reconceptualize the "origins story" of these ideas from within the historiography of radicalized Protestant religious culture. Religion's place within contemporary globalization has received extensive commentary in both academic and nonacademic discourse, in no small part fuelled by the perceived rise in fundamentalist and activist religious political activity and military insurgency around the world. Such discussion takes as a starting point the idea that religion persists within secularism, that it quite possibly enables aspects of secularist thought, and that "religion" becomes a vessel and marker for identity when other discursive categories of global

---

34. The following work has influenced my thinking about specifically U.S.-centered accounts of secularism and the enlightenment: Henry May, *The Enlightenment in America* (Oxford: Oxford University Press, 1976); Robert Wokler, "The Enlightenment, the Nation-State and the Primal Patricide of Modernity," in *The Enlightenment and Modernity*, ed. Norman Geras and Robert Wokler (Basingstoke: Macmillan, 2000), 161–83; J. G. A. Pocock, *The Machiavellian Moment: Florentine Political Thought and the Atlantic Republican Tradition* (Princeton, NJ: Princeton University Press, 1975), 333–48; Jay Fliegelman, *Prodigals and Pilgrims: The American Revolution against Patriarchal Authority, 1750–1800* (Cambridge: Cambridge University Press, 1982); Michael Warner, *Letters of the Republic*; and Gillian Brown, *The Consent of the Governed: The Lockean Legacy in Early American Culture* (Cambridge, MA: Harvard University Press, 2001). In a brilliant revision to Henry May's "American Enlightenment" thesis, Leigh Schmidt suggests that one sign of the modern Enlightenment is the "endeavor of establishing 'religion' as an abstracted object for historical and philosophical study." See Schmidt, *Hearing Things: Religion, Illusion, and the American Enlightenment* (Cambridge, MA: Harvard University Press, 2000), 84.

personhood attenuate or fail altogether.³⁵ Rather than merely returning to religion so as to recuperate American exceptionalism, we will consider how a broadened understanding of American religious history might help us see beyond the confines of the static nation. A close reading of the seventeenth-century New England archive will contribute not just to scholarly conversations within the broader field of American studies, but also to ongoing engagements with religion's persistence within secularism, and modern secularism's continuing indebtedness to religious history.³⁶

American Puritanism exists in complicated and paradoxical relation to reigning nationalist paradigms of the United States. Anne Hutchinson, for example, was banished and excommunicated *from* the very colony that would become first Puritan and then Revolutionary Massachusetts; the Puritanism whose misogynist intolerance we reject in modernity emerged around her dissenting performance. At the same time, "American Puritanism" continues to anchor a national myth of independence and freedom from religious and other kinds of enforced compliance.³⁷ This book considers more closely how both women and notions of femininity contributed to the production of a national religious myth whose coherence seems impervious to its own internal contradictions. The following pages consider intense feminine religiosity as both excessive and constitutive of social norms, as both a distortion of civil authority and the foundation of authority's political legitimacy. A deeply religious set of commitments expressed or enacted by Protestant women became the conceptual core of the "American Puritanism" we both identify and disavow today as *both* a story of profound and controlling American religiosity *and* an equally American story of religious tolerance and secularism.³⁸

---

35. See, for example, Pasquale Ferrara, "Globalization and Post-secularism: Religions and a Universal Common Identity," *Claritas: Journal of Dialogue and Culture* 1, no. 1 (2012): Article 7; and José Casanova, *Public Religions in the Modern World* (Chicago: University of Chicago Press, 1994).

36. For another approach to such questions, see Sarah Rivett, *The Science of the Soul in Colonial New England* (Chapel Hill: University of North Carolina Press for the Omohundro Institute of Early America, 2011).

37. For a recent historical treatment of New England Congregationalism as the origin of religious freedom, see Michael Winship, *Godly Republicanism: Puritans, Pilgrims, and a City on the Hill* (Cambridge, MA: Harvard University Press, 2012).

38. Tracy Fessenden has persuasively argued that "secular" American history, culture, and even jurisprudence depend on an unacknowledged Protestantism residing inside of these

This study employs a number of terms to enable its reading of this seventeenth-century archive, and there will be, inevitably, some slippage in their use. "Piety" indicates, broadly speaking, individual religious practice, including representational practices like confession, accusation, and autobiography. It also refers to the devotional life practices of lay individuals whose pursuit of spiritual experience gets reported as personally realized vernacular theology. Piety signals communal spirituality as well, be it the epistolary correspondence of the Quakers, the complex authorship of Mary Rowlandson's *Sovereignty and Goodness of God*, or the composite voice of Salem's so-called confessing witches and their accusers. Because this book is interested in how these two concepts of piety interact—how public or communal orders interact with inwardly realized experiences of spirit—I use the term frequently and, wherever possible, I attempt to indicate which kind of pietistic experience we are considering, be it a report of devotional practice, a theologically based remonstrance against state authority, a confessional report of spiritual perseverance, or a narrative of diabolism.

"Interiority" plays a crucial mediating role for thinking about these different kinds of pietistic practices and how the inner life of spirit manifests itself in the world. As part of this book's critical vocabulary, "interiority" indicates a variety of personally located cognitive and spiritual experiences and practices, as well as the ways in which those experiences achieve textual—that is, worldly or representational—status in relation to individual accounts about the inner life of religion. Spiritual interiority has long been a concern for religious studies scholars and theologians, particularly in relation to the analysis of mystical, contemplative, and ascetic traditions in Christianity.[39] It has, at times problematically, supplied a metaphor for anthropomorphic declarations of national or cultural identity,

---

domains. She notes that, for example, "Protestantism's emancipation from Catholicism both provides the blueprint for, and sets the limits of, secularism's emancipation from 'religion' itself... To consider the career of secularization in American culture," she goes on to say, "is therefore also necessarily to consider the consolidation of a Protestant ideology that has grown more entrenched and controlling even as its manifestations have become less visibly religious." See *Culture and Redemption*, 5.

39. On mysticism, particularly as it relates to women, see Caroline Walker Bynum, *Holy Feast and Holy Fast: The Religious Significance of Food to Medieval Women* (Berkeley: University of California Press, 1987); the most sustained discussion of mysticism and women in the American tradition is Ann Taves, *Fits, Trances, and Visions: Experiencing Religion and Explaining Experience from Wesley to James* (Princeton, NJ: Princeton University Press, 1999). On asceticism, see Geoffrey Harpham, *The Ascetic Imperative in Culture and Criticism* (Chicago: University of

as for example in Perry Miller's famous formulation of how, faced with the failure of the "errand into the wilderness," the Puritans of the late seventeenth century "found they had no other place to search but within themselves" for validation and understanding of their undertaking.[40] So when we consider Anne Hutchinson's claim to direct revelation, or the Quaker description of the "inner light," Mary Rowlandson's contemplative biblicism, or the reports of invisible affliction from Salem, we are making claims not merely about their sense but their worlds' sense of what spiritual experience really is and means, how that experience can be adequately reported, and the manner in which its claims to authenticity can be evaluated by the persons and institutions concerned with such things. The historical subjects of this study tell us about religion's aspect, contours, and shape; about its consolations and its insufficiencies; about its contributions, more broadly speaking, to gendered subjectivity and desire. Such appraisals constitute the prehistory of "reason" and the "modern individual" and are fundamental to the Enlightenment's attempted differentiation of itself from religion. Interiority thus marks a concept of an emergent modern individual whose inner life might be understood in the languages of both spiritual and psychological self-understanding and self-extension; interiority can refer to both premodern "religious melancholy" and modern states of "depression," for example. It marks the cognitive space of religious contemplation at the heart of mystical Christianity and devotional practice, as well as the faculty of sensory perception increasingly privileged in what Sarah Rivett has called the "science of the soul." As we move historically from the early modern to modern periods, the bourgeois concept of "privacy," and particularly female privacy, comes to indicate and even replace the idea of interiority. The idea of privacy itself came into being through what Jill Lepore calls "the secularization of mystery": the process by which humanity learned to solve what had formerly been the secrets of a sovereign God. These are all resonant terms for a study interested in exploring the religious roots of modern concepts of secular personhood and culture, and in the historical and philosophical connections between them.[41]

Chicago Press, 1987), whose analysis of "desire" as the object and product of ascetic discipline informs my understanding of interiority.
    40. Perry Miller, *Errand into the Wilderness*, 15.
    41. Jill Lepore, "The Prism: Annals of Surveillance," *New Yorker*, June 24, 2013. Academic discussion of privacy and reading in early America is extensive. Representative treatments

There were a number of theological variables that made the female religious experiences of these seventeenth-century women "radical," including mystical inwardness, spiritist piety, and resistant mediation. Where not typically being treated as potentially or plainly unorthodox, female piety was more aggressively seen to be either blasphemous or heretical threat to ecclesiastical and masculine authority. In the Protestant and more specifically Calvinist or radical reformation, we speak less of "heresy" than of "dissent" for the reason that "heresy" is a formal religious crime prosecuted by ecclesiastical juridical structures that the radical Reformation openly rejected. To be sure, Protestant ecclesiology was hardly more welcoming to female spiritual assertiveness than was the medieval church—far from it. Indeed, one could argue that the gendered cloistering of medieval monasticism was in some ways more welcoming to women than was the ecclesiastical emptiness of early modern reformed Protestantism, whose commitment to Presbyterian concepts of church governance and equality did not initially extend into the domain of female religious authorization. At least in the Catholic church, religious women had somewhere to go and specific orders in which to pursue spiritual fulfilment, whereas the undifferentiated spiritual space and liturgical restraint of the Reformation may well have contributed to misogynistic fears about female spiritual puissance. For some women and men in the seventeenth century, the primacy of "conscience" exploited the potential residing *within* Protestantism to authorize religious experiences that might exceed social and political expectations. The gendered exploitation of such Protestant possibility in New England is one of this book's primary considerations, as is the contribution of sexual difference and radical spirituality to secular discourses of rights, revolution, and liberty. The "radicalism" of the women and experiences considered in this book is complex and varied, to be sure, but the extraordinary relation of spiritual radicalism to its insufficient management by institutional and orthodox authority constitutes an important connective thread.[42]

---

include Warner, *Letters of the Republic*; and Cathy Davidson, *Revolution and the Word: The Rise of the Novel in America* (New York: Oxford University Press, 1986). For an acutely argued critique of Foucault influenced discussion of reading and interiority, see Gillian Brown, *Consent of the Governed*.

42. On women and mysticism in the Christian long view, see Grace Jantzen, *Power, Gender, and Christian Mysticism* (Cambridge: Cambridge University Press, 1995). Important historical treatments of gender issues in seventeenth-to-eighteenth-century Protestantism include Philip Greven, *The Protestant Temperament: Patterns of Child-Rearing, Religious Experience, and the Self in Early America* (New York: Knopf, 1977); Susan Juster, *Disorderly Women*;

This book, therefore, employs the term "female piety" to identify spiritual experiences and histories associated with both women and men over the course of the seventeenth century. By drawing out and developing a more detailed anatomy of seventeenth-century female piety in New England, I hope to build on the work of Amanda Porterfield, Ivy Schweitzer, Amy Lang, and Elizabeth Dillon among others, all of whom contend that different ideas about femininity and gender significantly contributed to discourses of salvation, dissent, and liberalism, which in turn contributed to our sense of "femininity" residing within American Puritanism. While much has been made, over the years, about how the Puritan "errand into the wilderness" prompted the erection of a "City on the Hill" in New England, the significant contributions of women and female piety to these projects—and not just as distraction or critique—have received less comment. Consider briefly the connection of the feminine to so central a concept as the "City on the Hill," a term famously theorized in Protestant and American protonational terms by John Winthrop. As Abram van Engen has argued, Catholic and Protestant polemicists alike claimed the term as belonging to Rome or the Reformation respectively. One of the scriptural truth-texts for Protestant apologia was Revelation 12, whose vision recounts the fleeing of the woman into the wilderness, for whom a place of safety is prepared while she and her people await the coming messiah. Against the Roman Catholic position that Rome, the "city on seven hills," was *the* City on the Hill described in Matthew 5:14, Protestant polemicists like Humphrey Lynde would claim early in the seventeenth century that the wilderness refuge of Revelation would become the visible location of the "invisible" remnant of God's elect. Even before radical Protestant

---

Louise Breen, *Transgressing the Bounds: Subversive Enterprises among the Puritan Elite in Massachusetts, 1630–1692* (New York: Oxford University Press, 2001); Catherine Berkus, *Strangers and Pilgrims: Female Preaching in America, 1740–1845* (Chapel Hill: University of North Carolina Press, 1998); and Jane Kamensky, *Governing the Tongue: The Politics of Speech in Early New England* (New York: Oxford University Press, 1997). Amy Shrager Lang takes the longer view in *Prophetic Woman: Anne Hutchinson and the Problem of Dissent in the Literature of New England* (Berkeley: University of California Press, 1987), a book that moves into the eighteenth- and nineteenth-century traditions. Laura Henigman also discusses the role of women in the later seventeenth and eighteenth centuries in *Coming into Communion: Pastoral Dialogues in Colonial New England* (Albany: State University of New York Press, 1999). Other important literary critical studies of the role of female gender over the course of the seventeenth century belong to Ivy Schweitzer, *The Work of Self-Representation: Lyric Poetry in Colonial New England* (Chapel Hill: University of North Carolina Press, 1991); and Amanda Porterfield, *Female Piety in Puritan New England*.

women found themselves asserting their faith from a marginal space or condition of enforced remove or formal exile, Protestant polemic claimed a feminized condition of embattlement and proleptic martyrdom as a fundamental condition for the emergence of spiritual truth and the erection of a visible "city upon the hill."[43] One of this book's broader claims is that female piety functioned as a kind of insufficiently suppressed voice within colonial Puritanism. This incomplete quieting of radical belief anticipates the political life of embattled victimhood in secular America as well.

"Female piety" designates a variety of female experiences in seventeenth-century New England and, in doing so, this book runs the risk of collapsing what are, in fact, quite different religious experiences into a singular conceptual category. Even a first-time reader of the Antinomian Crisis and the *Sovereignty and Goodness of God* would not confuse the outspoken critique of Anne Hutchinson with the exemplaristic ambitions of Mary Rowlandson. This study pays close attention to the "varieties of religious experience" found within this archive, even as it attempts to locate what Susan Juster has called "a distinctive female presence and voice within American Protestantism."[44] We can think of this presence as both historically connective and conceptually distinct, and where we used to assign what is essentially an exercise in "tolerance" to the secular ambitions of Enlightened modernity, we will by this book's end have a better sense of how "religious toleration" might also have taken up residence in the house of American Puritanism as well.

One obvious and "unfeminine" source of seventeenth-century Protestant radicalism can be found in the career of Roger Williams, whose adventures in New England have been well documented. He is often credited with "inventing" the idea of the separation of church and state, if not the broader concept of religious toleration that informs it. Arguably one of the most aggressive Protestant iconoclasts of the seventeenth century, he famously attacked the "hireling ministry" of Boston's early civil settlement as a presumptuous incursion into God's sovereignty, and a dangerous assertion of civil authority into matters exclusively spiritual. His

---

43. Sir Humphrey Lynde, *Via Devia, or The By-Way* (London: A. Matthews, 1630), 9. I am grateful to Van Engen for sharing his essay "Claiming the High Ground: Catholics, Protestants, and the City on the Hill," which is part of a forthcoming essay collection.

44. Susan Juster, "The Spirit and the Flesh: Gender, Language, and Sexuality in American Protestantism," in *New Directions in American Religious History*, ed. Harry S. Stout and D. G. Hart (New York: Oxford University Press, 1997), 335.

polemic clearly promoted an "antinomian" theology whose privileging of *sola scriptura* and denunciation of civil authority so annoyed the architects of New England Congregationalism that he was banished even before Anne Hutchinson. One way to think about this is to suggest that Williams was a great theorist of a practice of piety we have not yet considered to be feminine in its performance. This oversight, to call it that, is a bit curious, given that our modern regard of Protestant religion views it as being fundamentally and even wonderfully "private," and so by our secular perspective "naturally" or "essentially" associated with the feminine. In privileging Hutchinson and other prominent religious women in New England, this study does not want to minimize Williams's contribution to what has been called the "spiritist" strain in seventeenth-century New England. Rather, it proposes that we understand his contribution as being part of a religious tradition largely populated by women or by performances marked as feminine in their realization. Rather than place Roger Williams off to the theological sidelines (or worse, in Rhode Island), *Female Piety and the Invention of American Puritanism* identifies his renegade theology, and the English dissenting tradition of which he is a part, as one important starting point for understanding the gendered inscriptions of a radicalized Protestant piety that would eventually promote modern and secular discourses of privacy as feminine and secretive.

Although largely focused on women and their religious experiences, this study takes seriously the idea that gender is a category of identity that can and often does exist independent of sexual difference. We are interested here in what Sandra Gustafson in her analysis of eighteenth-century evangelical minister Jonathan Edwards has called "gender in performance," the idea that gender both establishes and disestablishes itself in and through religious experience. Thus Edwards might evoke "the affective power of . . . liminal feminine speech" in his conversion relation and claim the authenticity of grace as a feminine submission to divine will.[45] While a number of important studies of gender and American culture have argued that a "feminization" of piety, literature, or culture was a consequence of secularizing trends and post-Enlightenment political ideas, this book traces the productive contribution of the feminine to seventeenth-century notions of religious authenticity and power. We shall see in this analysis how the "female piety" of men like Roger Williams, Humphrey

---

45. Gustafson, *Eloquence Is Power*, 64.

Norton, George Fox, and Cotton Mather might be better understood as part of the gendered matrix of seventeenth-century religious culture in New England.

No doubt in response to the "feminization" of church attendance, scholars have found that the later-seventeenth- and early-eighteenth-century sermonic style tended to spend more time individuating the saint and the sinner than did an early funereal tradition that privileged doctrine. The individuation of faith was a key gesture not merely in the vernacular female piety of seventeenth-century Puritan New England, but in the representation of such piety within the secularizing eighteenth century as well. For example, the prevailing association of the funeral sermon with the female subject was remarkable precisely because it was a text grounded in the life experiences of a woman, and yet aimed at the general religious population. In the transformation of the female saint into sermonic text, the life of female piety becomes the text of the Protestant church's own historical narrativization and homiletic future.[46] Not only had colonial church attendance become increasingly female over the course of the seventeenth century, but to some extent the exegetical text of Puritan discipline had become female-identified as well. Just as women came increasingly to sit in the pews of the meeting-house, so did a spiritual femininity reside inside the exhortational address of late-seventeenth-century Congregationalism. By the end of the seventeenth century, female piety had become the marrow of Puritan divinity in New England, and would become in later years for both religious and nonreligious commentators in the United States, an important touch-point for situating the religious culture of New England within competing paradigms of national history and political narrative.

Neither radical female piety nor orthodox clerical authority—taken alone—could be said to be the one "true" American Puritanism captured in this seventeenth-century story of female piety and historiographical containment. Rather, they together produced this construct. This book

---

46. On the evolution of the New England Puritan funeral sermon, see Emory Elliott, "The Development of the Puritan Funeral Sermon and Elegy: 1660–1750," *Early American Literature* 15, no. 2 (1980): 151–64; and Sarah Rivett, "Tokenography: Narration and the Science of Dying in Puritan Deathbed Testimonies," *Early American Literature* 42, no. 3 (2007): 471–94. On the scaffold tradition, see Daniel Cohen, *Pillars of Salt, Monuments of Grace: New England Crime Literature and the Origins of American Popular Culture, 1674–1860* (New York: Oxford University Press, 1993); and, more recently, Jodi Schorb, "Hard-Hearted Women: Sentiment and the Scaffold," *Legacy: A Journal of American Women Writers* 28, no. 2 (2011): 290–311.

returns to these voices—to the assured independence of Hutchinson and the orthodox reply from Cotton; the angry zeal of the Quakers and the punitive response of Boston's authorities; the melancholy protest of Rowlandson and the exemplary demands of Increase Mather; and, finally, the embodied claims of the Salem afflicted and the anxious management of their clerical observers. In considering how these voices interacted, we shall see how they together invented the text that is American Puritanism. The many voices of this complicated text continue to be heard in some of the most preoccupying political, cultural, and social debates of the contemporary United States. Viewed as cultural history and as historical construct, this condition is the invention of American Puritanism.

ONE

The Woman Who Gave Birth *to* America

PERHAPS THE BEST-KNOWN BIRTH in colonial New England belongs to Anne Bradstreet. Her well-known and widely anthologized "The Author to her Book" apostrophizes her completed poetry as a recently born child: "Thou ill-formed offspring of my feeble brain, / Who after birth didst by my side remain."[1] Written after the London publication of the *Tenth Muse* in 1650, "The Author to Her Book" engages in a fairly routine form of female authorial self-deprecation—that of appearing indifferent to her poetic achievement—in order to assert the value of her work indirectly. She shows off her poetic skill—"I stretched thy joints to make thee even feet" is followed by a line whose iambic feet collapse into a series of spondees—and so folds the agency of poetic correction into the actions of child-rearing. The tension created and sustained over the course of the poem draws attention to gendered aspects of both poetic and parental activities. The poem's staged ambivalence about its literary merit, because tied to the language of childbirth and described in terms of unsuccessful parenting, implies a similar ambivalence about the speaker's relation to domestic labor, and to maternal agency as well. She has, after all, given birth to a monster, which she re-describes as an "afterbirth," and instinctively tries to hide from view, where "all may judge." By employing the

---

1. Anne Bradstreet, *The Works of Anne Bradstreet*, ed. Adrienne Rich (Cambridge, MA: Belknap Press of Harvard University Press, 1967), 221.

monstrous birth imagery in the 1650s, Bradstreet recalls Anne Hutchinson's and Mary Dyer's infamously recorded monstrous births of 1637 and 1638 and, with that recollection, registers some of the ideological work these parturitions had already performed (and would continue to perform) in early-seventeenth-century New England, and in the historiography of the Antinomian Controversy that was to come.[2]

In her depiction of the "kidnapping" of the poem by "friends, less wise than true," Bradstreet recalls the moment when Anne Hutchinson's private conversations with several Bay Colony ministers became public testimony against her during her November 1637 "Examination" before the General Court of the Massachusetts Bay Colony. "It is one thing," Hutchinson admonished Governor John Winthrop and the Court, "for me to come before a public magistracy and there to speak what they would have me speak, and another when a man comes to me in a way of friendship privately; there is a difference in that" (AC, "Civil," 319). At stake for both women is the violation of intimate life: for Bradstreet, the exposure "to public view" of her damaged, "halting," "rambling brat"; for Hutchinson, the betrayal of pastoral confidence. For Bradstreet, as for Hutchinson several decades earlier, the crime refers both to monstrous object and its exposure: "I cast thee by as one unfit for light, / Thy visage was so irksome in my sight," writes Bradstreet. "Yet being mine own, at length affection would / Thy blemishes amend, if so I could."[3] Winthrop's rejoinder to Hutchinson's objection—"What if the matter be all one," meaning that Hutchinson's beliefs are the same whether communicated privately or publicly—to some extent misses the point both of these women attempt to make: that private visions have their own integrity, and should be free from coercion (AC 319). At the conclusion of her civil examination and quasi-trial, Hutchinson asks "wherefore I am banished" merely for speaking divinely revealed truths (AC 348). Her elocutionary assertiveness claims her coerced status in much the same way that Bradstreet's authorial diffidence asserts her potential victimization by

---

2. Following David Hall, this book uses the term "Antinomian Controversy" to describe the events sometimes called the "Antinomian Crisis" and the "Free Grace Controversy." See Hall, *The Antinomian Controversy, 1636–1638: A Documentary History* (1968; repr., Durham, NC: Duke University Press, 1990). All references to the controversy from this source are noted parenthetically with the abbreviation AC.

3. Bradstreet, *Works*, 221.

actual friend and imagined foe alike.[4] Both women identify and protest the exposed afterlife of what had formerly been their interior life, whether as the unauthorized revelation of imaginative agency in Bradstreet's case, or the casuistical manipulation of contemplative piety in Hutchinson's. The problem here is not merely that the public display of private meaning fails to access what Emily Dickinson would a few centuries later call the interior place "where the meanings are." It is also the case, and more significantly so, that these pious women understand themselves to possess a spiritual experience whose integrity has in some sense been violated. At least in Hutchinson's case, spirit sponsors a form of Protestant selfhood that is able to experience and articulate its own coercion. A self conceived in these terms, as we know from Michel Foucault's account of "discipline," is one commensurate with secular understandings of individuality, and one whose feminine performance in particular connects gendered Protestant religious discipline to incipient discourses of modern personhood.

Against Hutchinson's assertion of divinely direct inspiration, the Massachusetts Bay authorities ensured that Hutchinson's theological crimes remained firmly tied to a female body deemed heretical in its unseemly productivity and expressivity. Forty years later, Mary Rowlandson would loosen those ties and assert the power of the female contemplative to imagine religious piety as a form of female independence. These women, and others including men like Roger Williams, manifested a tension inherent in the Reformed Protestant tradition between extraordinary and emblematic spirituality. The troubled relation between these two practices—between an antiworldly contemplative piety on the one hand, and, on the other, a devotional practice that found expression within congregation and community—informed the New England Antinomian Controversy to the extent that it was a theological dispute whose very "revelation" turned it into a social and political one.[5] As faithful adherent to a deeply conserva-

---

4. Bethany Reid argues that Bradstreet's poem reveals the poet's late-career preoccupation with "women and illegitimacy," and that with this poem and others "Bradstreet enters a female discourse that extended well beyond womanly fears of childbirth to embrace charges of illegitimacy not unlike those leveled at Anne Hutchinson." See Reid, "'Unfit for Light'": Anne Bradstreet's Monstrous Birth," *The New England Quarterly* 71 (1998): 518–19.

5. There has been much debate over the years about what the Antinomian Controversy was "really" about, and detailing the scholarly record here would be impossible. For a recent book-length treatment that warns against overemphasizing Anne Hutchinson's role in the episode, see Michael Winship, *The Times and Trials of Anne Hutchinson: Puritans Divided* (Lawrence: University of Kansas Press, 2005). In the area of feminist critique and gender studies approaches,

tive reading of reformation theology, Hutchinson came to represent a form of transgressive social identity derived from her radical spiritual autonomy. The eruption of feminized spirit, this chapter suggests, structured the political life of the colony in these years, and its feminine performance broadly determined the controversy's historiographical legacy in the years to come. The attempted management of her behavior by both civil and clerical authority took unspoken issue with the Calvinism it was claiming to defend and, in doing so, began sketching in New England the cultural and theological entity we today know as "American Puritanism." Together with a postsecular historiography that placed Hutchinson within an American political discourse of "dissent" and "liberty," the discursive organization of a state-identified Puritanism anchored post-Puritan-era narratives of American national identity in histories of radicalized female spirituality. In this way, American history and culture could both claim and deny Hutchinson in a contradictory gesture that acknowledged and suppressed both feminine piety and its critique on behalf of secular national history. What was crucial about Anne Hutchinson's example was as much the political chaos her spiritual radicalism implied in the 1630s, as it was the legacies her theological dissent helped imagine. Taken together—her religious radicalism and its worldly management—invented the construct we call American Puritanism, otherwise known as Anne Hutchinson's monstrous birth.[6]

FEMALE TROUBLE

One important rhetoric of the controversy describes Hutchinson's religious appeal as both bodily and mental illness. Her critics' fixation on the language of infection, on the contagious spread of her error, on the

---

see Elizabeth Dillon, *The Gender of Freedom*, particularly chapter 2; Lyle Koehler, "The Case of the American Jezebels: Anne Hutchinson and Female Agitation During the Years of Antinomian Turmoil, 1636–1640," *William and Mary Quarterly* 31, no. 4 (1974): 55–80; Ann Kibbey, *The Interpretation of Material Shapes in Puritanism: A Study of Rhetoric, Prejudice, and Violence* (Cambridge: Cambridge University Press, 1986); and Amy Shrager Lang, *Prophetic Woman*. Michelle Burnham argues an important reading of the economic life of religion in "Anne Hutchinson and the Economics of Antinomian Selfhood in Colonial New England," *Criticism* 39, no. 3 (1997): 337–58. For a recent corrective to the historical reification of the controversy, see Jonathan Beecher Field, "The Antinomian Controversy Did Not Take Place," *Early American Studies* 6, no. 2 (2008): 448–63.

    6. For a reading of the monstrous birth in relation to the emergence of liberalism, see Dillon, *The Gender of Freedom*, 83–102. Michael Kaufmann reads the monstrous birth as a usurpation of patriarchy and the "inversion" of conversion from saint to sinner. See Kaufmann, *Institutional Individualism*, 89–91.

seductive eroticism of her influence, and on the dangers of mere proximity to their source, indicated not just the satanic origins of Antinomianism but the ease with which it might communicate itself from the one to the many. In Winthrop's notice of Mary Dyer's "monstrous birth," we read of Dyer being "notoriously infected with Mrs. Hutchinson's errours."[7] In their co-authored coda to the controversy, *The Short Story of the Rise, Reign and Ruin of the Antinomians* (1648), Winthrop and Thomas Welde would later develop a more elaborate metaphor of medicinal infection to characterize the evangelical power of the Antinomians: "this was ever their method, to drop a little at once into their followers as there were capable, and never would administer their Physicke, till they had first given good preparatives to make it worke, and then stronger & stronger potions, as they the patient able to beare" (AC 206). "The number of these infectious persons increasing now," Edward Johnson would later write in his retrospective account of the controversy, "and having drawn a great party on their side and some considerable persons they grow bold, and question the sound and wholesome truths deliver in publick by Ministers of Christ." This "Woman of another kinde of spirit, who hath had many Revelations of things to come" sprouts a populist legion of emboldened lay theologians, either seduced or infected by "their owne conceited Revelation, ulcerating and bringing little less then [sic] frenzy or madness to the patient, the Congregation of the people of God began to be forsaken, and the weaker Sex prevailed so farre, that they set up a Priest of their own Profession and Sex."[8] In Johnson's often quite funny invective, the causal relations between Hutchinson and her followers become blurred. The source of the people's infection—Hutchinson's preaching—becomes the symptom of their illness—they set her up as their minister. She "represents" the people and so becomes representative of them, their many conceits, professions, and madnesses reduced to the singular point of Hutchinson's body. It is worth noting Johnson's recognition of the parody here of the Congregational practice of a meeting house "calling" its minister, who then becomes their pastoral leader. Although the Presbyterian practice of a congregation "electing" its

---

7. John Winthrop, *The Journal of John Winthrop, 1630–1649*, ed. James Hosmer (New York: Scribner's, 1908), 1: 266.

8. Edward Johnson, *The History of New England, or Wonder-Working Providence* (London: Nathan Brooks, 1653), 99–100, 96 and 100. Janice Knight's discussion of "orthodoxy" helpfully demonstrates that there was no single orthodoxy in the early years of New England. See Knight, *Orthodoxies in Massachusetts: Rereading American Puritanism* (Cambridge, MA: Harvard University Press, 1994).

pastor was an anti-ecclesiastical gesture, the "orthodox party" denounced the self-authorizing "libertinism" of Hutchinson and her followers. In any case, the Antinomian parody of ministerial appointment claimed its dissenting authority from some of the reformation's anti-ecclesiastical theological positions, and in doing so connected theories of church and political governance to a populism contaminated by the feminine. It is worth remarking, in this respect, that Johnson's problem here is not with populist democratic church governance per se, but rather with Hutchinson's apparent subversion of it.[9]

Hutchinson's Protestantism construed religious life in a vernacular language of mystical agency that would be emulated by successive generations of radical dissenters and spiritual enthusiasts. Precisely because Calvinist Protestantism proclaimed a God whose message could be heard in the language of everyday life, Hutchinson's claims of divinely inspired knowledge conjured the spectacle of inscrutable piety passing as legitimate public spirituality. She is, according to her supporters, "a Woman that Preaches better Gospell then [sic] any of your black-coates that have been at the Ninneversity."[10] Her story, moreover, tells us she had always been something of a seeker, "being much troubled," she told the General Court at her civil trial in 1637, "to see the falseness of the constitution of the church of England, I had like to have turned separatist." But at a particular moment in time, she "kept a day of solemn humiliations and pondering of the thing; this scripture was brought unto me" (AC 336). As she reports it, anybody armed with faith and the Bible can commune with God in an equally private and exclusive manner, notwithstanding the preparationist doctrines of public devotion, self-examination, religious education, pastoral authority, the confessional culture of church election, and Puritan salvation theory.[11] In both her civil examination and the subsequent church trial, to say nothing of the lay conventicles of which no

---

9. For the contrary reading—that the "lay rebellion" was no such thing—see James Cooper, "Anne Hutchinson and the 'Lay Rebellion' against the Clergy," *The New England Quarterly* 61, no. 3 (1988): 381–97. Part of the complicated political life of the controversy had to do with the calling of John Wheelwright, Anne Hutchinson's brother-in-law, to the ministry of Boston's First Church, a move Winthrop successfully blocked, but in doing so only increased the antipathy between the Hutchinsonian faction and Winthrop's own.

10. Johnson, *History of New England*, 96.

11. Lisa Gordis argues that John Cotton and other early preachers practiced a form of sermonic artistry that provided a sense of "interpretive inevitability" to its listeners. See Gordis, *Opening Scripture*, 38.

written record is known to survive, it appears Hutchinson extemporized a theology of internally practiced spiritist piety remarkable for its articulation outside of pulpit and synod. Hutchinson, as well as other midcentury radical Protestants like the familists, Brownists, and, as we shall see later in some detail, the Quakers, took the "election" of the soul's justification seriously enough to believe it made them different from and more special than their overly preparationist brethren. Hutchinson's "radical spiritism," to borrow a phrase from Philip Gura, forecast the emergence of a modern individual for whom religion would become a compelling aspect of private self-realization. In the United States, the self-elevation of Calvinistic soteriology that Hutchinson theorized would become a key element of secular discourses of the exceptional nation.[12]

The articulation of the privatization of religion is consistent with the standard secularization thesis—that religion "goes private" in the new public order of the secular—but what is important to keep in mind is radical spirit's contribution to an emergent secularism. As Hutchinson would put it herself: "Now if you do condemn me for speaking what in my conscience I know to be truth I must commit myself to the Lord" (AC 337). Hutchinson separates the credible, internally apprehended self from its falsification in a public order. She implies further that the world's rejection of her spiritual agency merely amplifies its divinely conferred authority and helps sponsor a moral, psychological, and eventually political theory of inviolable selfhood defined through its victimization by the state. This idea of impregnable martyrdom, it need hardly be pointed out, remains a powerful trope in contemporary American political life, and Hutchinson was nothing if not prescient in her embattled self-understanding. Finally, in her turn away from the condemnatory gaze of the court, she establishes the boundary of a self not merely as religious, but specifically defined as such through a gesture of worldly renunciation. The increase rather than the surcease of what Mary Douglas has called boundary management in religious cosmology created the conditions for a coming modernity premised on the sequestering

---

12. Philip Gura, *A Glimpse of Sion's Glory: Puritan Radicalism in New England, 1620–1660* (Middletown, CT: Wesleyan University Press, 1984), 49–92. Eventually, the evaluation and authority of divinely and empirically inspired states of belief would start to look very similar, as Sarah Rivett argues in *The Science of the Soul in Colonial New England*. For the important statement on Puritanism's contribution to exceptionalism, see Sacvan Bercovitch, *The Puritan Origins of the American Self*, a book in which neither Antinomianism nor Anne Hutchinson play a large role.

of religious from other modes of life, and here Hutchinson performs this gesture as a specifically female act of boundary management.[13]

Although there has been some controversy over the historiographical significance of the "monstrous birth" episodes of Hutchinson and her friend, the early Quaker martyr Mary Dyer (to whose story we return in the next chapter), the frequency with which the episodes appear in both early and latter-day histories is as inarguable as it is unremarked. Nearly every pre-1800 narrative history of New England makes reference to them. In his *General History of New England*, Ipswich Minister William Hubbard returns repeatedly to Hutchinson and her propagation of "divers errours" following her 1638 banishment and removal to Rhode Island. In spite of repeated attempts by the Boston Church to convince the exiles of "their errors and disturbances to the peace here" and of "how the church had been wronged by them," each successive year witnessed the broaching of "new errors, the issues of their depraved minds, more misshapen than those monsters, which were credibly reported to be born of the bodies of some of them." Even a Hutchinson supporter like Samuel Gorton makes reference to the miscarriage, criticizing the "rage and envy of this professing generation" for imprisoning Hutchinson through the winter of 1638, whereupon "the woman miscarried, upon which they grounded their abominable untruths." John Oldmixon's 1708 *The British Empire in America* professes not to know the truth of the matter, but nonetheless reports "some of the more Orthodox Writers against her did, in affirming she was brought to Bed of many monstrous Births, as if she was deliver'd of a Monster for every erroneous Tenet she held, and that her Companion Mrs. Dyer was brought to bed of such an ill shap'd Thing, as frightn'd and astonish'd all the Spectators." Thomas Hutchinson, the last Royal Governor of Massachusetts, lets Samuel Gorton do the dirty work of referring to his distant maternal predecessor's monstrous birth, only to dismiss Winthrop's renditions of the birth as being "as credible as that of the Flanders Countess, who is said to have as many children at a birth, as there are days in the year."[14]

---

13. Mary Douglas, *Purity and Danger: An Analysis of Concepts of Pollution and Taboo* (1966; repr., London: Routledge, 2002).

14. William Hubbard, *Chronological History of New England in the Form of Annals to 1680* (1682; repr., Boston: Little, Brown, 1848), 342; quoted in Thomas Hutchinson, *The History of the Colony and Province of Massachusetts-Bay* (1936; repr., Cambridge, MA: Harvard University Press, 1970), 1:64; John Oldmixon, *The British Empire in America* (1708; reissue London: Brotherton, 1741), 76; Hutchinson, *History*, 64.

Arguably the most influential seventeenth-century use of Hutchinson's and Dyer's extraordinary deliveries belongs to Cotton Mather, whose account of the Antinomian Controversy in the *Magnalia Christi Americana* concludes, in memorable crescendo, with his depiction of the "surprizing prodigies, which were lookt upon as testimonies from Heaven."[15] Mather laces his prose with the languages of maternal malnourishment, sexual defilement, and bodily infection, all rhetorical tendencies clearly attached to an overarching discourse of debased maternity, if not a more generalized misogyny against female carnality in Western philosophy and religious thought.[16] Beginning with a standard recollection of Eve's seductive part in the Fall, Mather goes on to observe that "a poysen does never insinuate so quickly, nore operate so strongly, as when women's milk is the vehicle wherein 'tis given."[17] There is little here that is original in Mather's history of infection, seduction, and teratology. Suffice to observe that his *fin-de-siècle* historiographical extension of these terms forwards the logic of understanding female piety as a problem requiring representative disfiguration, which under Mather's control attempts to replace the mysteries of spirit with the excesses of the body. These rich if repulsive iconographic framings attempt to identify and "mirror" a piety that both resists and solicits publication. In so doing, they serve to reinforce the inside-outside structure of spirit's relation to visible externals that, in his view, her constantly radiating spirit was threatening to collapse. The desire to keep this loudmouthed woman in her proper place thus overwrote a conflict over spiritual authenticity with a story of gender transgression, thereby inventing a narrative—and, importantly, telling that narrative as history—of spirit's waning and replacement by a modern discourse of embodiment.

Our default reliance on the Winthrop-Mather archive has resulted in a historical scholarship on Hutchinson that has repeatedly reproduced their assumptions about the interaction of gender and theology in the

---

15. Cotton Mather, *Magnalia Christi Americana*, 2 vols. (1702; repr., New York: Russell and Russell, 1852), 519.

16. For discussion and critique of this tradition, see Sallie McFague, *Metaphorical Theology: Models of God in Religious Language* (Philadelphia: Fortress, 1982); and Grace Jantzen, *Becoming Divine: Towards a Feminist Philosophy of Religion* (Bloomington: Indiana University Press, 1999).

17. Mather, *Magnalia Christi Americana*, 516. I thank Lisa Gordis for pointing out the oddness of implying in this passage a sexual connotation to breastfeeding. For a feminist analysis of the language of "spiritual milk" in Quakerism, see Michele Tarter, "Nursing the New Wor(l)d: The Writings of Quaker Women in Early America," *Women and Language* 16, no. 1 (1993): 22–35.

early-seventeenth-century Bay Colony. These assumptions dominate the historiography of Anne Hutchinson and the Antinomianism synonymous with her name. Consider, as a modern example of an unavoidably Winthrop-Mather influenced historical commentary, Emery Battis's *Saints and Sectaries: Anne Hutchinson and the Antinomian Controversy in the Massachusetts Bay Colony*. Battis recounts the birthing experience of the early New England Quaker Mary Dyer, the wife of the Boston milliner. Attended by Boston's midwife, Jane Hawkins, and Anne Hutchinson, the "travailing" Mary Dyer delivers what Winthrop later came to call a "monstrous birth." As Battis tells it:

> This was not going well at all. Mary was a strong woman with two healthy children, and a seven-month baby should be a light load to deliver . . . Hours ago there had been life evident, delivery seemed imminent. Still Mary strained and gasped, the terrible animal groans tearing through her clenched teeth . . . Anne held Mary tightly in her strong arms, wrestling her to stillness against the agony as Goody Hawkins turned the child . . . Anne was oblivious to the sweat which soaked her from her own efforts and the heat of the fire which must be kept burning in the closed room . . . The last frightful scream tore from Mary's throat and she fell back, mercifully unconscious. It was for Anne and Goody Hawkins to see the hideous fruit of Mary's labors. A creature so horrible in its malformation as to bear only the slightest terrifying resemblance to mankind. It was most mercifully dead.[18]

Battis's dramatization of the "monstrous birth" is something of a historical fiction. As he brings his narrative focus to bear equally, if not predominately, on Anne Hutchinson's semiconspiratorial participation in Mary Dyer's abortive delivery, his history remains essentially consistent with the historiography of Antinomianism that holds Anne Hutchinson to be the origin, cause, center, and resolution of the dispute's theological and social disturbances. Recall Winthrop's triumphalist speech at Hutchinson's November 1637 examination before the General Court at Newtown: "We have been hearkening about the trial of this thing and now the mercy of God by a providence hath answered our desires and made her to lay open her self and the ground of all these disturbances to be revelations" (AC 341). Through

---

18. Emery Battis, *Saints and Sectaries: Anne Hutchinson and the Antinomian Controversy in the Massachusetts Bay Colony* (Chapel Hill: University of North Carolina Press, 1962), 178.

a sleight of hand consistent with Winthrop's and Mather's depictions of the controversy, Battis's Hutchinson becomes responsible for somebody *else's* monstrosities. The modern version assumes with Winthrop an essential connection between the laboring female body and the theology of radical femininity.[19] In the reduction of Mary Dyer to avatar for Hutchinson's radicalism, Battis reproduces the misogyny inherent in Winthrop's and Mather's descriptions of the multiple transgressions of the Antinomians and their cause as the singular "monstrous birth" of Anne Hutchinson.[20]

This revisionary gesture was central not merely to the 1637 "Examination" and 1638 church trial; it factored crucially in John Winthrop's first notice of the event in his *Journal*:

> The wife of one William Dyer, a milliner in the New Exchange, a very proper and fair woman, and both of them notoriously infected with Mrs. Hutchinson's errours, and very censorious and troublesome, (she being of a very proud spirit, and much addicted to revelations,) had been delivered of a child some few months before, October 17 (1637), and the child buried, (being stillborn,) and viewed of none but Mrs. Hutchinson and the midwife, one Hawkins's wife, a rank familist also; and another woman had a glimpse of it, who, not being able to keep counsel, as the other two did, some rumour began to spread, that the child was a monster. One of the elders hearing of it, asked Mrs. Hutchinson, when she was ready to depart; whereupon she told him how it was, and said she meant to have it chronicled, but excused her concealing of it till then, (by advice, as she said, of Mr. Cotton), which coming to the governor's knowledge, he called another of the magistrates and that elder, and sent for the midwife, and examined her about it. At first she confessed only, that the head was defective and misplaced, but being told that Mrs. Hutchinson had revealed all, and that he intended to have it taken up and viewed, she made this report of it, viz . . .[21]

---

19. Susan Juster has suggested that the "intense physicality of the female body" became a model for piety more generally, as the female mystic's bodily excitement reached "beyond the finite" into the ineffable. See Juster, "Mystical Pregnancy and Holy Bleeding: Visionary Experience in Early Modern Britain and America," *William and Mary Quarterly* 57, no. 2 (2000): 254–55.

20. Hutchinson's ability to twist the normal into the abnormal appears in even sympathetic critical discussion, for example Michael Winship, *Times and Trials of Anne Hutchinson*: "Hutchinson only needed to bend his [John Cotton's] ideas slightly and surround them with a fog of questions to insinuate her own position" (39).

21. Winthrop, *Journal*, 266–67.

Written on the eve of Hutchinson's departure from the Bay Colony, the passage revisits the scene of the General Court examination of Hutchinson's transgressive "revelations." Indeed, Hutchinson's explanation for her concealment of the aborted delivery—John Cotton advised her thus—indirectly reasserts her old theological alliance with Cotton, whose "influence" on Hutchinson's errors was one of the central problems of the controversy's social and political life. Disentangling Hutchinsonian error from Cottonian pastoralism, in other words, was the unspoken aim of both the civil examination and the church trials.[22] Yet in the monstrous birth's concealment, the alarming theological association of Hutchinson with Cotton re-emerges as a conspiracy of monstrous parturition, in which Cotton finds himself once again needing to explain his doubtful intimacy with Hutchinson's errors to the Bay Colony authorities. The story of radical spirit's promiscuous "mingling" with all good order becomes the story of Cotton's mingling with Hutchinson. The always difficult to manage lines between a spiritual agency prone to self-direction and one more amenable to clerical guidance becomes a drama of interpersonal entanglement defined by gender and sexual difference. Untangling these improper admixtures drives the official narrative of the controversy, whose prosecution and outcome serve as something of an origin story for the nation's contradictory religious and revolutionary historiographies. The monstrous birth's revelation, its rhetorical autopsy if you will, thus contributed to the production of "American Puritanism" as a legitimate discourse of New England's Protestant settler culture and American pre-nationhood. In so domesticating Anne Hutchinson's theology to a rhetorically framed monstrous body, New England's civil and clerical leadership unwittingly made that monster the foundation of the New England Way.

PERSONALIZING PIETY

Hutchinson's story has consistently provoked and frustrated a desire to "know" her better. Surely the same woman who inspired what James Cooper has called the "lay rebellion" against the clergy; who either duped or voiced the opinions of no less rigorous a Calvinist theologian than John Cotton; who so admirably parried, in one legal and theological melee after

---

22. Cf. Winship, *Times and Trials*: "Blaming Hutchinson for the entire controversy allowed much else to be swept under the rug" (4).

another, the attacks of her inquisitors, accusers, and judges; who did all of this because, as she put the matter so acutely in her civil trial, God "hath let me to distinguish between the voice of my beloved and the voice of Moses, the voice of John Baptist and the voice of antichrist" (AC 336–37) and who made all of these remarkably public and political gestures of personal belief having born fourteen children and expecting at the time, she believed, a fifteenth: surely this person invites the kind of historical desire that produces not only great history, but great fiction as well.[23] Rightly or wrongly, Hutchinson has become the primary focus of the scholarly inquiry into the theological quagmire of the "Free Grace Controversy" in New England. The argument for what Timothy Wood has called an "intimate spirituality" may help us appreciate the way in which our interest in Hutchinson has become "personal," that is, focused on the idea of a person as much as the ideas of that person.[24] Hutchinson's theological opinion has come to be "personalized." Because a religious experience enclosed within and reported by means of unaided experiential interiority, Hutchinson's quasi-mystical religion presents itself as a curiously personality-driven subject for inquiry: to know the person, we might say, is to know her religion, and vice versa. Marilyn Westerkamp argues in this regard that Hutchinson's theology was primarily mystical, and that "in communicating directly with the individual female believer ... the Spirit affirmed that personhood denied by the established church."[25] The personal rather than the pontificate becomes the focus of both theological and scholarly desire. The promise of accessible piety provides notional access to the "individual" or even a "self" indicating a condition of recognizable "personhood" roughly a century before Benjamin Franklin, to take a well-known example of

---

23. And sometimes both at the same time, as we can see from any number of purported "histories" that indulge in various forms of hagiography, invention, and wishful thinking, most famously Nathaniel Hawthorne's nineteenth-century portrait of her, "Mrs. Hutchinson." See, for example, Edward More's essay on Hutchinson's role in the emergence of American religious freedom, in which one learns that Hutchinson "found her happiness in gathering society about her" and that the "personal element" defined her role in the struggle. More, "Questions of Religious Freedom," in *Commonwealth History of Massachusetts: Colony, Province, and State*, ed. Albert Hart Bushnell (New York: Russell and Russell, 1927), 395. For the still definitive reading of Hutchinson as historical source for Hawthorne, see Michael Colacurcio, "Footsteps of Ann Hutchinson: The Context of *The Scarlet Letter*," *English Literary History* 39, no. 5 (1972): 459–94.

24. Timothy Wood, "'Whosoever Will be Great Among You': The Leadership of John Cotton During the Antinomian Crisis," *Christian Scholars Review* 35, no. 1 (2005): 85.

25. Marilyn Westerkamp, "Anne Hutchinson, Sectarian Mysticism, and the Puritan Order," *Church History* 59, no. 4 (1990): 496.

American secular achievement, conceived of republican selfhood in relation to the denial of personality as the condition of political effectiveness. It was a woman, Anne Hutchinson, who insisted that her beliefs, while realized inwardly, stemmed from a most antipersonal source, that is, God, and it was institutional and historiographical authority that attempted to dismiss those beliefs by insisting on their female, embodied, and so personal origin. Franklin's secular rationalism was as much the product of spiritual radicalism as it was of religion's subordination to Republican politics.[26]

Another way to get at the "personal" element is to suggest that a homiletic theology of intimacy emerges from Hutchinson's radical spirituality. In this reading, her Antinomianism is "feminine" because performatively enacted as an exercise of spiritual "intimacy" rather than merely because spoken by a woman.[27] We can think of her as being part of what Sarah Ahmed calls an "affective econom[y], where feelings do not reside in subjects of objects, but are produced as effects of circulation." Our desire to "know" Hutchinson need not serve as an example of the misogynistic trivialization of women, women's history, or feminine spirit as "merely personal" adornments to important historical narrative. Rather, we might in following Ahmed's lead here come to understand our own position, as contemporary readers of early modern spiritual and social experience, to be conditioned by the affective economy of gender, spirit, and representation found in the seventeenth-century New England archive. Our responses today, the relationships we imagine between our now and our then, include all of these components. We might even push this analysis further and consider the provocation to "personalize" our reading of Hutchinson in light of what Eve Sedgwick calls "reparative reading." As we saw with Emery Battis's critique of the monstrous birth episodes, the suspicious skepticism of the paranoid style still informs the scholarly view of the past, which is to say, following Sedgwick, that we would be wise to resist employing paranoid hermeneutics to read the text of Anne Hutchinson and the broader "Puritanism" within which that text took shape. If we

---

26. For a broader argument connecting Puritan religion to Franklinian republicanism see Mitchell Robert Breitwieser, *Cotton Mather and Benjamin Franklin: The Price of Representative Personality* (Cambridge: Cambridge University Press, 1984). For an argument that assumes Franklin as a successful secularist, see Michael Warner, *Letters of the Republic*, particularly chapter 3.

27. Sandra Gustafson makes a similar point in relation to Jonathan Edwards's performative femininity. See Gustafson, *Eloquence Is Power*, 61, 64–67.

consider the invitational intimacies of Hutchinson's life—her deeply personal theology, her victimization by authority, the disadvantaged status of her femininity—we can reclaim those experiences as integral to her piety, and their uncovering as integral to our understanding of American Puritanism. We need not, in other words, perform a kind of violence to the text of "American Puritanism" that repeats the interpretive violence done to Hutchinson and other radicals like her in the seventeenth century. In the words of Heather Love, we might in our approach to this archive and the historiographical narratives we derive from it, come to "diagnose, not punish" that past and its actants in our desire to reframe our understanding of it now.[28]

Our "feelings" today about religion, gender, and secularism's history are, at least in part, the effects of the circulation of affect in the seventeenth century, which is another way of rethinking secularism's understanding of its paranoid relation to its own religious past. Her many critics, as we know, subjected her experiences to interpretive engagements intended to call out the secret truths of her claimed spiritual experiences. "Paranoia," writes Sedgwick, "places its faith in exposure," an idea whose ambition describes both New England's and our own relation to Anne Hutchinson, and does so using a word ("faith") whose religious connotation is unavoidable. This is to say that to the extent a culture of close examination characterized seventeenth-century New England Congregationalism, it also outlines a secular understanding of modernity's relation to both itself and to its religious past. Again following Sedgwick, the paranoid style is committed to "exposing and problematizing hidden violences in the genealogy of the modern liberal subject." At the same time, our view of the religious past depends on an arsenal of critical approaches—"subversive and demystifying parody, suspicious archeologies of the present, the detection of hidden patterns"—that deeply religious Christians in the seventeenth century practiced as part of a committed devotional life.[29] This is not merely to say that something like "Puritan introspection" looks like secular cultural hermeneutics. It is to say, additionally, that the "paranoid style" of Puritan New England enabled such a secular cultural hermeneutic to emerge at all.

---

28. Sara Ahmed, *The Cultural Politics of Emotion* (New York: Routledge, 2004), 8; Eve Sedgwick, *Touching Feeling: Affect, Pedagogy, and Performativity* (Durham, NC: Duke University Press, 2003), 130; and Heather Love, *Feeling Backward: Loss and the Politics of Queer History* (Cambridge, MA: Harvard University Press, 2007), 149.

29. Sedgwick *Touching Feeling*, 131.

Indeed, the conservative reformation may fairly be viewed as an invitation to employ a hermeneutic of suspicion intended, paradoxically enough, to provide interpretive certainty about spiritual meaning where by definition there could be none. In the Congregational churches of New England, would-be members petitioned to be accepted into full church covenant by submitting their confession of spiritual experience to examination by both the minister and the congregation's already admitted members. The confessional culture of New England Congregationalism located these narratives within a skeptical interpretive economy that sought to evaluate the credibility of the penitent's spiritual confession, or as Thomas Weld put it in 1651: "his effectual calling to Christ, and how God hath carried on the work of grace . . . to the satisfaction of the Brethren present, they give testimony of the Godly and approved life and conversation of each other."[30] Anne Hutchinson's claim to direct and unmediated spiritual experience was in this sense entirely consistent with the basic culture of confession, and its eventual evaluation and judgment by first the Civil and then church tribunals in Boston mimicked the congregational examination understood to be a normative component of church discipline.

Part of Hutchinson's radicalism lay in her refusal to consent to the terms of her interpretation by her community: her refusal, that is, to serve as an emerging Puritanism's "text." Take for example the following brief exchange between Hutchinson and John Winthrop during the 1637 civil trial:

> Gov.: Well, we see how it is. We must therefore put it away from you or restrain you from maintaining this course.
>
> Mrs. H.: If you have a rule for it from God's word you may.
>
> Gov.: We are your judges, and not you ours and we must compel you to it. (AC 316)

Here, Hutchinson claims that only God may determine the terms of spiritual interpretation, which Winthrop denies on the basis of the court's authority. Hutchinson's appeal to divine sovereignty—a statement of religious

---

30. Thomas Welde, *A Brief Narration on the Practice of the Churches in New-England* (Boston, 1651), 2–3.

belief if ever there was one—results in the articulation of the state's power to regulate public religious carriage. Hutchinson's banishment—or, at the very least, its rationalization—may well have followed from her being recognized as a disturbance to the public, but Hutchinson's claim here is that the privately revealed word of God carries equal if not greater force than the laws of the magistracy. She challenges her interlocutors to disprove her claims, which, of course, they cannot. She thereby becomes occasion for paranoid reading, for the production of critique and reification more broadly. Radical religion serves as modern skepticism's cause.[31]

It is worth asking at this point: is there anything specifically *feminine* about her religious practice? There is a reasonable case to be made that her gender is contingent with respect to her spiritual agency and even history. Christianity, at least as it manifests itself in Protestant salvation theory, has a long if somewhat unevenly applied tradition of holding that the soul doesn't have a gender or, at the very least, that one's gender does not determine God's decision making. This is different from observing, as some have, that gender explains the causality of her persecution and banishment, which in the end could have little or nothing to do with her religious beliefs and practices. It is also the case that men could hold beliefs similar to those we associate with Anne Hutchinson; indeed, we shall see shortly that at least one New England minister probably did, and there were other prominent men like John Wheelwright and Henry Vane who were identified as being of the Antinomian party. So, at least in the case of Hutchinson, how do we assign gender to faith?

One reason why questions of gender persist is because Hutchinson's identity as a woman was itself consistently cited by both her defenders and her detractors, as well as in subsequent historiography and critique, including our own today. A significant portion of her civil trial was concerned with the lay "conventicles" in her house where this woman of "ready wit and bold spirit" led women and probably men in lay discussions of the week's sermons in the putatively feminine space of the home. Magistrates like Winthrop and ministers like Thomas Shepard repeatedly drew

---

31. In saying so, I am drawing on the collective authorship of *Is Critique Secular? Blasphemy, Injury, and Free Speech*, ed. Wendy Brown and Saba Mahmood (Berkeley: University of California Press for the Townsend Center of the Humanities, 2009). Each of the essays in this volume takes issue with the assumption that critique is necessarily a secular activity because it is animated by the spirits of empiricism and human reason, rather than by the desire for salvation and divine intimacy.

attention to her violation of Paul's injunction against a female ministry.[32] In the church trial held in the late winter of 1638, which was more concerned with her religious views than with their social and political impact, her Congregation summarily excommunicated her family on the grounds that their "natural affection" for her would tincture their ability to judge her objectively. At least one commentator implied Hutchinson's concupiscence played a role in the controversy, and yet another even called her husband's virility and therefore masculinity into question. Then there are the "monstrous births" (both hers and her friend Mary Dyer's), which both contemporary and latter-day commentators have consistently cited as either explanation or cause (or both) for her troubles. Given how much fuss Hutchinson's contemporaries made about her gender, it is no surprise to find historiography and scholarship doing so as well. Whether we like it or not, it is today impossible to consider the episode and its outcome without considering the significance of gender—of both genders, in fact.[33]

Consider, as a counterexample, Roger Williams's very brief career as a Congregationalist minister in New England. Like Anne Hutchinson, Williams was a better Calvinist and theologian than Winthrop, whose muddled confusion of civil with gospel law led the eventual leader of Rhode Island to aver Winthrop's "hireling ministry" to be "none of Christ's." The Massachusetts Bay Colony banished Williams in the fall of 1635, fully a year before Hutchinson seriously ran afoul of the magistrates and the clerics, and in its banishment order cited the "diverse new and dangerous opinions" of the Salem minister as cause for his necessary removal. The same language appears in the reception of Hutchinson, whose championing of the laws of the gospel over the laws of the state had similarly motivated Williams to reject the state's demand for religious conformity. To be sure, Williams was also motivated in his polemic by what he took to be an abrogation of political responsibility toward indigenous peoples on the part of the colonists. Nan Goodman finds, for example, that the banishment order came on the heels of a series of provocations and unanswered charges including abusing

---

32. 1 Corinthians 14:34–35 contains the famous injunction against women's preaching in a chapter more generally preoccupied with discerning the difference between true and false prophecy. For a discussion of the importance of prophecy to the trial, see Louise Breen, *Transgressing the Bounds*, 17–19.

33. The famous comment about Hutchinson's verbal prowess belongs to Winthrop, *Journal*, 195. John Cotton makes an indirect adultery accusation in his admonishment to her at the end of the church trial (AC 372). The comment about her husband's failures comes, again, from Winthrop, *Journal*, 195.

the magistrates for their unconvincing separatism and political toadyism, attacking the Bay Colony for exploitative land-grabs, and, interestingly for this study, being "vociferously on the side of requiring women to wear veils in church." It was not that Williams's theological views were much different from those of the Bay ministry so much as it was the case that he took more seriously the inherent political separatism of the radical reformation when it came to judging the state's fitness to supervise religious practices, or religion's fitness to authorize or legitimize state authority.[34] Williams's important if contested place in the history of religious toleration and the "separation of church and state" enshrined in the American Bill of Rights parallels the contribution Hutchinson and her successors would make to a dissenting discourse of "religious liberty." Both Williams and Hutchinson were committed to the integrity of religious belief as a facet of self claimed separately from the claims made on and by the state. In both cases, we see that religious motivations had what we might call secular results, a logic we will see repeated in the experiences of seventeenth-century Quakers in New England.[35]

Still more so than Williams, Hutchinson's apparently mystical theology implied femininity in its performance, and that performance's historical recollection in the postsecular historiographical imagination specifically cites the feminine as a key epistemological terrain of historical knowledge. The beckoning gesture of Hutchinson and her theology—that provocation to "know" and reveal her—might usefully be seen as the effect of religious mystery itself. Mysticism's "personalized" relations between believer and deity depended not only on a powerfully private experience of divine closeness, but on negative theology's logic of the emptied self. Although the effusive language of mystical writing has become one of its defining characteristics, the moment itself, as William James observed in the *Varieties of Religious Experience*, "defies expression . . . no adequate report of its

---

34. Nan Goodman, *Banished: Common Law and the Rhetoric of Social Exclusion in Early New England* (Philadelphia: University of Pennsylvania Press, 2012), 71. Goodman intriguingly suggests that Hutchinson's willingness to "entertain strangers" violated a broader prohibition against letting outsiders into the fledgling colony (44–49). See also John M. Barry, *Roger Williams and the Creation of the American Soul* (New York: Viking, 2012).

35. The minister John Wheelwright was another "male Antinomian." His infamous Fast-Day sermon criticized the idea of state-ordered religious celebrations and observances, arguing that any such gesture denied the sovereign primacy of Christ and God in the conferral of grace and so brought the community into a "Covenant of Works." See Wheelwright, "A Fast Day Sermon," AC 168–70.

contents can be given in words . . . it cannot be imparted or transferred to others."[36] Given that mystical experience interrupts the circuitry by which self and other might become known to each other, we might initially regard suspiciously the notion that mysticism's "personal" quality makes the mystic more immediately knowable. The braiding of self and divine unity theorized a split between the "agency" of mystical involvement, and a historically knowable self temporarily shed in the mystical moment. Patricia Caldwell notes for example that "Mrs. Hutchinson's extreme piety leads her inexorably into the ineffable divine," a path traveled often enough by the (often female) mystics whose visionary and linguistic excesses ultimately referred to divinity's co-optation of the mystic's otherwise evacuated human faculties.[37] "The Lord knows that I could not open scripture," Hutchinson points out during her civil examination, "he must by his prophetical office open it unto me" (AC 337). Exactly what we can "know" about Anne Hutchinson's religious experience (to say nothing of her "personality"), or whom we are claiming to know through representations made about her, is circumscribed by the structure of the theological views she appears to have held. Strictly speaking, we don't know anything about her religious experiences, notwithstanding the shortened conversion and emigration narratives that survive from the 1637 trial. There is, in this early modern instance of the secularization of mystery into "secrecy," both everything and nothing to know about her travels with God. The nature of her spirituality resists translation into the register of comprehensible language, to say nothing of orthodox theological convention. Female piety thus resists even as it invites its own interpretation, and in this sense female piety comes to stand as a primary symbol not merely for the practice of religious belief in the seventeenth century, but for our postsecular investigation of such historical practices as well.[38]

---

36. William James, *The Varieties of Religious Experience* (1902; repr., New York: Library of America, 1990), 343.

37. Patricia Caldwell, "The Antinomian Language Controversy," *Harvard Theological Review* 69, no. 3 (1976): 363. On the development of Christian mysticism out of Platonist philosophy, and the gendered implications of early Christianity's incorporation of Platonism, see Grace Jantzen, *Power, Gender, and Christian Mysticism*, 26–58.

38. Jantzen takes strong issue with the modern assumption of "ineffability" as the governing trope of the mystic's attempt to describe her experiences with divinity, arguing instead that what characterizes the writing of mystical women is verbosity rather than silence. Jantzen's critique notwithstanding, there is a long association of mysticism's characteristically resistant relation to language. William James, of course, makes this argument. For a modern version, see Geoffrey Harpham, *The Ascetic Imperative in Culture and Criticism*, 19–44.

Hutchinson was and perhaps still is the text that must be opened. "But now having seen him which is invisible," she tells the court, "I fear not what man can do to me," a statement whose claim of direct access to God was not lost on a religious culture struggling with the paradoxical ambiguities born of God's sovereignty over a fallen world from which he had absented himself (AC 338). The threat of Hutchinson's mysticism was as much the political anarchy her detractors feared such theological innovations would foster as it was the resistance to explication her theology sustained.[39] The problem, to put it differently, is that in her resistant spiritual assertions, she effectively placed herself at the center of New England's hermeneutic interpretive culture—only to decline her interpretation by that culture. To many detractors then and now, her confident biblicism appeared to be little other than an unseemly arrogation of divine power to herself: a delusional—possibly satanic—confusion of the Holy Spirit's direct operation on the soul with the devil's distraction of the mind. Her claims of unverifiable knowledge derived through mystical communication prompted their aggressive assignation of quasi-heretical practice to her. The paranoid readers of Hutchinson's time "revealed" her secrets so as to reject them. In doing so, they effectively secured her centrality as interpretive cause to the theological ambitions of New England settlement culture in a gesture that simultaneously called the social and political credibility of those ambitions into question.

Antinomianism is "feminine," then, in a variety of ways, no one of which can be assigned specifically to sexual difference, but all of which can be understood in relation to their performance by both men and women claiming to be animated by the spirit of God. Historically, her mystical spiritual agency recalls a long tradition of female prophetic and visionary Christians. In terms of her contemporary Protestant context, her anti-ecclesiastical and interior piety coordinates with the subordination of women in the seventeenth century.[40] From the perspective of social history, her religious agency's manifestation in both the home and in the church (to say nothing of her examinations and trials) collapsed a vision of female independence with one of theological autonomy. Even where

---

39. In this line of thinking, I am indebted to Elisa New's ideas regarding the shared "feminist invisibility" of Hutchinson and Anne Bradstreet. See her "Feminist Invisibility: The Examples of Anne Bradstreet and Ann Hutchinson," *Common Knowledge* 2, no. 1 (1993): 99–117.

40. For each of these views in turn, see Caroline Walker Bynum, *Holy Feast and Holy Fast*; and Ivy Schweitzer, *The Work of Self-Representation*.

one might wish to "rescue" a "free grace controversy" from its overdetermined association with Anne Hutchinson, such a gesture uncomfortably recreates the conditions of her attempted marginalization by her contemporary authorities, to say nothing of ignoring her centrality to an actual historiographical tradition that more or less "forgot" male Antinomian peers like Henry Vane and John Wheelwright. Finally, the forgetting of Hutchinson and the piety she represented uncritically replicates the logic of secularism's forgetting of its own religious origins narrative, and in particular its gendered origins.

JOHN COTTON'S MISCARRIAGE

If part of the problem of Hutchinson's appeal was that it borrowed from—and was in turn enabled by—the Calvinism embraced by the English reformation, then the contemporary *and* modern response has been to labor mightily on behalf of the Puritan cause of unscrambling Hutchinsonianism from Congregationalism.[41] It may well be for this if for no other reason that the "orthodox party" took a second run at Hutchinson in the early spring of 1638, conducting a "church trial" whose unspoken aim was to disentangle Cotton from Hutchinson. From the vantage point of legal history, the civil trial reached the verdict it did because Hutchinson's "dayngerous" religious views had come to cause a public disturbance. Her banishment, along with the banishment orders entered against her followers, reflected a broader desire to restore something approaching political cohesion following the various upheavals of the mid-1630s.[42] If the late 1637 civil trial stumbled on spiritual heresy while trying to get a troublesome woman to keep her mouth shut, the April 1638 church trial sought to define that spiritual heresy more clearly and remove its unpleasant association with Cotton. In any case, the problem for both trials was not merely Hutchinson's privately realized beliefs but their marked similarity to John Cotton's publicly professed and so "official" theology.

---

41. Both contemporary and modern-day readers have found Hutchinson's theology to be everything from scandalously heretical to rigorously consistent with the best teachings of the English reformation. For a capaciously drawn discussion, see Winship, *Times and Trials*, 6–20.

42. A good narrative of those years can be found in David Hall's introduction to *The Antinomian Controversy*, 4–20. For discussion of the legal issues of the controversy, see Goodman, *Banished*, 27–54.

John Cotton was Hutchinson's pastoral confidante and a leading theological light in New England's attempted reformation of the English church. In one of his journal entries referring to Hutchinson's civil trial, John Winthrop infamously remarked the similarity between Hutchinson's perceived theology and that practiced as the church discipline of Congregational Boston; according to Winthrop, "no man could tell (except some few, who knew the bottom of the matter) where any difference was" (AC 208). Winthrop's befuddlement notwithstanding, just about all of the confusions eventually attributed to Hutchinson had been hotly disputed within the New England ministry around the same time Hutchinson began spreading her "errors." Carried on through exchanges of letters, Cotton's theological dispute with his brethren was neither slight nor resolved, and its irresolution dramatically impacted the trials of Anne Hutchinson. One question put to Cotton regarded the "immediate witness" of the Spirit on a believer, whether or not, that is to say, saving justification was "so cleare" that there need not be a corresponding "Worke" either performed by the convert or witnessed by the church to verify it (AC 49). The ministers' concern is that without some external frame within which to assess the integrity of spiritual claims, there may be "a seed of much hypocrisie and delusion in the Churches" (AC, "Elder's Reply," 65). In his response to the "Reply," Cotton maintains that the soul's justification exists "without respect to the merit or worth of a work" (meaning there is no phenomenological account of conversion); that the Spirit "witnesseth without sight of any work of ours foregoing as any way preparing us therunto" (which could mean that neither the agency of conversion nor its assessment lay within the purview of the church); and, finally, that Christ alone "is the cause of our faith, and the good works that follow from it" (AC, "Rejoynder," 87). It is easy to get bogged down in the causal fog of Puritan salvation theory, but jumping ahead to Hutchinson's civil trial in November 1637, we can see Cotton maintaining this position of the essential inaccessibility of spiritual agency in his testimony "That she may have some special providence of God to help her is a thing I cannot bear witness against" (AC, "Civil," 341). Although the archive can't confirm this, there is good reason to suspect that Anne Hutchinson was only following pastoral instructions when she claimed special and direct access to God independent of ministerial verification and instruction. Ironically, we might say, the Cotton archive provides access to Hutchinson's theology.

She certainly appears to have believed that her spiritist theology was entirely in keeping with his teachings. In sustaining the integrity of her theological positions against the attacks of both a preparationist ministry and its political allies, Hutchinson may well have had Cotton's own sermons in mind, perhaps something like the following, taken from his magisterial sermon cycle *Christ the Fountain of Life,* published in 1651, although probably preached in England in 1628:

> God poures out his spirit in a rich and plentifull measure; he poures out his spirit upon all flesh; whence it comes to passe, that the servants of God understand many secrets of Gods counsell. . . . that many a godly man by the same spirit discernes many secret hidden mysteries, and meanings of the Holy Ghost in Scripture more then ever he could by any reading, or instruction; and many times discernes some speciall work of the spirit of God, which inables them to fore-see some speciall blessings, . . . and so leads them on to many good things which they did little thinke of, and so makes them Propheticall spirits, and bowes them to teach others also, to lead on others of their neighbours in the Wayes of God.[43]

In this one selection, we see a number of theological tenets that would appear before, during, and after the trials of Anne Hutchinson.[44] While it appears true that Cotton for the most part sustained a ministry which emphasized constant introspection and maintained the discipline of sanctification along preparationist lines, this passage clearly relaxes the pieties of preparationism to make room for the spiritual agency for which Hutchinson was condemned. Whether or not she heard Cotton preach *Christ the Fountaine of Life* in 1628 or read the sermon in manuscript form is a question we will probably never answer. There is, however, sufficient evidence on both sides of Cotton's migration to allow for the possibility that she learned some of her more "desperate enthusiasms" from her favorite minister and spiritual advisor.

---

43. John Cotton, *Christ the Fountaine of Life* (1651; facsimile repr., New York: Arno, 1972), 62.

44. Theodore Bozeman has recently argued that Cotton went from being a strict pietist in England before he migrated, to being something of a potential spiritist after his settlement in New England. See *To Live Ancient Lives: The Primitivist Dimension in Puritanism* (Chapel Hill: University of North Carolina Press for the Omohundro Institute of Early America, 1988), 218–21 and 230.

First, Cotton emphasizes the agency of the Spirit in conversion, which is itself something of a departure from Trinitarian theology's typical focus on the authority of God as recorded in the scripture. He also maintains the need for penitents to imitate the example of Christ's pietistic purging of the body of Sin prior to salvation. The precise place of spiritual agency in conversion was part of the dispute with the Bay ministers prior to Hutchinson's trial. Asked "whether Sanctification being discerned, may not be, and often is a ground of Primitive Comfort, as it is an Evidence of our being in Christ," Cotton replied (with uncharacteristic succinctness): "I doe not beleeve that this Sanctification being discerned, is a ground of Primitive Comfort, though when it is evidently discerned, it be an Evidence of our being in Christ." (AC, "Sixteene," 51–52). Although affirming the preparationist position that sanctified behavior gives cause for the self and others to have evidence of salvation, it simultaneously refuses to grant certainty ("comfort") to the individual. Furthermore, Cotton's answer does not put the experience of sanctification, or its perception of "Comfort," to the test of scripture, suggesting that a convert might consider their estate from the point of view of spiritual experience before anything else. The problem is not merely that of the willful hypocrite trying to fake his way into full church membership; it is, more troublingly, that of the unwitting hypocrite: the would-be convert who wants to be saved, who prepares for salvation through the disciplined exercise of the pieties, who acts as if he were saved, and yet still may not be one of the chosen. In response to a final question put by the Ministers in early 1637, asking whether or not "practical reasoning" may not safely be used to consider the state of the soul, Cotton replies that such reasoning is "a lawfull way to conclude a mans [sic] safe Estate..so [be it] the Reason be not Carnall but spirituall" (AC 58). By using the scripture with the mind, and by "the Experimentall observation of a good Conscience, enlightened by the Spirit of God, and looking up to Christ to cleare the Conclusion from both," the convert may well take comfort in his salvation. Here Cotton returns to a Trinitarian theologian's position (that salvation is performed by the three-person God), but the emphasis on the spirit is clear: practical reasoning and good conscience cannot suffice without "the *Witnesse* of the spirit" (AC 58).

Second, Cotton emphasizes the superior and exceptional instruction offered by the Spirit to the penitent. Spiritist self-instruction augured sociopolitical fears of anarchy, as such a practice could potentially release the elect from their obligations to natural and civil laws. The emancipation of the individual spirit from the mortal experience of the "carnal" self was not only a precept Cotton advanced from the pulpit; it was, more generally, an outcome of the Protestant reformation's liberation of faith from the worldly authority of Catholic ecclesiastical power. The agency of the Spirit necessarily introduced a powerful, unpredictable, sudden, and interventionary element into the mechanics of salvation. "The power of miraculous intervention," as Mary Douglas has called it, "was no mere magical sideshow in European Christianity."[45] It was, within the history of Protestantism, a crucial agent in the reformation's ongoing polemic against the deadened externals of Catholic ritual. Spirit was the agent of religious feeling, of revolutionary resistance to "encrusted" institutional authority, and of emancipation from the deadened life of inherited sin, observance of form, and empty works. Indeed, Cotton even suggested that the soul, once saved, was freed from all earthly forms of instruction: in his response to Question VI of the "Sixteene Questions," Cotton answered that "the assurance of a mans good Estate, may be maintained to him, when the frame of his Spirit is growne much degenerate" (AC 50). This idea is entirely consistent with the Synod of Dort's position on the unquestionable perseverance of the Saints, which is to say that the fear of anarchy imagined in Antinomianism's emancipation of self from social authority was as much the product of synodical theology as it was of the "fervid" imagination of the hysterical woman and her guileful misinterpretations of the scripture. Score another point for Hutchinson.

Third, Cotton clearly authorizes the agency of prophecy and, moreover, connects prophetically derived spiritual authority to the emergence of a legitimate lay ministry. He implicitly defended her claim of direct revelation at the civil trial: a claim his ministerial brethren disputed at that trial and Winthrop altogether ignored when declaring her revelatory reports to be "the most desperate enthusiasm in the world" which "may breed more if they be let alone" (AC, "Civil," 342). Winthrop goes on to assert "that the revelation she brings forth is delusion" to which "*All the Court but some two or three ministers cry out, we all believe it—we all believe it*" (AC, "Civil," 343; italics original). Here, Winthrop affirms not that revelation is itself always delusional, but rather that Hutchinson's particular prophecies

---

45. Douglas, *Purity and Danger*, 76.

and claims to divine knowledge are. Perhaps Winthrop's phrasing was an attempt to make room for Cotton in the leaders' tent by conceding the principle of direct revelation while condemning Hutchinson's particular performance of it, a concession which, as the examination record goes on to show, failed to keep some of the ministers from wanting to scrutinize Cotton still further. Given the history of Christ's own gospel ministry, which consisted of the transformation of ordinary men, women, sinners, and unbelievers (including the Apostle Paul himself) into the efficacious servants of the one true God, a New Testament minister as able as John Cotton would indeed be careful about placing limits on what God could or could not do with respect to the gospel's evangelizing imperative. The transformation of the ordinary sinner into the extraordinary convert capable of direct access to God was not merely the story of the emergence of the primitive church's earliest ministry; it was the story of Christ himself. Hutchinson's spiritist insurgency derived its authority from a New Testament theology derived from one of the English reformation's most able ministers.[46]

Hutchinson performed what might be called a Puritan vernacular theology based partly on the teachings of John Cotton, and partly on her individual readings of scripture. Her "Antinomian" practices derived from credible theological positions found within seventeenth-century dissenting Protestantism, and taught within John Cotton's New England pastoral work; they found a most receptive arena in New England. This communicative arena, moreover, was one famously theorized in a political theory of the Christian state: John Winthrop's "Modell of Christian Charitie," one of the most influential lay sermons ever written by an English Puritan. Winthrop's sermon proposes the formation of a government at once "civil and ecclesiastical," defined by the relation between the natural law of the Old Testament's Mosaic covenant of works on the one hand, and the gospel law of the New Testament's Christian covenant of grace on the other. These two orders of law, like the men and women whose lives they will govern in the coming Christian commonwealth, are necessarily

---

46. Julie Sievers offers a concise discussion of Cotton's perceived and actual theological differences from his peers, including Winthrop. See "Refiguring the Song of Songs: John Cotton's 1655 Sermon and the Antinomian Controversy," *The New England Quarterly* 76, no. 1 (2003): 73–107.

interactive: the Pentateuch regulates the postlapsarian conditions of fallen humanity, thereby giving rise to the need for Christ's delivery of grace, the requirement for an agency defined by mercy, and the possibility of humanity's salvation through Christ's willing sacrifice. The law of Moses is dead without the law of Jesus; the former is required in the state of degeneracy, while the latter defines the hope of human regeneracy and provides an ameliatory power in human affairs prior to the soul's redemption.

Winthrop spends some time discussing "the exercise of this love [Christ's law] which is twofold, inward or outward."[47] Strife between professing Christians emerges from "the contrary or different nature of the things themselves," that is, from the apprehension that the hidden nature of one person is of a fundamentally different order from the other. In other words, a truly saved Christian *feels* there is some difference between himself and the other he perceives to be unsaved, just as God "loves his elect because they are like Himself, He beholds them in His beloved son." Not through submission to Mosaic or natural law but through the gift of heightened perception and spiritual comprehension bestowed on the elect through God, does the true Christian come to exercise his earthly duties and, in doing so, manifest the invisible power of God in the external world. Winthrop goes on to develop and detail this operation through a maternal analogy predictably derived from Genesis:

> So a mother loves her child, she thoroughly conceives a resemblance of herself in it. Thus it is between the members of Christ. Each discerns, by the work of the spirit, his own image and resemblance in another, and therefore cannot but love him as he loves himself. Now when the soul, which is of a sociable nature, finds anything like to itself, it is like Adam when Eve was brought to him. She must have it one with herself. This is flesh of my flesh (saith the soul) and bone of my bone. She conceives a great delight in it, therefore she desires nearness and familiarity with it. She hath a great propensity to do it good and receives such content in it, as fearing the miscarriage of her beloved she bestows it in the inmost closet of her heart.[48]

---

47. John Winthrop, "A Model of Christian Charity," in *The Norton Anthology of American Literature*, vol. A, 7th ed. (New York: Norton, 2009), 148.

48. Ibid., 154.

If this passage did not create then it certainly describes the logic of Anne Hutchinson's exercise of the spirit. Although a good deal of the dispute recounted during the civil and church trials focused on Hutchinson having found fault with various ministers preaching a covenant of works, she ultimately assigned the origin of her critique to the immediate voice of God. She defended her truths by claiming they were not hers, and excused (to the extent she did) her errors by claiming her human frailty as the culprit rather than any particular willful misreading on her part. Winthrop's comparison of the exercise of gospel mercy to the creation of Eve, moreover, theorizes Christian love as stemming from the direct operation of the creator on this created: a Christian cannot help but act in such a way that honors the spirit in their heart as it reflects the bestowal of grace by the creator upon his or her created. To do otherwise would be, in Winthrop's own words, to produce a "miscarriage": a bastardized theology of externals that would extinguish the light of this "City on the Hill" and engulf the reformation in papal darkness. Even before the monstrous birth episodes, Winthrop conceived a model of New England's success and failure partly dependent on a vocabulary of gestation and (mis)birth. We might in light of this reading note the persistent use of Winthrop's sermon, if not its central conceit of the "City on the Hill," over the course of the political history of the United States. From municipal to federal levels of government, politicians have seized on the sermon to describe, however nostalgically, the ongoing ambitions of the United States, a secular employment of the historical text of American Puritanism that also neatly reproduces the suppression of the feminine undertaken by New England's clerical and political authorities.

It is no surprise, then, that Winthrop seized on the monstrous birth episodes. Precisely because the kinds of things Hutchinson was saying—whether in the space of the conventicle or in the privacy of the pastoral confessional—were consistent with what others had either said or practiced, his management of the monstrous births served the useful rhetorical function of separating, once and for all, the heretics from the saints. The theological niceties on which the controversy was founded restaged the unknowable status of true conversion in the abstract realm of theology. Arguably, the theory of state Winthrop propounds in the "Model of Christian Charity" was driven by the ambiguous epistemology of the conservative reformation. One reason why the theological hairsplitting cut so deep, in other words, was because it publicized a problem inherent in Congregational salvation theory and practice: that the state of the soul was, finally, unknowable. The need to "knit" the mystery of faith into the charity of "brotherly love" was another way to subsume feminine piety within orthodox community and thereby serve as the condition of the Christian state's emergence. Whether miscarried, monstrous, or natural birth, the future of the reformation is to be read through signs generated by female excess and, just as importantly, its containment.

The hidden mysteries of female spirituality and childbirth alike are thus ripped from her body and exposed, not unlike Anne Bradstreet's poetry, so "all may view." Monstrosity becomes the public sign of mystical piety, the unmistakable revelation of a corruption hidden beneath the inscrutable mask of faith. Unlike a politician like Henry Vane or a minister like John Wheelwright, whose public acts and words were subject to scrutiny and consideration because constitutive of public life and political arrangements more generally, Hutchinson could only be read through a religious logic of inner experience and coerced exposure. To the extent that Winthrop's theory of Christian agency defined the power of the indwelling spirit in relation to a maternal logic of creation, it is little wonder that he later found cause to define Hutchinson's heresy as being a form of miscarried theology, a determination that simply couldn't be applied to male Antinomians like Roger Williams, Henry Vane, John Wheelwright—and John Cotton. Just as Hutchinson's mystical inwardness instanced a visage of female power simultaneously visible and inaccessible, so did the representation of the monstrous births insist on a similar dialectic of private sin and material display. This isn't to say, of course, that these women "intended" these birthing experiences to anchor theology in the experiences of parturition, or even that they understood their religious experiences in terms of their experiences of childbirth. It is rather to observe that Winthrop's and Welde's depictions of the monstrous birth episodes of Hutchinson and Dyer, while intended to justify their harsh treatment at the hands of Bay Colony authority and Congregational orthodoxy alike, unwittingly established a parallax of monstrous birth and pious faith that would go on to found a historiographical tradition of writing about Hutchinson as the progenitor of one of America's most cherished stories of a revolutionary identity premised on religious victimization. Winthrop's handling of the "monstrous" birth, we might say, produced something of an historical afterbirth, a (mal)formation of the City on a Hill we have named "American Puritanism."

FROM ANTINOMIANISM TO ADULTERY

Histories of Anne Hutchinson started to be written before she even left Boston. Some of those early histories became the source material for later incarnations of an American historiographical and literary imagination that remained focused on Anne Hutchinson and the radicalism she represented. Nathaniel Hawthorne's famous Hester Prynne traces the footsteps of the "sainted Ann Hutchinson" as she exits the prison door to stand on the threshold of *The Scarlet Letter*. Later in the novel, we read that Hester "might have come down to us in history, hand in hand with Ann [sic] Hutchinson, as the foundress of a religious sect." It is possible to read these two references together as ironizing the historical source who, as the "foundress" of a new religion, quite naturally "sainted" herself. Such a reading would be in keeping with Hawthorne's other published musing on Hester's possible historical source, "Mrs. Hutchinson," which the younger Hawthorne published in 1830. This sallow entry from Hawthorne's juvenilia aggressively satirizes where it doesn't more simply attack Hutchinson as the historical author of a contemporary "feminine ambition" the young male author had come to resent and envy early in his career.[49] To the extent that Hawthorne's 1850 novel champions the fictional recasting of this seventeenth-century source—and there is rather a lot of debate about this, as Hawthorne scholars well know—we can nonetheless observe that Anne Hutchinson has come to trudge at least two contrary paths in the American literary and historical imaginations.[50] On the one hand, she seems to serve as a feminist-identified provocation and resistance to institutionalized, and male-identified, formations of social and political authority; in this reading, she serves as the origin of what Amy Shrager Lang has called a "logic of dissent" in American social and political thought. On the other, she is a politically empty gesture, neither feminist nor socially activist either in her time or when invoked as historical source. In this reading of Hutchinson, we find not a source for political liberalism so much as one giving voice to a radically undisciplined self tied to an essentialist reading of feminine hysteria. What is intriguing in particular about the "negative"

---

49. Nathaniel Hawthorne, *The Scarlet Letter*, ed. and introd. Leland Person (1850; repr., New York: Norton, 2005), 36, 108, 167.

50. For a recent review of feminist debate about Hawthorne and *The Scarlet Letter* in particular, see Nina Baym, "Revisiting Hawthorne's Feminism," *Nathaniel Hawthorne Review* 30, no. 1 (2004): 32–55.

version of Hutchinson is that much of what this more "secular" critique identifies as problematical is what Winthrop and the ministers found to be so in the seventeenth century. The suspicious reading of Hutchinson is what the secularization narrative finds troubling about its own religious past: namely that religion is irrational, feminine in its performance and, in its commitment to inner experience, opposed to the political life of public rationality that is an important ideal of modern secularism itself, not just in the United States, but in other countries committed to the ascendancy of the secular state. Female piety thus remains a problem on either side of an imagined religious/secular divide.

The contemporary debate about Hester Prynne's feminism thus translates a theological debate about Hutchinson's religious beliefs into a debate about her political meaning: deciding whether or not she is a "feminist" largely repeats the terms of asking whether or not Hutchinson was a legitimate religious pioneer. Hester Prynne's protest against the novel's grim beadles was a distinctly nineteenth-century commentary on female sexual agency, which is to say that Hawthorne transposed seventeenth-century theology into the key of nineteenth-century sexual politics and, in doing so, revived even as he deplored the misogynistic rhetoric of the seventeenth century. Modern critical meditation on Hester Prynne at times also replaces "the religious" with "the feminist" and, in so doing, rewrites what was once a debate about religious righteousness into a frankly political narrative more dear to secularism: the legitimacy of women's agency and voice as a key discourse of the modern. "Most self-identified Hawthorne feminists . . . stress the way Hawthorne inevitably punishes and/or silences unconventional women," Nina Baym observes, thereby identifying a contemporary critical discourse that would apply with equal force to the historical outcome of the Antinomian Controversy: surely a "silencing" of the "unconventional woman" if ever there was one.[51] If it is fair to say that talking about Hester Prynne is like talking about Anne Hutchinson, then the specific terms of that comparative discussion would replace theology with sexuality or, in keeping with the novel's own commitment to shifting signifiers, Antinomianism with Adultery. This isn't to say that nobody today talks about "religion in Hawthorne"; we have plenty of that. We also want to take care not to unduly privilege the "more Protestant" *Scarlet Letter* over, say, the "more Catholic" *Marble Faun*; both texts engage with the

---

51. Ibid., 40.

anti-Catholic discourse of nineteenth-century Protestant America.[52] The more purposive historical setting of *The Scarlet Letter*, to say nothing of its more significant cultural work, invites a closer look at how the backward glance of American secular culture in the nineteenth century furthers our analysis of Puritanism's feminine contours in the colonial period. Indeed, the very terms of our modern approach to the novel's fictional heroine and that character's likely historical source replicates the structure of secularism's relation to its religious past; what "used to be" religious is now understand as modern feminist discourse; what "used to be" religious life is now the life of sexual politics. We now consider the seventeenth-century spirituality that made Anne Hutchinson radical to be the naturally occurring preoccupations of secularist critique: sexuality, female agency, the sovereignty of the body, and the conflict between social and legal tribunals.

My point is that this perspective is, in and of itself, what Talal Asad calls a "formation of the secular," a view that coordinates religious and nonreligious ideas into culture, broadly conceived. Religion becomes a "text" of culture rather than an avenue out of the human into the transcendent. Culture's articulation as such becomes an aspect of meaning production, even as it depends on residual concepts of sacrality as its enabling condition. That religion ("Antinomianism") could mean something else ("Adultery") is a thought possible only in "a secular age," as Charles Taylor might put it. The brilliance of Hawthorne's novel is that he records this relation as the historical setting and content of the plot, which enacts the translation of radical female piety into recognizable acts of modern political and sexual dissent. The novel invites a modern perspective to see how intimately connected our Americanized secularism is to the seventeenth-century radical female piety that gave rise to it.

The transformation of Antinomianism's religious content into the secular political and social content of Hawthorne's America can be seen not merely in *The Scarlet Letter* and its critical afterlife, but in the national historiography of the Antinomian crisis itself. American historiography's embrace of Hutchinson replays the religious anxieties of Antinomianism as if they are the postreligious political concerns that dominate the nation's historiography more generally. It is a remarkable because largely unremarked fact of the Antinomian Controversy that nearly every history of the United

---

52. See Jenny Franchot, *Roads to Rome: The Antebellum Protestant Encounter with Catholicism* (Berkeley: University of California Press, 1994), 260–69; 350–58.

States at least mentions the incident, and most discuss it and Hutchinson in some detail. As early as 1644, in the first transnational history of the recently concluded strife, John Winthrop's and Thomas Welde's *A Short Story of the Rise, Reign, and Ruine of the Antinomians, Familists, and Libertines* (1644), the crisis begins to take on the aspect of founding national trauma:

> And when our Common-wealth began to be founded, and our Churches sweetely settled in Peace . . . Lest we should, now, grow secure, our wise God (who seldome suffers his owne, in this their weary-some Pilgrimage to be long without trouble) sent a new storme after us, which proved the sorest tryall that ever befell us since we left our Native soyle. (AC, "Short," 201)

The passage notes the exceptional success and suffering enjoyed by the chosen: an infamous theology of election and abandonment that would soon enough become a colonial and national aesthetic. Roughly thirty-five years later, William Hubbard's *Chronological History of New England in the Form of Annals to 1680* would similarly suppose Anne Hutchinson "to be the occasion of all the formentioned commotions in the colony of Massachusetts" that had, prior to her fomentings, been a place of the Lord's beauty and of a new Primitive Church.[53] By 1680, of course, following the Pequot War and other conflicts with indigenous peoples, there was more of a story to tell, especially given the recently concluded war with Massasoit ("King Philip"), yet Hubbard's framing comment impresses commotion and colony onto the abstraction ("occasion") which Hutchinson had by this point become.[54] With the publication of the *Magnalia Christi Americana* in 1702, Cotton Mather extended this seventeenth-century, triumphalist, and originary trauma-narrative of Hutchinson's rise and ruin into the eighteenth century as well. That history infamously records the slaying of Hutchinson as the Hydra, and cattily sponsors woman in general as the sower of all discord and sectarianism: *"Dux femina factae."*[55] For Mather, as we have seen, radical female piety anchors his understanding of Puritanism's historical afterlife.

---

53. Hubbard, *History of New England*, 283, 280.
54. For a discussion of Hubbard's ambiguous place in mid-seventeenth-century historiography, see Dennis Perry, "'Novelties and Stile Which All Out-Do': William Hubbard's Historiography Reconsidered," *Early American Literature* 29, no. 2 (1994): 166–82. Perry also finds Hubbard to be a harsh critic of Hutchinson and even of Winthrop's "moderationism" (175).
55. Mather, *Magnalia*, 517.

Eighteenth-century historians and divines continued to cite the significance of the Antinomian Controversy and Anne Hutchinson to the history of colonial New England. William Douglass's *Summary, Historical and Political, of the British Settlements in North America* (1749) implicitly registers the importance of the crisis not merely to the founding of Rhode Island but to the founding of a surprisingly recognizable mythology of religious tolerance: "Banished from [Massachusetts], because of dissenting from the generally received Way of religious Worship; these Emigrants were Puritans of Puritans, and by Degrees refined so much that all their Religion was almost vanished, afterwards it became a Receptacle of any People without Regard to Religion of social Worship."[56] Puritan radicalism in the seventeenth century becomes an indifferent secularism in the eighteenth. Established early by Roger Williams in Providence, the open-door policy of Rhode Island would later—as the next chapter's discussion of the Quaker invasion suggests—become a key rhetoric of dissenting American Protestant, sectional, and liberal historiography. In *A Summary History of New-England* (1799), post-Revolutionary historian Hannah Adams makes this connection between Antinomian exile and United States religious identity even more explicit, repeatedly noting the "intolerance" of Massachusetts while describing the founding of Rhode Island in terms entirely consistent with the story of America's revolutionary destiny, a narrative increasingly central to early republic and national understandings of American liberal democratic self-invention: "The exiles from Massachusetts found a comfortable asylum in that country, and soon effected a settlement. They formed themselves into a body politic, and entered into a voluntary association for government."[57] Rhode Island, the haven of schismatic error, serves as the political history of the new secular nation.

Not merely in colonial but in postnational American historiography does the Antinomian crisis work as an organizing principle of American

---

56. William Douglass, *Summary, Historical and Political, of the British Settlements in North America* (Boston: Rogers and Fowle, 1749; repr., New York: Arno, 1972), 76.

57. Hannah Adams, *A Summary History of New England* (Boston, 1799), 53, 61. Michael Vella discusses Adams's depiction of Hutchinson and the controversy as a kind of translation of religious dispute into ideological debate between early national Republicans (spiritists) and Federalists (Congregationalists): "Any discussion of religious dissension in the colonies, especially that of the Antinomians and the Quakers, was important because it provoked ideological tropisms that enunciated contemporary differences between theological parties as well as Federalists and Republicans." See Vella, "Theology, Genre, and Gender: The Precarious Place of Hannah Adams in American Literary History," *Early American Literature* 28, no. 1 (1993): 30.

political and historical development. No less a celebrated historian than George Bancroft credits Hutchinson with the colonial invention of democratic institutions first theorized by Descartes, "who did but promulgate, under the philosophic form of free reflection, the same truth which Anne Hutchinson, with the fanaticism of impassioned conviction, avowed under the form of inward reflections." For Bancroft, Hutchinson represents a "natural consequence" of the reformation, whose privileging of free conscience perforce imagined the Anglo-American nineteenth century's triumphalist narrative of democratic institution-making. "The true tendency of the principles of Anne Hutchinson," continues Bancroft, "is best established by examining the institutions which were founded by her followers," among them Henry Vane, but also the founders of Rhode Island, who for Bancroft emerge as the true signatories of the wilderness compact enshrined in American nationalist mythology. The Rhode Island constitution established by these "voluntary exiles" installed "Democracie, or popular government" alongside "liberty of conscience" to produce a "little community held together by the bonds of affection and freedom of opinion."[58] In Bancroft's rewriting of Winthrop's "Modell of Christian Charity," Anne Hutchinson gives birth to a leveling populism, a sentiment which, although celebrated in the heyday of nineteenth-century political liberalism, was of course denounced at the time as one of if not *the* most dangerous "offsprings" of her dangerous errors: "These Opinions being thus spread, and growne to their full ripenesse and latitude, through the nimbleness and activity of their fomenters, began now to lift up their heads full high, to stare us in the face, and to confront all that opposed them" (AC, "Short," 208). The point here is not to settle once and for all whether Anne Hutchinson was or was not a "protodemocrat" (or feminist, or even human rights crusader). Rather we are seeing how American historians have positioned her relation to the emergence of a key narrative—the story of victimized religious freedom—told and retold in the historiography of American secular nationalism.

From the magisterial multivolume works of great nineteenth-century nationalist historians like Bancroft and Charles Francis Adams, to Nathaniel Hawthorne's posthumously published cheeky history for children (*Grandfather's Chair*, 1904), the episode occupies center stage

---

58. George Bancroft, *History of the Colonization of the United States*, vol. 1 (Boston: Little, Brown, 1844), 391–93.

in the ongoing attempt to understand the origins and, according to mid-nineteenth-century historian John Palfrey, the "influences exerted by the people of New England on the fortunes of the nation of which it now makes a part."[59] Far from occupying an exclusively dissenting position in American intellectual history, Hutchinson and Antinomianism have functioned as a key indication of uniquely American and often contradictory tendencies within broadly progressive readings of national development. This three-hundred-year historical preoccupation with the theological hairsplitting of seventeenth-century radical Protestantism has not confined itself to the writing of national histories. Local histories of New England, Massachusetts, and, as one might expect, Rhode Island, devote considerable attention to the crisis. Religious and denominational historiography have since 1642 been debating the theological merits and shortcomings of the "Antinomian heresy," arguing for and against the "truth" of Hutchinson's religiosity within the framework of the Protestant reformation. More recently, as we have seen, feminist historians and critics have read Hutchinson and her experiences as a watershed moment in American women's history. The controversy has featured prominently in literary histories of the United States, and in cultural studies of colonial New England. Given the diversity of approaches, it would be inadvisable, if not altogether impossible, to characterize a single attitude toward Hutchinson and the crisis taken up by historians and critics over the years. How Hutchinson and other women who came after her managed to vanish either into the exemplarity of their imitable piety or the offensiveness of their radical *extremis* will remain of interest to us over the course of this book. The spiritual life she appears to have led, and which we know she defended to the last, has played a powerful and ongoing role in the emergence not only of the historical institutions of seventeenth-century Congregational practices, but in the national if not nationalist narratives of America.

As with Roger Williams, whose refusal to grant colonial civil actions divine sanction led to his removal to (and founding of) the state of religious multiplicity known as Providence, Rhode Island, Hutchinson has come to stand at the head of a tradition of religious independence, if not a tradition of American dissenting liberty more generally. One late-nineteenth-century popular history, Samuel Drake's *A Book of New England Legends and Folklore* (1883), prefaces its entry on Hutchinson by invoking, with

---

59. John Palfrey, *History of New England*, vol. 1 (Boston: Little, Brown, 1859), xi.

others, the language of maternity to describe the development of the colonies; Drake observes that "New England was the child of a superstitious mother," before going on to attack the Bay Colony's leaders for condemning Hutchinson.[60] After defending her theology, praising her public demeanor, and castigating "the mockery of a trial, in which the judges expounded theology instead of law, and in which no rule of evidence was respected," the history concludes that "to succeeding generations she is an amazing example of the intolerance of the day."[61] Many histories sound the clarion call of religious persecution in similar fashion. Williston Walker's *A History of Congregational Churches in the United States* connects the "spirit of persecution" evidenced in the trial of Anne Hutchinson to the "far more violent forms" of intolerance the Bay Colony authorities would visit upon Baptists and Quakers.[62] Even defenses of the Bay Colony authorities on the grounds of political expediency could invoke the language of religious persecution: for this reason, John Fiske concedes that Hutchinson's treatment was an "odious act of persecution."[63] Still others insist wholeheartedly on the intolerant bigotry of Winthrop and the other authority figures. Vernon Parrington refers to the "admirable courage of Mistress Hutchinson," and suggests that "New England democracy owes no debt to her godly magistrates." Far from it: "From Connecticut and Rhode Island, it must be recalled, rather than from the Bay Colony, came those democratic principles and institutions that were to spread widely in later years and create the New England that after generations have like to remember."[64] In *The Emancipation of Massachusetts*, Brooks Adams tells the story of the state's emergence and eventual liberation from a "theocracy." This progressive narrative of growing religious toleration and political liberalism begins with Anne Hutchinson, whose fate, according to Adams, "make a fit ending to this sad tale of oppression and wrong."[65]

---

60. Samuel Adams Drake, *A Book of New England Legends and Folklore* (Boston, 1883; repr., Boston: Little, Brown, 1901), vi.

61. Ibid., 21–22.

62. Williston Walker, *A History of Congregational Churches in the United States* (Boston, 1894), 147.

63. John Fiske, *The Beginnings of New England, or the Puritan Theocracy in Its Relations to Civil and Religious Liberty* (1889; repr., Boston, 1898), 129.

64. Vernon Parrington, *Main Currents in American Thought: An Interpretation of American Literature from the Beginnings to 1920* (New York: Harcourt Brace, 1927), I: 50, 53.

65. Brooks Adams, *The Emancipation of Massachusetts* (Boston: Houghton Mifflin, 1887), 235.

At stake in the historiographical rescue of Anne Hutchinson from her contemporary and even latter-day persecutors is, among other things, secular America's mythological fantasia of the origins and the righteousness of religious freedom, a fantasia the nation has not been shy about making available to other countries. Early-twentieth-century historian James Truslow Adams argues in the preface to his influential *The Founding of New England* that early religious dissent was a crucial factor in the emergence of all varieties of uniquely U.S. liberties: his work "has also endeavored to exhibit the workings of the theocracy, and to show how, in the period treated, the domestic struggle against the tyranny exercised by the theocratic party." The appearance of Anne Hutchinson, and the description of her hopeless protest, achieves nearly mythic dimension in this treatment, "as it was evident now that no voice could be raised in criticism of any acts of the civil ecclesiastical authorities, and that the words and lives of the ten thousand or more inhabitants of Massachusetts had come wholly under the control of their rulers." Recovering religious dissent from its corrupt persecution, Adams implies an account of the origin of religious freedom not in the orthodox narrative of the "Bay Colony fathers" and their perspicacious exercise of moderate political authority in the early years of the colony-nation. Rather, we hear "America" in the suppressed voice of inspirited righteousness and belief. "The voices that had pleaded for religious toleration, for civil liberty, and the religion of love, were silenced."[66] The "true" voice of America belongs to the martyred woman, whose tragic "disappearance" from history lodged that lonely voice of belief at the heart of a culture that would eventually produce the Bill of Rights and its self-evident truths. The revolutionary origins of American life are to be found in the inspired dissent of precisely those troublemakers deemed "heretics" by authority. Little wonder that such a narrative would install itself, in both political and religious domains, at the heart of early national projects of American myth-making. "Thus," writes George Bancroft in the *History of the United States*, "was Rhode Island the offspring of Massachusetts."[67] The (il)logic of maternity that we have seen in Bradstreet and in negative accounts of Hutchinson's "monstrous" opinionating appears in the romantic historian's sympathetic rescuing of Antinomianism from the

---

66. James Truslow Adams, *The Founding of New England* (Boston: Atlantic Monthly, 1922), x, 174, 171.
67. Bancroft, *United States*, 381.

trash of religious radicalism. The secular fantasy of religious toleration as the product of reason's progress or religion's surcease fails to account for the persistent association of radical Protestantism with this fundamental account of American revolutionary origins.

At the same time that a Hutchinson-identified Antinomianism serves as a convenient origin for narratives of American national identity, it also serves as a fixed point of America's realization as ideological necessity. That is, the "gift" of Hutchinson's dissent and suppression is the self-evident legacy of the freedom to dissent and to be free from state suppression. We enjoy this legacy today and understand it as a truth of American national identity even if we don't know anything about the history of Antinomianism or Anne Hutchinson. Understood today as a kind of righteously self-realized and enacted performance of "freedom," religious radicalism continues to define a uniquely American identity that continues to criticize an American nation that has deviated from its "true" course or origin. Hutchinson's spiritual independence underwrites both versions, serving either as an identifiable historical tradition of uncontainable religious power from which the state sought to distance itself, or as a fixed idea of radical spirit causing a revolution that will remain unfinished until the arrival of the eschaton itself.

We might therefore read Hester Prynne's refusal to disclose the identity of her co-adulterer as a position made possible by Anne Hutchinson's defense of her own spiritual inviolability. The potential for an independent and still dangerous feminist politics to become one of the most representative stories of nineteenth-century America (and beyond) makes sense when we view the translation of radical spirit into radical politics as a continuous rather than discontinuous narrative of American secularism. A profoundly religious idea like spiritual inviolability comes to imply emergent notions of personal sovereignty, natural rights, and self-ownership, all key elements of an American modernity manufactured in relation to a humanly rather than divinely centered account of the world. What we have come to identify as the secular discourse of American Puritanism depended on a female-identified spiritist piety residing at its core. As we shall in subsequent chapters, neither Hutchinson nor her historical descendants were content to reside there quietly.

TWO

The Quakers' New England Bodies

THE BROAD THEOLOGICAL DEBATES of the Antinomian Controversy are familiar to students of colonial New England. When we approach some of the specific charges brought against Hutchinson during the civil examination and the church trials, however, the picture blurs somewhat. Between the remoteness and the complexity of seventeenth-century scholastic rhetoric and theology, we might be forgiven for wondering, along with John Winthrop, just what all the fuss was really about.[1] Additionally, other aspects of the controversy have seemed more pressing to many scholars, who have produced a trove of studies rich with insights into the social and political meaning of the controversy and its impact on New England's and America's histories more generally. Whether or not this interest elsewhere than religion is another sign of the secular, the Antinomian Controversy's elusive theological quandary is still worth pursuing precisely because the theology of Antinomian spirituality became a suppressed and abiding trace within the construct of American Puritanism. Both a radical piety voiced in feminized spiritual language and its assiduous management by a male-identified civil and clerical authority established a dominant historiographical tradition that ultimately issued key narratives of American dissenting and national identity. This chapter tells the next segment of this story.

---

1. In his diary Winthrop noted, "no man could tell (except some few, who knew the bottom of the matter) where any difference was." See Winthrop, *Journal of John Winthrop*, 208.

In colonial Boston, some of the immediate successors to Anne Hutchinson arrived as immigrants and departed as martyrs, thereby forwarding a hermeneutic of embattled Protestant spirituality into the latter half of the seventeenth century. These successors were members of the Society of Friends, otherwise known as Quakers, who believed themselves compelled by God to take his received Truth from England to the plantations of the New World. Like Anne Hutchinson before them, these early Quakers rejected even the mildest ecclesiastical arrangements of the reformation, claiming instead to experience God through direct revelation and personal witness. The liturgical emptiness of Quakerism made each of them a vernacular theologian—even, on occasion, implying that their personal revelations transcended the authority of Scripture itself. Their theology of personal immediacy and revelation recalls what Catherine Smith has called the "ancient language" of mysticism. Christian mysticism, of course, has a long history, arguably beginning with Christ's experiences in the wilderness, and later associated with the famous medieval and female mystics Julian of Norwich and Marjory Kempe in England, Christine de Pisan, and Catherine of Siena in Europe. While seventeenth-century Quakers did not directly cite their medieval predecessors—as dedicated antischolastics they hardly cited anyone—their performed religion had much in common with historical Christian mysticism, including the importance of prophecy, the agency of religious speech, and the pre-eminence of women in their community. "During the English revolution," as Christina Berg and Philippa Berry put it, "the prophetic medium afforded several women a vehicle for imaginative self-expression which was considerably less restricted than those media of verse and prose formerly available to them." In its recollection of this extra-ecclesiastical, primitivistic, and feminized spirituality, early Quakerism offered not only old but "ancient" spirituality as corrective to the theological failures of the reformation. Curiously, this backward glance ended up looking ahead to an epicene all too comfortable with claiming such radical and gendered spirituality as its rejected other.[2]

The experiential life of faith reported by the Quakers and punished by the Puritans together produced a history of spiritual vitality and suffering

---

2. Catherine Smith, "Jane Lead: the Feminist Mind and Art of a Seventeenth-Century Protestant Mystic," in *Women of Spirit: Female Leadership in the Jewish and Christian Traditions*, ed. Rosemary Ruether and Eleanor McLaughlin (New York: Simon and Schuster, 1979), 200; Christine Berg and Philippa Berry, "'Spiritual Whoredom': An Essay on Female Prophets in the Seventeenth Century," in *1642: Literature and Power in the Seventeenth Century*, ed. Francis Barker (Essex: University of Essex, 1981).

ultimately claimed within the history of secularism. This chapter continues our discussion of female piety's contribution to the construction of American Puritanism through a reading of the so-called Quaker Invasion of New England that took place in the late 1650s. The unapologetic and aggressive evangelism of the Quakers provoked state-identified penal responses from New English political and religious authorities.[3] Although banishment and excommunication were harsh penalties for Anne Hutchinson to pay for merely questioning aspects of ministerial authority, they pale in comparison to the Puritan treatment of visiting and local Quakers. In serving as the site of both devotion and discipline, the Quaker's body sponsored a theology and politics of suspicious embodiment, precisely the monstrous birth Hutchinson's contemporaries had feared and painstakingly elaborated as deviant some two decades prior. As was the case with Hutchinson, ideas about gender informed this midcentury theological and political conflict, leading to a construal of early modern personhood defined simultaneously by divine inspiration and state-sponsored victimization. The punished body of the Quakers ironically furthered the idea of the state's own "sacred" differentiation from religion, a differentiation that took the form of the state claiming the authority to punish religious dissidence through formally adopted statute.[4]

In the punished body of belief, religious faith found its limit. Our analysis considers how the judicially sanctioned assault on the dissident religious body provided new ways for nonreligious ideas of selfhood to express themselves through religious experiences. Whether seized by the violence of the spirit or the violence of the courts, the Quaker's body came to signal a configuration of modern personhood. Driven to a condition of human

---

3. This chapter focuses on the Quaker experiences in Boston and Rhode Island, which were the primary colonial centers of Quaker agitation in the 1650s. For more comprehensive discussion of the Quaker presence in New England, see Arthur J. Worrall, *Quakers in the Colonial Northeast* (Boston: University Press of New England, 1980), chapter 1; Rufus Jones, *The Quakers in the American Colonies* (New York: Norton, 1966); and Frederick Tolles, *Quakers in the Atlantic Colonies* (New York: Macmillan, 1960). For a recent literary approach, see James Emmett Ryan, *Imaginary Friends: Representing Quakers in American Culture* (Madison: University of Wisconsin Press, 2009).

4. Nan Goodman similarly argues that "the story of the Quaker presence in the Massachusetts Bay Colony is largely of Puritan lawmaking and of the Quakers' legal protest against it, all of which emanated from the many efforts that were made to banish them." Where Goodman argues that the New England Quakers were ultimately more interested in "community formation and . . . legal membership," this chapter stresses how the theology of Quakerism fundamentally informed both early Quakerism and the state's attempted management of it. See Goodman, *Banished*, 91, 88.

extremis by the inhumanity of their Puritan tormentors, the Quakers wrote narratives of affliction that supplied a vocabulary of human suffering that could not be contained within their own spiritual hermeneutic. An insufficient religious epistemology thereby produced a recognizable language of the "human" coterminous with American secularism's most ambitious moral and political project: the elaboration of natural and eventually "human rights" whose integrity and universal applicability derived from an essentially religious set of commitments. This isn't to say that the state's legal rendition and discipline of its religious foes somehow subsumed actual Quakers into a reconfigured body-politic. Rather, the imprisonment, corporal punishment, banishment, and execution of the Quakers enabled the idea of the state to consolidate itself in relation to an embodied religion's abasement. In certain familiar narratives of modernity, this is the ontology of secularism.

SPIRITUALIZING THE PROFANE

Religious scholars in many traditions have debated what it means to call religious faith "experiential." Experiential religion, as Christopher Hill among others has found, was a significant feature of the Protestant religious enterprises collectively identified as the radical reformation of seventeenth-century England.[5] Robert Sharf has recently argued that, historically speaking, "The characteristics of immediacy and indubitability galvanized the 'hermeneutic of experience.'" This hermeneutic "promised to ground the meaning of religious texts and performances through an appeal to the experiences to which they refer."[6] The experientialism of Hutchinson and the early Quakers was consistent with aspects of what would become an important component of New England's religious culture.[7] Given Hutchinson's commentary on the experiential immediacy

---

5. Christopher Hill, *The World Turned Upside Down: Radical Ideas During the English Revolution* (New York: Viking, 1972), 366.

6. Robert Sharf, "Experience," in *Critical Terms for Religious Studies*, ed. Mark C. Taylor (Chicago: University of Chicago Press, 1998), 104.

7. Andrew Delbanco, *The Puritan Ordeal* (Cambridge, MA: Harvard University Press, 1989), 41–80. Andrea Knutson argues that the principle of "indwelling" grace "gave rise to an experiential piety that was not viewed as separate from biblical religion but was one and the same." See Knutson, *American Spaces of Conversion: The Conductive Imaginaries of Edwards, Emerson, and James* (New York: Oxford University Press, 2010), 5. Understandably, critics and historians have suggested that Anne Hutchinson would have been at home with the Quakers.

of the convert's resurrection, moreover, we might directly link her theology to the Quaker doctrine of the inner light and the need, further, for the individual to experience the soul's rebirth into Christ.[8] Whether or not Hutchinson was a "pre-Quaker" is beside the more important point that she shared with Quakers theological tendencies that defined religious authenticity in terms of the personalized realization of divine spirit. During the 1650s and '60s, this theology of inwardly realized and embodied spiritual meaning came to be tied to ideas about the feminine, thereby continuing the trajectory of female piety's centrality to Puritan culture initially established in the Antinomian Controversy.

While the Quakers may have been very interested in publicity, they weren't in it for the sake of aligning their religious beliefs with even a nominal concept of the state. Their commitment to realizing a radically personal theology would appear in seventeenth-century colonial New England as an itinerant transatlantic spiritual activism that promised universal spiritual regeneration by faith and experience alone. In 1659 George Fox provided this account of what became the Quaker concept of the inner light:

> First the Lord brought us by his power, and wisdome, and the word by which all things are made to know and understand, and see perfectly that God had given to us, everie one of us in particular, a Light from himselfe shining in our harts & consciences, which Light, Christ his Son, the Saviour, of the world had lighted every man, and all mankind withall; which Light in us we found sufficient to reprove us, and convince us of every evil deed, word, and thought, and by it, in us, we come to know good from evil . . . and also by the Light in us, we perfectlie came to know the way of restauration, and the meanes to be restored, these things to us were

---

See, e.g., Norman Petit, *The Heart Prepared: Grace and Conversion in Spiritual Life* (New Haven, CT: Yale University Press, 1966), 155; and Philip Gura, *A Glimpse of Sion's Glory*, 61–63. Quaker historians and hagiographers routinely associated Hutchinson with the Friends; see, e.g., Hugh Barbour, *The Quakers in Puritan England* (1964; repr., London: Friends United Press, 1985), 132.

8. Perry Miller makes the connection explicit in *Errand into the Wilderness*: "From the theory that a regenerate soul receives an influx of divine spirit, and is joined to God by a direct infusion of His grace, we might deduce the possibility of receiving all instruction immediately from the indwelling spirit, through an inward communication which is essentially mystical. Such was exactly the deduction of Mistress Anne Hutchinson, for which she was expelled to Rhode Island. It was exactly the conclusion of the Quakers, who added that every man naturally susceptible to this inward communication" (190).

revealed by the Light within us, which Christ had given us, and lightened us withall, what man was before transgression.[9]

The early modern soul is a dark interior in need of divine illumination. Here, the light is direct revelation itself: the divine disclosure of the "true" nature of the creation and with it the ability properly to understand the role of the Created in God's ordering of the universe. Quakers relied on light not only as the primary metaphor of universal regeneration, but as the primary metaphor for all forms of genuine spiritual knowledge. God's bestowal of an inner light also permits, through its regenerative power, the soul to be convinced of its actual commission of sin. With that "convincement," as the Quakers put it, the convert would know the nature of good and evil more generally. Conversion is the basis of all real knowledge, and is furthermore available to every created person through the presence of the Light in all of us. To the idea of spiritual election they shared with the Dissenting traditions of English Protestantism, the Quakers added the principle of a universal salvation. As such, they rejected the doctrine of limited atonement promoted so strenuously by New England's ministerial and political leadership, even as they asserted the exceptional status conferred on those heeding the inner light. The possibility of universal salvation, it is worth noting, was a theological "innovation" Protestant theologians debated actively in the seventeenth and eighteenth centuries and still debate today, but which both religious and secular thinkers—Emerson's transcendentalism is one such example—identified as an important part of the continuing appeal of Christianity in an otherwise secularizing world.[10] In their privileging of exclusive and total divine sovereignty, early Quakers nonetheless implied a limit to all worldly authority, as for example when Anne Gilman describes the light as that "secret witness of God, which reproves thee secretly when no mortal eye seeth."[11] By observing a standard Christian distinction between revelation and mystery, Gilman also provides a notional separation of public and private forms of experience that state-identified religion

---

9. George Fox, *The Great Mystery of the Great Whore Unfolded: and AntiChrist's Kingdom Revealed unto Destruction* . . . (London: Thomas Simmons, 1659), preface.

10. Peter Field suggests that Emerson had a "spiritual affinity" with the Quakers and believed that the idea of the "Inner Light" secured the universalist ambition of his own democratic metaphysics. See Field, *Ralph Waldo Emerson: The Making of a Democratic Intellectual* (Lanham, MD: Rowman & Littlefield, 2002), 113–14.

11. Anne Gilman, *Epistle to Friends* . . . (London, 1662), 8.

sought to align. Of course, an "election" both special and universal—one unique to Americans but available for the world—anticipates an extant ideology of American national mythology familiar to us today.

As spiritist theologians, seventeenth-century Quakers, as they came to be known at first pejoratively and later more positively, rejected even the highly abstemious sacerdotalism of Low Church Puritans and the New England Congregationalists.[12] Friends waited to be moved by extraworldly spirit to worldly action, and they did so without the assistance of ordinance. In their commitment to the idea of *sola scriptura*, they were not antitext or more generally antirepresentational so much as they lived for and according to a testimony *lived within*, the word and spirit of God as personally experienced, communicated with other Quakers, and read in accordance with a hermeneutic at least loosely defined by scripture. Individual Quaker spirituality achieved a kind of communal materiality in the discursive network of correspondence that structured seventeenth-century Quaker witness. By broadcasting the light beyond themselves and into the world, such witness manifested a form of individualized, and yet still public and even collective, spiritual agency.

And move them the spirit did, as virtually every seventeenth-century Quaker who wrote of his or her spiritual experience testified. Robert Fowler, the ship captain who transported the largest contingent of the "Quaker Invasion" to New England, described his motivation to carry these missionaries this way: "The power of the Lord fell much upon us, *and an irresistible word came unto us*, that the seed in American [sic] shall be like the sands in the sea. It was published in the ears of the brethren, which caused tears to break forth in the fullness of joy."[13] Ann Audland recounts that in 1654 "the next day being the first day of the week, we went to a meeting which we heard of in the Towne; and when the meeting ended, *we were moved* to the Steeple-House, to speak the word of the Lord to Priest and People; and in obedience to the Lord, we went" (italics added). A few years later, Dorothy White would testify:

---

12. Quakers both objected to and carefully cultivated the use of the term "Quaker" in the 1650s and 1660s, as Kate Peters shows in *Print Culture and the Early Quakers* (New York: Cambridge University Press, 2005), 91–123. For a still durable and succinct discussion of Quaker theology in the context of radical English Protestantism, see Christopher Hill, *The World Turned Upside Down*, 231–58.

13. Robert Fowler, *A True Relation of the Voyage Undertaken by Me, Robert Fowler*, September 1657, Swarthmore Collection, Friends House Library, London, 2.

And again on the eight day of the same month as I was waiting upon the Lord with his people, the Word of the Lord came to me, and it stuck close in me, about the space of two hours, saying, I will overturn, I will overturn the powers of the earth; and the word of the Lord came to me, saying, write again once more to them that are sitting in Counsel, to Judges and Rulers.

Joan Vokins, a missionary of the Society of Friends who travelled extensively in New England and the Caribbean, consistently portrayed herself as the reluctant witness repeatedly moved by the spirit to testify for the truth: "but the *overcoming Power* of the true and living God wrought so strongly with me, that *I was made willing* to take up the Cross, and follow Jesus through many Tribulations, and he (magnified be his Power) most wonderfully supported and conducted me all along."[14] The irresistibility of grace led to its publication in the world. Quakers happily took up their place in the objective position of a divine grammar of obedience, and their representational agency assumed what Nancy Ruttenburg has called a rhetoric of "humble self-enlargement."[15]

Quakers developed an identifiable vernacular style. As radical dissenters from established episcopacy, they extemporized their own liturgical scripts with material borrowed from Scripture (David's dream, for example), Protestant conversion narrative, medieval mystic writing, and the spiritual testimonies (both spoken and written) of other Quakers, especially their leader, George Fox. They conceived of their conversion as a "convincement," the persuasive overcoming of a reluctance born of sin to accept the direction of the Spirit, and they published the power of the Spirit over the world and its inhabitants. In their letters, the "Children of the Light," as they often styled themselves, emphasized such familiar motifs of Protestant conversion discourse as a sense of personal sinfulness, the deadening or hardening of heart, the kindled desire for salvation, feelings of hope following such a quickening, and a desire to experience God's perfect beauty and love. Quaker witnesses more particularly emphasized

---

14. Anne Audland, *A True Declaration of the Suffering of the Innocent* (London, 1654), 1; Dorothy White, *Counsellors Counsel; A Warning from the Lord* (London: Thomas Simmons, 1659), 2; Joan Vokins, *God's Mighty Power Magnified: As Revealed in His Faithful Handmaid Joan Vokins* (London: Thomas Northcott, 1691), 38.

15. Nancy Ruttenburg, *Democratic Personality: Popular Voice and the Trial of American Authorship* (Stanford, CA: Stanford University Press, 1998), 115–19. For a discussion of Quakerism's print aggression, see Kate Peters, *Print Culture and the Early Quakers*, 15–43.

and shared the experience of what they called "a new birth," a momentous and discernible spiritual natality of the adult soul's regeneration within the light emanating from an inwardly realized spirit. From this second "inspiriting," as Lydia Fairman would put it in a letter dated in 1656, "you wait and feel the power dwell with it, that you may witness its workings in you, to the destroying of the power of sin."[16] Individual Quakers modeled this structure of witness to themselves and conveyed such elocutionary ambition to each other. One could enumerate this formula in the extent writings of seventeenth-century Quakers of both genders. In their projection of spirit outward, Quakers published their experiences of "that Light of God" in places other than the circumscribed precincts of church, ordinance, and episcopacy.[17]

Quite deliberately, they published sacred text in profane space, and they did so in order to extend holiness into the fallen world. In a 1656 letter to Margaret Fell—one of the earliest archived letters describing the Quaker mission in the New World—Henry Fell reports: "Some there are, as I hear, convinced who meet in silence at a place called Salem. Oh truly great is the desire of my soule towards them and the love that flows out after them daily, for I see in the Eternal Light the Lord hath a great worke to do in that nation."[18] In the marketplaces, on the pillories, in letters to royalty, on the outskirts of towns and cities, Quakers transmitted their light-filled message, hoping their writing would be "hasteninge a place for the Redemption of it from under Bondage."[19] In appearing to deny distinctions between sacred and profane, Quakers advanced the more radical proposition that the entire world and all of its inhabitants could be saved. The evangelical ambitions of these early friends were thus global and universal in scope, anticipating the important role that missionary Christianity would come to play in European expansion and empire-building in the eighteenth and nineteenth centuries. The millennial dream of universal conversion extends into contemporary global discourses of religious "fundamentalism" whose relation to secularism has come into question. Fundamental to a revised critique of secularism is a respect for religious

---

16. Lydia Fairman, *A Few Lines and True Testimony* (London: Thomas Simmons, 1659), 1.
17. Margaret Fell to Charles II, 1660, Spence Collection, Friends House Library, London, 3/94.
18. Henry Fell to Margaret Fell, 1656, Swarthmore Collection, Friends House Library, London, 1/66.
19. Ibid., 1/69.

agency that not only is both universal and universalizable but more crucially can be practiced in relation to religious positions that are extreme and threatening to secularism's political and cultural arrangements. Toleration, to put the matter differently, only possesses meaning in relation to its ability to accommodate what might in another analysis be considered intolerable. Today's global secular is constituted by a discourse of "tolerance" that still attempts to place reasonable limits on acceptable and unacceptable forms of religion and religiously motivated behavior. This ambivalence can also be located within the experiences of seventeenth-century Quakers. Although they believed their own spiritual activism to be part of God's plan for a universal salvation for a darkened world, they also insisted that the same God who licensed their efforts also placed limits on their acceptability. Secularism's "faith" in its own powers of accurate discernment, if we can put it that way, found a premodern articulation in the committed religious agency of the Quakers.[20]

Motivated by their inwardly realized experience of the "Light," Quakers "published" mystically apprehended truths as a public spirituality across the early modern Atlantic world. Their evangelical and epistolary homiletics were transcripts of mystical self-extension that staged Quaker faith as a transatlantic missionary drama. Such "publication events," to borrow a term from Matt Cohen, brought inwardly realized religion into dialogue with the public worlds of Restoration politics and transatlantic colonialism.[21] "Moved of the lord," begins Margaret Fell in one of nineteen surviving letters she wrote to Charles II in the latter half of 1660, "by the eternall spirit of life to speak to that in thy conscience which is eternal," Fell assumes that the "light" which moves her to write is the same light shining within the King's conscience as he reads her letter.[22] The power of God does not merely transcend the worldly exigencies of space, political identity, class, or gender but, more significantly, anchors these worldly effects in a knowable sacred authority. What the King "knows" is what Fell herself "knows," and both forms of worldly knowing emanate from the

---

20. Charles Taylor, "Why We Need a Radical Redefinition of Secularism," in *The Power of Religion in the Public Sphere*, ed. Eduardo Mendieta and Jonathan Vanantwerpen (New York: Columbia University Press, 2011), 56 and 35. For broad treatment of "political theology" and global secularism, see Mark Lilla, *The Stillborn God: Religion, Politics and the Modern West* (New York: Knopf, 2007). On toleration as a response to pain, see Lars Tonder, *Tolerance: A Sensorial Orientation to Politics* (New York: Oxford University Press, 2013).
21. Matt Cohen, *The Networked Wilderness*.
22. Margaret Fell to Charles II, Spence Collection, Friends House Library, London, 3/93.

same eternal power of the Spirit. Although separated from each other by both time and space, Quakers imagined a simultaneity of experience made possible through their individual encounters with a collectively knowable God. Whether petitioning the newly crowned King to make good on an earlier promise of tolerance, or writing to Friends stationed in Barbados or imprisoned in New England, the spiritual community of early Quakerism imagined a collapse of both time and distance—a shortening of the way, as it were—in the reception and broadcast of the Truth. The universal Light from within would make a wide world intimately knowable, thereby serving as a newer language of modern "discovery" intimately tied to a language of dissent in the pre-Revolutionary Atlantic. Although the Quaker "light" was primarily mystical in its origin, it also anticipated the emergence of "light" as a keyword of the coming Enlightenment.[23]

One of the original itinerant ministries of the colonial Atlantic world, Quakerism linked England, New England, Northern Africa, and the Caribbean in a circumatlantic network of divinely shared inspiration. Frederick Tolles described the geographical zone of Quaker activity as "the enormous area bordering the North Atlantic basin. The culture we are dealing with therefore is the culture of the 'Atlantic Community.'" The "calling" was, in fact, incomplete without the convert's conveyance of the message to others, and there appear to have been few geographical limits for the "Children of the Light," many of whom believed that their effectual calling to preach and to travel were intimately connected to global eschatology. The urgency of the individual's own calling translated into an urgency to communicate that message to others. George Fox explicitly directed his followers to carry the Truth "all over the world" and to all persons, "professors, Jews, Christians and heathens" alike. These early friends honored their election by carrying the news to the far expanses of the seventeenth-century Anglo-colonial world. Seventeenth-century Quakers helped create their own version of "a spiritual *imperium in imperio*," a contact zone of sorts in which cultural, ethnic, and geographical differences

---

23. For this formulation of the "sacred past" as a resource for modern religion, I am indebted to Mircea Eliade, *The Sacred and the Profane: The Nature of Religion*, trans. William R. Trask (1957; repr., New York: Harcourt, 1987), especially 68–115. For a discussion of "wonder" as an early modern discourse, see Stephen Greenblatt, *Marvelous Possessions: The Wonder of the New World* (Chicago: University of Chicago Press, 1991). Vernon Parrington connected Quaker mysticism to a "doctrine of democracy" unconsciously spread "in an autocratic world" in *Main Currents of American Thought*, 2:362. For a discussion of religion's contribution to eighteenth-century Enlightenment discourses in the colonial world, see Sarah Rivett, *The Science of the Soul*.

met and formed a prenational aggregate of early modern spiritual connectedness.[24] At the very moment when the postreligious modern nation-state was becoming a possibility in England, radical English Protestants like the Quakers were trying to reformat the world into a spiritual empire modeled on their received truths. The Quakers' spiritual imperialism criticized even as it furthered the elaboration of the modern English (and eventually American) imperial nation.[25]

The Quaker's body, whether "quaking" in Hertfordshire or Boston, became a site of transatlantic revelation and prophecy, and until the actual "invasion" of New England and the statutory sanctions and executions it provoked, it is more or less impossible to distinguish between reports of spiritual experience made on one side of the Atlantic or the other. From the perspective of theology and evangelical engagement, there is little to no difference between English and New English Quakerism in the seventeenth century. This is in no small part due to the abstemiousness of Quaker liturgical and devotional practices; fewer rules meant fewer reasons to dissent, at least from each other. In addition, the small size of the Anglophone Quaker community promoted an affective and intimate network that took no notice of national or geopolitical discretions. Relatedly, this network of seventeenth-century Quakerism was thoroughly mediated by an epistolary correspondence that constantly shared and mirrored experiences reflexively between them. We shall shortly see that English and New World–based Quakers had different experiences, but these experiences differentiated themselves along primarily legal and political rather than theological lines. The "management" of a universally transcendent spiritual ambition by the local exigencies of politics, law, and custom was, of course, a fundamental tension within these communities, but that tension was produced largely in relation to nonreligious (i.e., state-based) intervention. Quakerism was always part of the world it only seemed to renounce, and its ambivalent negotiation of Anglo-American imperial and settlement cultures contributed to cultural and religious formations that would eventually differentiate along protonational lines.

Far from being "antiworldly"—in the sense that it rejected all interplay with carnal, natural, or visible things—Quaker witness insisted on worldly

---

24. Frederick Tolles, *Quakers in the Atlantic Colonies*, 3, 22.
25. On contact zones, see Mary Louise Pratt, *Imperial Eyes: Travel Writing and Transculturation* (London: Routledge, 1992).

interaction. This is less to reject than to qualify the ascetic dimension of Quakerism's theological abstemiousness and commitment to social (albeit not religious) austerity. Not only did a will-to-textuality inhere within the anti-sacerdotalism of Quakerism, but this impulse to representation constituted the discursive community that was the Society of Friends in the seventeenth century. Quaker apologist and missionary Francis Howgill frames the continuum between spiritual interiority and testimonial representation as a relation sponsored

> but by the Spirit, if truth which gave forth the words of truth, which may manifest and doth manifest itself as it will, when it will, where it will, and how it will, for it is unlimited and it will not be limiited [sic] by its own words as to be found, but may speak words which it never spoke before.[26]

Howgill proposes a form of spiritual testimony defined by its very uncontainability and granted credibility in direct proportion to his own contribution's diminishment. Against a "hireling ministry" that sought to control and dispense a ministry through ordinance, liturgy, and ritual, the Friends sought to blanket the world with a layer of words directly apprehended from God himself. In fact, God is himself the source of what would come to be known more widely as human imagination: the ability to "speak words which it never spoke before." One historian has called this the Quaker doctrine of "celestial inhabitation," by which the transformation of the individual sinner into the saint became another expressive node in an expanding network of revealed truth in the world.[27] George Fox believed that the inward dwelling of the spirit "literally transformed and perfected the saints so they became flesh of His flesh and bone of His bone," earthly vessels for celestial words which would eventually rearrange the world into a more perfect image of a now more powerfully visible God. If the power of an omnipotent God could remake the sinner into a saint, then the power of his word as revealed by Quaker witness could remake the world itself. Considered from the perspective of the story modernity likes to tell about the impact of the philosophical Enlightenment on the

---

26. Francis Howgill, *The Heart of New-England Hardened through Wickedness* (London: Thomas Simmons, 1659), 17.
27. See Richard Bailey, *New Light on George Fox and Early Quakerism: The Making and Unmaking of a God* (New York: Mellen, 1992).

modern world, it might be difficult to find a more ambitious statement of this claim than the Quaker commitment to the universal power of the inwardly realized Light.

In the perfectionist and expressive zeal of these early modern Protestant mystics, we can see an incipient if untheorized assertion of one of the Enlightenment's favorite stories of human progress. What we might call the "civilizational impulse" in Western secularism emerged in relation both to early Quakerism's engagement with politics and law and to more broadly epistemic issues captured in the Quaker reliance on the terms "Light" and "Truth" to describe their religious experiences. Part of that "Truth," then, is to improve the world through its articulation. It was not so simply the case that the mystical, self-involved Quakers clung tenaciously to what Enlightenment thought would later describe as a superstitious and enchanted world. The Quakers strove to bring the Light into the shadows and recesses of a corrupt world for the purpose of improving a world so found. The certainties of ancient spiritual practice thus promoted the desires of progressive modernity in more ways than one. Far from being the quasi-separatist religious crackers that establishmentarian polemic and even modern scholarship have found them to be, seventeenth-century Friends saw themselves engaging profoundly and continuously with a world they would, through their divinely licensed exertions, make better. In the standard narrative of the modern, this story typically issues in a progressive historiography of self-privileging Protestantism and rational social organization—otherwise known as the modern nation. The seventeenth-century Quakers experience disrupts any simple progressive historical narrative which holds that secular progress is measured by the distance found between religious and nonreligious understandings of the self, or even by the proliferation of spiritual "options" as a prominent philosopher of secularism has argued.[28] Instead, New England Quakerism's refusal to be extinguished created conditions by which an American secularism could report that it still retains a soul.

QUAKERISM'S FEMININE BODIES

In both the Judeo-Christian and Western philosophical traditions, spirit and carnality attached themselves to male and female bodies respectively.

---

28. Charles Taylor, *A Secular Age* (Cambridge, MA: Harvard University Press, 2007).

Both Augustine and Aquinas, for example, imported a gendered duality into the confessional and scholastic traditions of medieval Christian spirituality. The association of carnality with the feminine and transcendent spirit with the masculine continued into the reformation and beyond, as feminist intellectual and religious historiography has also found.[29] The embodied spirituality of early Friends' devotional life, of course, became its chief identificatory feature, nominalized in its pejorative assignment of the very term "Quaker." Because associated with embodied life, Quaker practice opened itself to two charges simultaneously. The first, often voiced as a critique of religious libertinism, was the idea that Quakers embraced their sinful carnality and so were little more than deluded hypocrites, if not and more egregiously, witches. Thomas Jenner's anti-Quaker polemic, *Quakerism Anatomiz'd*, accuses the Quakers and particularly Quaker women of having carnal relations with Satan himself:

> That since their imprisonment, he [Satan] hath frequently appeared, and actually possessed them, bruising, tearing, tossing them up and down the prison, and tormenting them with strange fits, convulsions, quakings, shakings in all their joynts, and swelling in their whole bodies, their skins ready to break, which made them cry out with great horror, as eye-witnesses of Quality can attest to it.[30]

Jenner asserts that diabolism resides at the core of Quakerism's "testimonial" practices, but in doing so he describes the relation as turning on possession rather than consent. The distinction between these two forms of diabolic agency may seem slight, but as we shall see in chapter 4, such slight distinction becomes a crucial feature in the accusatory confessional culture of the Salem trials.

The second frequently voiced critique of Quakerism attacked its "feminine" identity, a gendered spirituality most famously theorized and performed by the redoubtable Margaret Fell, an undisputed leader of English

---

29. Michele Lise Tarter, "Quaking in the Light: The Politics of Quaker Women's Corporeal Prophecy in the Seventeenth-Century Transatlantic World," in *A Centre of Wonders: The Body in Early America*, ed. Janet Moore Lindman and Michele Lise Tarter (Ithaca, NY: Cornell University Press, 2001), 148; and Grace Jantzen, *Power, Gender, and Christian Mysticism*, 141–55. For one such discussion of these issues relative to the seventeenth-century English Protestant experience, see Phyllis Mack, *Visionary Women*, 15–50.

30. Thomas Jenner, *Quakerism Anatomiz'd and Confuted* (London, 1670), 161.

Quakerism. In the gender polemic, Quakerism's theological radicalism implied where it did not more directly assert a rearrangement of worldly social relations so as to accord with the spiritual order of God's domain as the Quakers understood it. Quakerism very quickly acquired a reputation for being disruptive and aggressive, as Friends frequently "testified" against the "hireling priests" during and after church services, to say nothing of staging frequent and controversial public demonstrations of their spiritual gifts. Theological, social, and political revolution conjoined in Quaker spirituality, and did so in ways that set the bodies and persons of women in particularly dramatic relief.[31] In James Nayler's famous Palm Sunday demonstration, for example, women accompanied him, to scandalous outrage, singing "Holy Holy Holy" as he entered the city of Bristol in 1656 in a re-enactment of Jesus's Palm Sunday arrival in Jerusalem. The scandal derived as much from the perceived sacrilege of Nayler's theatricalization of one of Christ's most important Holy Week acts, as from the sexually suggestive activities of the women who participated in the stunt.[32] Quakers in New England, both men and women, similarly vexed clerical and civil authorities with their strident interruptions of and attacks on ordained clergy, their public demonstrations, and their willing martyrdom. There was in Quakerism a continuum between spiritual and social agency, and the historical record left from this period in New England's colonial history prominently featured women assuming vital spiritual and political roles.

As one of the first Christian groups to advocate consistently on behalf of female religious leadership, the sect only became more notorious. Perhaps as important as Margaret Fell's cultivation of this public leadership role was the consistent participation of women in Quaker acts of public agitation and evangelism. As a consequence, female Friends suffered persecution during the Interregnum and early Restoration years nearly as much as did men, which is to say that to the extent that the persecution of

---

31. Cf. Lilla: "Every revolution in the soul contains potential revolution in the world," *Stillborn God*, 28.

32. Hugh Barbour, *Quakers in Puritan England*, 63. In the history of disruptive Quaker activities (and their severe repression), the story of James Nayler's 1656 "re-enactment of Jesus' entry into Jerusalem on Palm Sunday" is one of the better known. An early example of charismatic pastoral leadership, Nayler's controversial relations with Quaker women and with George Fox himself led to one of the earliest schisms within the Society of Friends. For a fuller discussion of Nayler and his trial for blasphemy by Parliament, see Barbour, *Quakers in Puritan England*, 62–67.

Quakers amounted to a form of publicity, then the visible face of Quakerism was as often as not that of a woman. Critics, and there were many, frequently focused on the prominence of women in Quaker missionary work. Jenner again provides a good example of this critique in his description of a Quaker meeting in which "A Woman also, being at a Quakers meeting in Buckinghamshire, was suddenly transported with great raptures for about two dayes, but after fell into grievous cursing, swearing, and blaspheming, Crying For a devil, for a devil, till she died: divers were there who saw and heard it."[33] Here the possessed body leads to the production of irrational voice, as the "inspirited" body becomes little more than a suicidal catastrophe of satanic delusion. In the description of the female Quaker, the theological and social agency of Quaker spirituality collapses into a familiarly misogynist image of female spirituality's excessive corporeality.[34]

Quakers nonetheless both embraced and complicated the gendering of embodied spirituality, routinely testifying to the power of the Word to overcome any person's bodily self-command. Indeed, the loss of bodily self-control premised the notion of the soul's absolute submission to God as much as it presented the problem of excessive carnality decried in Western theological and philosophical misogyny. William Robinson, who was executed in Boston on October 27, 1659 (and to whose story we will return), wrote a letter to the Boston court prior to his sentencing in which he describes his conversion: "The Word of the Lord came Expressly unto me which did fill me Immediately with Life and power and heavenly love; By which he constrained and Commanded me, to pass to the Town of Boston."[35] Henry Fell, who was finally unable to travel to New England from Barbados in 1657, told his sister Margaret Fell that the desire to bring the Light to New England manifested itself as his own body's contortion: "oh I cannot mention that place, but my bowells yearnes towards them."[36] Quaker inspiration could take the form of the parent subduing the rebel-

---

33. Jenner, *Quakerism Anatomiz'd and Confuted*, 159.

34. Feminist discussions of Quakerism include Tarter, "Nursing the New Wor(l)d," 22–35; Carla Pestana, "The Quaker Executions as Myth and History," *Journal of American History* 80, no. 2 (1993): 441–69; and Anne Myles, "From Monster to Martyr: Re-presenting Mary Dyer," *Early American Literature* 36, no. 1 (2001): 1–30.

35. Quoted in Joseph Besse, *Sufferings of Early Quakers: America* (1753; facsimile repr., York, England: Sessions Book Trust, 2001), 199. All further references to this text are made parenthetically with the abbreviation SA.

36. Henry Fell to Margaret Fell, May 1757, Swarthmore Collection, Friends House Library, London.

lious child, as Robinson informs his executioners: "the Lord, who filled me with Living Strength and power from his heavenly presence which at that time did mightily overthrow me . . . and willingly was I given up from that time to this day, the will of the Lord God to do and to perform whatever become of my body" (SA 200). One might think that in a Puritan religious and parenting culture that often enough insisted on the need to break the sinner's and (or) child's rebellious will, such a sentiment might gain some traction.[37] As with John Donne's poetic rendition of the soul under divine siege ("Batter My Heart"), Robinson's defense of the body's evidentiary authority takes the form of God, through the Holy Spirit, laying siege to the reluctant believer: "By his Almighty Power and everlasting Love, constrained me and laid this Thing upon me, and truly I could not deny the Lord, much less resist the Holy One of Israel" (SA 200). Constraint leads to spiritual extension; the ascetical body's confinement, punishment, and imminent death produce ever greater occasion for speech, for "publishing" the power of the Lord in a sinful world and, in doing so, blurring the line between sacred and profane terrains of human truth and thereby enabling the former to illuminate the latter.

Within Puritan Christological discourse, the idea of union with Christ was frequently expressed in matrimonial terms wherein the convert, male or female, was always bride to Christ as bridegroom. Viewed in this regard, early Quakerism's advocacy of spiritual equality was consistent with one of Christianity's most persistent salvational allegories; Quakerism's embodiment of this idea only carried it one step further. One might say that a body so "feminized," whether in respect to theological or sociological discourses, becomes the essential condition of all Quaker identity. In this sense, it sustained the idea of radical piety's "feminine" identity as a performative concept that, in its availability to men and women alike, reasserted the universalism of the "ungendered" soul.

The loss, interruption, supercession, or even dispossession of bodily control advanced the worldly work of the spirit. Seventeenth-century Friends not only embraced the testimony of the ecstatically involved body but deployed that testimony in a variety of ways as part of their evangelical work. Female and male Quakers consistently invoked a vocabulary of embodiment in their Gospel efforts, often positioning the specifically

---

37. For a discussion of Puritan attitudes toward child-rearing, see Philip Greven, *The Protestant Temperament*.

female body in familiar if potentially controversial discourses of sex, marriage, and birthing. Mary Howgill testified that in 1660:

> I was at the Town of Colchester at my Friend's house, and in the evening season, I went to my Bed to take my rest in God, where refreshment from him I did receive to my soul, and also my naturals, having at that time but little strength as to my natural life; And so according to God's will, and the mind of the Lord, I gave up my self, and lay down upon my Bed, in God's Will and Word, in which Word I was kept and preserved.[38]

In a clearly undisguised metaphor of intercourse, Howgill claims that the weakened and supine body renders the soul available to spirit, just as the embedded supine female body is available to male penetration. In a focused critique of the Pauline interdiction on female preaching, Margaret Fell invokes the familiar biblical metaphor of the "seed" in such a way as to imply another metaphorical reading of the term as reproductive physiology: "Thus much may prove that the Church of Christ is a woman, and those that speak against the womans speaking, speak against the Church of Christ, and the Seed of the Woman, which Seed is Christ."[39] The reproductive logic of birth and the body complements the scriptural logic of female religious speech. Quaker spirituality also expressed itself through sexually charged language, as in the following extraordinary letter written by Joseph Nicholson to Margaret Fell dated at Boston in 1660:

> Oh thou fairest among women thy voice is sweet and thy countenance is comely. There's non like thee for comlyness, which the lord hath put upon thee. Happy are they which hear the pleasant sound which proceedeth from the fountain of life in thee. If she therein partake with thee and so continue on in the faith amoung women, there's non like thee whom the lord hath adorned. I am refreshed by night in my bed when I think of the sweet harmony that flows from thee. The daughters of Sion may rejoice in thee who hast fed with the food which is immortal; thou are strong indeed in the strength of the almighty.[40]

---

38. Mary Howgill, *The Vision of the Lord of Hosts. By a Handmaid of the Lord* (London, 1662), 3.
39. Margaret Fell, *Women's Speaking Justified by Scriptures* (London, 1667), 5.
40. Joseph Nicholson to Margaret Fell, January 7, 1660. Swarthmore Collection, Friends House Library, London, Trans. 2, 927.

The first line reads like a Petrarchan sonnet, as Nicholson severally speaks to the physical attractions of Quakerism's most important female spiritual leader, who provides nocturnal comforts to a supine Nicholson, whose rapt greeting of Fell identifies his experiences with those of Quakerism's female adherents. Neither the erotic imagery nor the cross-gender identification between Friends is particularly unusual here. Far from it: the personalized familiarity of Nicholson's greeting stood as potent reminder of the immediacy Quakers sought in their connection to Spirit. Indeed, the bodily charge between male and female Friend was another form of spiritual publication, as Nicholson and countless other Quaker writers registered the worldly presence of divine power as the affectionate and, on occasion, overwhelming spiritual broadcasts of their feminized piety.

Quakers not only linked the language of the female body to the language of vital spiritual experience and power. They also invoked the image of the female body to defend themselves against the established church's attacks. Francis Howgill, one of the leaders of Quakerism's first generation, began one of his two denunciations of New England's treatment of visiting friends by explicitly comparing the Quaker mission to New England to the "old Dragon" who, in a "foaming rage," has forever been trying "to overflow, and to drown, and to swallow up the woman, which was made to flye into the wilderness for many dates, having a retired place there God hath prepared for her . . . and a remnant of her seed hath he [Satan] made war with every where." Howgill's Quakers are "the free-woman and her seed," and their persecutors are "all the Nations" that "have drunk the Whores Cup of Fornication, and have been enflamed therewith."[41] Writing in post-Restoration London, the male Quaker Patrick Livingstone used slightly less aggressive rhetoric to make the same point; he asks a series of questions that connected the license of women's preaching to the matrimonial compact between Christ and the church, and Christ and the individual believer: "Was not Israel that went from her spiritual husband, called an Harlot, or a whorish woman? And were not there many Males and Females to make up this Woman that had forsaken her Husband? Is not Christ the Husband? is not this Church the Spouse of Christ? is not he as well the Husband of the males as of the Females, and of the Females as of the Males?" Joan Vokins locates the vital soul in the sick body when she writes

---

41. Francis Howgill, *The Popish Inquisition Newly Erected in New England* (London, 1659), a2. All further references to this work are made parenthetically with the abbreviation *PI*.

"Upon the Third Day of the Eleventh Month, 1669, as I lay very sick in my Bed, I felt the everlasting blessed powerful Life to arise and spring up in my Heart, which gave Dominion over my bodily weakness, and caused me to write these few Lines unto you, that so we may consider the large Love of our God, and praise his holy Name together."[42] Bodily abjection makes possible spiritual elevation, a familiar formula of mystical self-extension at least since the time of the medieval visionaries. It was not merely the case that Quakers rejected all episcopacy, liturgical discipline, and ordinance. Against the structuring order of legal abstraction, they asserted themselves and their embodied experiences of the holy as the only authentic location of religious experience. Seventeenth-century Quakerism's claim of the persecuted and specifically feminized body anticipated the secular discourse of "innocency's" victimization by illegitimate worldly authority.

Quakers organized their spiritual life around the feminized body rather than around the liturgical abstractions of ecclesiology. In this respect, Quakerism's emergent homiletic cited and, in doing so, claimed the rhetorical abjection of Anne Hutchinson's body as a positive feature of radically uncontainable and fecund spirituality. This reclaiming by Friends continued the transatlantic migrations of Anne Hutchinson, from Boston to London in Winthrop's *Short Story*, and now from London back to Boston, in the transnational ministry of itinerant Quakers. Arguing that Quakerism was just one of Anne Hutchinson's many "monstrous births" would miss the larger point here. Quakerism's radical spiritism inserted itself into an already circulating discourse of religious and social management. Early modern Quakers countered the ecclesiology and misogyny of established Christianity through the recollection of mysticism as well as through the embrace of embodied spirituality and promotion of women as recognized spiritual equals. The feminized embodiment of Quakerism both projected and invited a language of suffering that identified its theology with the afflictive traditions of Christianity. For all their presumptive differences, which both Quakers and their detractors aggressively asserted, these dissenting English Protestants (including the New England Puritans) both located spiritual integrity in close proximity to abjection. They each derived social and political power from spiritual and worldly degradation, and in their homiletic and scholastic productions, identified typologically

---

42. Patrick Livingstone, *Truth Owned and Deceit Denyed* (London, 1667), 46; Joan Vokins, *God's Mighty Power Magnified*, 1.

with the famous historical victims of the Bible, including Job, Jonah, and, of course, Christ himself.

One problem here is that in their claims to embattled victim-status, Quaker and Puritan were *too* similar. Most of the nationalist traditions of American history begin with the origin-as-victim story of the Puritans; they just as often end there, as well. The English church was to John Cotton as the First Church in Boston was to Anne Hutchinson; the threat of Catholic Charles no doubt prompted the New England Puritans to up the ante on their Quaker interlopers. As the seventeenth century progressed, the colonial purchase on its affliction at the hands of the imperial center became increasingly emphatic, which is to say that the identity of "persecusant" itself became a universalizing discourse of colonial self-understanding. In this respect, both Quaker and Puritan connected the hagiography of the persecuted early church through to the martyrs of Foxe's *Actes and Monuments* to the historical aftermath of the English Civil War. Both Quaker and Puritan martyrology contributed to an incipient language of embattled righteousness whose postnational articulations still reverberate with powerful affect in the secular.[43] As we shall see shortly, however, Quaker and Puritan mentalities developed different understandings of bodily pain and suffering, and the eruption of female-identified Quakerism in Puritan New England contributed crucially to the manufacture of the ideological edifice of later-seventeenth-century American Puritanism.

ANOTHER ERRAND

How might the Quaker invasion become part of the longer historical and ideological narrative of seventeenth-century New England? We might begin simply by telling some of the Quakers' story. Thomas Salthouse reported the following to the Quaker leadership in Swarthmore Hall, England: "Dorothy Waugh hath thoughts of taking shiping at Bristoll for New-England."[44] Although impossible to know exactly when these early Friends decided to bring the Light to New England, this 1656 letter to Margaret

---

43. For discussion of a contemporary version of religiously inflected victim-narrative, see Susan Faludi, *The Terror Dream: Myth and Misogyny in an Insecure America* (New York: Picador, 2007).

44. Thomas Salthouse to Margaret Fell, March 29, 1656, Caton Collection, Friends House Library, London, 3/93.

Fell is one of the earliest surviving references to what would become known as the "Quaker Invasion" of New England.[45] The first Friends to visit New England were two women, Anne Austin and Mary Fisher, who arrived in Boston via Barbados in July of 1656. Deputy-Governor Richard Bellingham, forewarned of the Quaker arrival by their London agent William Leverett, "immediately ordered them to be detained on board, and sen[t] officers who searched their Trunks and Chests, and took away about an Hundred Books . . . The Danger which was apprehended from the Arrival of these Women, and the Spreading of the Books." Austin and Fisher were imprisoned, forbidden to speak with any resident of Boston, and their "Books were burnt by the Hangman in the market-place." The Boston authorities appear further to have strip-searched their prisoners "under Pretence of searching whether they were Witches, and on that Occasion" the women "were barberously [sic] and immodestly used." After a five-week imprisonment, the women were ordered aboard a vessel, which returned them to Barbados. Compared with their treatment of subsequently arriving Friends, the Boston Council dealt with Austin and Fisher somewhat mildly, which is to say that lengthy incarceration, starvation, and privation were the gentlest measures the New England Puritans used to counter the first wave of the Quaker invasion. The attachment of "danger" and infection ("spreading") to women returns Puritan polemic

---

45. The "Quaker Invasion" of the later 1650s has remained little more than a sidebar in most the major discussions of seventeenth-century New England Puritanism. Perry Miller, *Errand into the Wilderness*, treats the Quaker invasion as a small early skirmish in the larger battle over "toleration" in the British empire that won't really be fought until the Restoration and then largely in London (122–25). Geoffrey Nuttall, *The Puritan Spirit: Essays and Addresses* (London: Epworth, 1967), discusses the Puritans' "unmitigated abhorrence" for all things Quaker in spite of their theological consanguinity (170–76). Philip Gura overstates the matter when he observes that the Quakers "threatened to undo three decades of foundation work for the New English Sion," but he does consider them to be one of several "varieties of New England Puritan radicalism"; see Gura, *A Glimpse of Sion's Glory*, 144–52. Stephen Foster discusses the Quakers as a "very tangible and very radical" problem but ultimately concludes that they failed to gain any real traction in New England; see Foster, *The Long Argument: English Puritanism and the Shaping of New England Culture, 1570–1700* (Chapel Hill: University of North Carolina Press, 1991), 190–94. Quaker-specific studies have produced a good deal of scholarship on the Quaker invasion; see Worrall, *Quakers in the Colonial Northeast*; Frederick Tolles, *Quakers in the Atlantic Colonies*; Rufus Jones, *Quakers in the American Colonies*; and Ryan, *Imaginary Friends*, 35–49. William G. McLoughlin, *New England Dissent, 1630–1833* (Cambridge, MA: Harvard University Press, 1971), and Carla Pestana, *Quakers and Baptists in Colonial Massachusetts* (New York: Cambridge University Press, 1991), quite specifically tell an "alternative" story of colonial Protestantism. For a more recent treatment of the New England Quakers from a legal history perspective, see Goodman, *Banished*, 86–114.

to the terrain of Anne Hutchinson's toxic appeal, ironically elevating by identifying women as a threat worth the state's official notice and exercise of juridical agency.

This initial skirmish in the Lamb's War prompted the first of what would become a series of increasingly severe anti-Quaker orders and statutes adopted by the reigning Boston Council to contain the spread of what the Council described in a July 1656 Order as the "very dangerous, heretical, and blasphemous Opinions" held by Quakers "contrary to the Truth of the Gospel here professed among us" (SA 177, 178). Only a few weeks later, in August of 1656, a larger group of Quakers arrived in Boston, among them several individuals (Christopher Holder, William Brend, and John Copeland) destined for especially grisly persecution and eventual martyrdom. Several women were among the group as well, including Dorothy Waugh, all of whom were imprisoned in Boston Gaol for nearly eleven weeks and forced to endure privations of food and contact with each other. During this lengthier imprisonment, the General Court at Boston passed its first of three general laws against the "cursed sect of Hereticks lately risen up in the World, which are commonly called Quakers." This law, proclaimed on October 14, 1656, held provisions for fining ship captains knowingly transporting Quakers to Massachusetts; for imprisoning any such Quakers upon arrival; for "severely" whipping and putting to work all such persons apprehended; and, finally, for fining, imprisoning, and banishing (on a second offense) any person who "shall take upon them to defend the Heretickal Opinions of the Quakers" or even read their books. The first Quaker subjected to the statutory penalty of corporal punishment was—unsurprisingly we can say now—a woman, Mary Clark, who, "moved of the spirit," travelled from London to Boston in early 1657 to "deliver her Message to Merciless men," only to be rewarded for her efforts "with twenty Stripes of a three-corded Whip on her naked Back, and detained . . . in prison about twelve Weeks." If Quakers believed in a fundamental spiritual equality between men and women, the Puritans believed in equal opportunity corporal punishment. While Quaker women, in principle, were whipped less severely than were men, there is good reason to suspect their punishments were comparatively worse, as the Puritans found Quaker women to be transgressors not just of religious discipline but of social discipline more generally (SA 179, 180, 181). To the extent that the critique of Quakerism was in no small part motivated by social concerns regarding proper behavior, the intense focus on women established that the relation between radical spiritism and Congregational pietism was in a fundamental way a gendered one. With her body exposed and physically abused, the degraded Quaker woman links mystically derived and inwardly realized religious life to the spectacle of public humiliation and torture. In doing so, she becomes the center around which the Puritan tribunal convened. Punished and feminine piety anchored the social politics of the Quaker invasion and became the condition that enabled the consolidation of legal power of a Puritan identified state.

Little over a year after these first missionaries arrived in Boston, Henry Fell would report to George Fox that "The powers of darkness are at worke in New England still against friends to the shedding of their blood." Perhaps unbeknownst to Fell at the time of writing this letter, the Boston Puritans were just getting started. Only one day after the proclamation of the first order, the General Court issued "an Addition to the late order, in Reference to the Coming or Bringing in any of the cursed Sect of Quakers into this Jurisdiction."[46] This second order also prescribed dismemberment for a second offense against a banishment order:

> And it is farther [sic] ordered, That if any Quaker or Quakers shall presume, after they have once suffered what the Law requires, to come into this Jurisdiction, every such Male Quaker shall for the first Offence, have one of his Ears cut off, and be kept at Work in the House of Correction till he can be sent away at his own Charge; and for the second Offence, shall have his other Ear cut off . . . And for every Quaker, he or she that shall a third Time herein again offend, they shall have their Tongues bored through with an hot Iron. (SA 183)

On September 16, 1658, the Boston jailer removed the right ears of three Quakers: John Copeland, Christopher Holder, and John Rouse. While awaiting the execution of the order, Rouse wrote the following to Margaret Fell: "I was moved to come to Boston, soe [yet] 5 weekes I was released, yet day 5 weekes at night I was put in againe; where was Christopher Holder and John Copeland 2 of the friends which came from England and we doe lie here according to their law to have each of us an ear cut off, but we are kept in the dominion of God and our enemies are under oure feet."

---

46. Henry Fell to George Fox, June 1658. Swarthmore Collection, Friends House Library, London.

Between the passage of the second Quaker law and the dismemberments of Copeland, Holder, and Rouse, Besse records seventeen separate instances of corporal punishment penalties served to both visiting and homegrown Quakers.[47]

About one month following the dismemberments, the General Court made capital punishment the statutory penalty for a third offense.[48] Four Friends would pay the ultimate price: Marmaduke Stephenson and William Robinson (executed together on October 27, 1659); Mary Dyer (executed in May of 1660), and William Leddra (executed in Boston, on March 14, 1661). Mary Dyer of Rhode Island, a friend of Anne Hutchinson with whose story her own was entangled back in 1638, had knowingly defied the banishment-on-pain-of-death provision of the last anti-Quaker act and had travelled to Boston against her family's wishes to protest the law itself. The General Court originally sentenced her to die with Stephenson and Robinson, but a last-minute intervention granted her a temporary reprieve. The scaffold drama is worth a look, this time from George Bishop's 1661 hagiographical polemic, *New England Judged*. Mary Dyer is the purported speaker in the first sentence:

> No Eye can see, No ear can hear, No Tongue can speak, No Heart can understand the sweet Incomes and Refreshings of the Spirit of the Lord which now I enjoy—I say, after she had parted joyfully with her Friends at the Foot of the Ladder, determined to dye, and saw her Friends at the Foot of the Ladder, determined to dye, and saw her Two Friends dead, and hanging before her, and had her Arms and Legs tied, and the Halter about her Neck, and her Face covered with a Handkerchief, which your Priest Wilson lent the Hangman for her Execution; and was even with the Lord in Joy and Peace, and so as it were out of the Body, an Order came from you for her Reprieve upon the petition of her Son, unknown to her, which being read, and the Halter taken off her Neck, and she loosened, she was desired to come down; which she not answering (because she staid to wait, on the Lord to know his Pleasure in so sudden a Change, she having given up her self to dye as aforesaid, and being so near to it); the People cryed

---

47. John Rouse to Margaret Fell, September 1658, Swarthmore Collection, Friends House Library, London, 1/82. Alternate spelling for Rouse is Rous. For the chronology of these punishments, see Besse, *SA*, 181–88.

48. For discussion of the progressive intensification of New England's anti-Quaker statutes, see Goodman, *Banished*, 97–101.

(for her Death they were against)—Pull her down; nor could she Prevail with them to stay a little (so earnest were they) whilst she might consider and know of the Lord what to do, but Ladder and she they were pulling down together.[49]

Mary Dyer's hagiographer frames the female mystic within an emerging discourse of the New England scaffold.[50] The words attributed to the condemned female Quaker verbosely draw attention to the impossibility of representing divine language in the world. Although radicalized as unreachable interiority, her spirit nonetheless achieves a kind of worldly publication, as unrepresentable spirit competes with the hortatory agency of her family and the assembled crowd seeking her reprieve. The proleptic martyrdom of Mary Dyer directly resists the desires of the crowd, which stalls her sainthood by pulling her down from the scaffold. There is another kind of contradiction as well. The compelling language of God, as she experiences it, sustains the punitive will of the Boston court, which is to say that radical spirit could further the goals of civic authority. Her performance locates the thematics of feminine piety—involved interiority, passive acceptance of divine authority, mystically apprehended language—at the center of a scaffold drama whose outcome publicized the idea of individual sovereignty even as it comes at the expense of Mary Dyer's mortal life. This conjoinment of female religious radicalism with the very apparatus of its suppression manufactures the martyr as the product of intertwined spiritual and secular discourses.

Michel de Certeau has offered that "individual bodies tell the story of the institutions of meaning," a claim that Mary Dyer and her fellow Quaker martyrs in Boston sustain not merely in their deaths but in the embodied theology that led to their condemnations.[51] Dyer returned to Boston in June of 1660, was again imprisoned, and a second time sentenced to death. On her second visit to the Boston scaffold, as Burrough and Besse each report it, several onlookers offered her yet a second reprieve if she would

---

49. George Bishop, *New England Judged, by the Spirit of the Lord, the First Part* (London: Robert Wilson, 1661), 109.

50. Daniel Cohen connects the early modern colonial scaffold to a uniquely American literary tradition in *Pillars of Salt, Monuments of Grace*. For a more focused discussion of the role of gender in later seventeenth- and early eighteenth-century colonial scaffold literature, see Laura Henigman, *Coming into Communion*, 19–87.

51. Michel de Certeau, *The Mystic Fable: The Sixteenth and Seventeenth Centuries*, trans. Michael Smith (Chicago: University of Chicago Press, 1986), 14.

depart Boston never to return, to which she replied, "Nay, I cannot, for in obedience to the Will of the Lord I came, and in his Will I abide faithful to the Death" (SA 206). In her more successful martyrdom, she protests the "unrighteous and unjust Law of Banishment upon pain of Death, made against the innocent Servants of the Lord."[52] A few commentators have suggested that the Puritans were in the end squeamish about executing a woman on religious grounds. They nonetheless carried out the sentence and, a short time later in March of 1661, they killed William Leddra, the last Quaker executed in New England.

The New England persecutions were exceptional. In terms of penal measures exercised by the state, they were far more severe than they had been in England, even if, in England, the suffering and death of persecuted Friends were fairly extensive in the later interregnum. To be sure, Friends in England suffered legal and extralegal consequences more or less from the start of George Fox's first evangelical activity in the late 1640s. He and nearly all members of the Quaker elite (including Fox's eventual wife, Margaret Fell) spent years imprisoned in jails all over England. During the 1650s and into the early Restoration, the gaols of London and most larger towns in southern England overflowed with Friends arrested on a variety of charges, who were subject to fines for refusing to attend Anglican church services; to property confiscation for refusing to pay clerical tithes; and to lengthy imprisonments for preaching in public, disrupting church services, and distributing literature. So long as the penal measure "fit" the crime, English Common Law gave sentencing judges a great deal of discretion in determining penalty. Generally speaking, the judiciary fined and imprisoned English Quakers, as there was no prescribed statutory penalty that called for corporal punishment. Those beatings and whippings endured by Quakers were essentially "sporadic . . . [and] essentially local in character" where not more directly the result of "popular hostility" against Friends.[53] Of course, officials and political figures implicitly licensed the excessive behavior of gaolers, constables, and ordinary persons, but the physical violence at times offered to Quakers in England was a matter of

---

52. Edward Burrough, *A Declaration of the Sad and Great Persecution and Martyrdom of the People of God, Called the Quakers, in New-England* (London: Robert Wilson, 1661), 29.
53. William C. Braithwaite, *The Beginnings of Quakerism* (1912; repr., Cambridge: Cambridge University Press, 1981), 445; Craig Horle, *The Quakers and the English Legal System, 1660–1688* (Philadelphia: University of Pennsylvania Press, 1988), 125.

customary practice and judicial license. In New England the situation was very different.

By the late 1650s there was nothing particularly unusual about New England Puritan authorities both imprisoning and exiling religious troublemakers. What is new about the Quaker invasion and the Puritan response, however, is that in the earlier episodes (including the banishments of William Lyford, Thomas Morton, Roger Williams, Anne Hutchinson, and Henry Vane) the decisions were not the result of statutory determination. Rather, they were ad-hoc decisions by local governing bodies acting on the basis of what the Charter and English common law permitted relative to the adjudication of religious crimes. Under the anti-Quaker regime in New England, the law identified Quakerism as a crime against the state's interests and prescribed specific statutory penalties. If, in 1638, few could tell what all the fuss was about, in 1656 no such indecision remained because neither the law nor its executors were at all interested in debating Quaker theology. Under the law, there was no such thing as a "theology of Quakerism" so much as there was a person whose religious life defined him or her in terms the state could first identify as "Quakerism," and then punish as a criminal. The anti-Quaker laws named the Quaker, yet altogether ignored her religious life, which is to say that under the terms of this regime, religion both mattered enough to warrant state management, yet did not matter enough for the state to engage with it as religion per se. Another way to conceptualize this would be to observe that, as an external manifestation of religiously motivated behavior, Quakerism solicited the authority of the state. The banishment regime of New England may have been theological in its motivation, in that the desire to identify and expel certain kinds of religious beliefs became possible only through the control of the bodies in which those beliefs resided. In its exercise of authority, however, the state allowed the origin of this behavior to become obscure. Banishment thus rendered the individual's religion socially and politically irrelevant—even "feminine" if you will—which is to say that banishment "reflected" the Quaker belief in the utter sovereignty of their religious beliefs, and in the fundamental separation of the agency practicing those beliefs from the authority of the secular state. By beating the spirit out of the punished Quaker body—or dismembering it, or hanging it—the Puritan regime perforce conceded the individual's claim on having an inwardly realized religious life at all. As a consequence, the legal "remedy" of corporal punishment, banishment, and execution enabled assertions of religiously motivated notions of personal sovereignty commensurate with the modern nation's eventual embrace of rights-based moral and judicial codes premised on the sovereignty of individual selfhood.

The retributive severity of New England's response to the Quakers came on the heels of one of the most important codifications of colonial law in seventeenth-century Massachusetts: the passage of the *Laws and Libertyes* in 1648. Legal scholars and historians have debated the significance of the *Laws and Libertyes*, but most are agreed that the revisions were mobilized on the part of a "desire to curb discretionary powers of the magistrates."[54] Indeed, the first article of what was sometimes called the *Body of Libertyes* expressly declares that "no man shall be arrested. Restrained, bannished, dismembered nor any wayes punished unless it be by the virtue or equity of some expresse law of the Country warranting the same established by a General Court and sufficiently published." The rule of law rather than the power of the magistrates or the theological belligerence of a ministry would determine the extent of the state's ability to punish transgression. The 1648 statutory revision also offered protection from cruel punishment and torture: "And for bodily punishments, wee allow amongst us none that are in-humane, barbarous or cruel." In a subsection on "Torture," moreover, the *Laws and Libertyes* implicitly defines "inhumane" whipping as a single beating "above fourty strips."[55] While we are not yet dealing with an episteme which would more or less define the "human" in some negative relation to "cruel and unusual," it is significant that the 1648 body of statutory laws quite precisely defined the point—more than forty lashes for a single offense—where the just exercise of authority becomes a form of injustice. The law defines the moment where a legitimate (and biblically prescribed) form of corporal punishment would exceed its own mandate: the moment where the human dispensation of justice becomes something other than what, today, we might call "humane."

The rationalization of the law, therefore, might be seen more generally as a provisional definition of the human as it would come to be understood in secular contexts of philosophy, law, and politics. The 1648 exercise was designed in part to remove the arbitrary element of the law: to remove,

---

54. Mark Cahn, "Punishment, Discretion, and the Codification of Prescribed Penalties in Colonial Massachusetts," *American Journal of Legal History* 33, no. 2 (1989): 108.

55. *Lawes and Libertyes Concerning the Inhabitants of Massachusetts* (Cambridge, 1648), 1, 46, 50.

in other words, the fallible judgment of men from the dispensation of merciful justice, and to promote what today we might call a "transparent" relation of the law's provisions to its worldly application. There was to be no "hidden life" for the law: its provisions had to be published to be enforced, and its enforcers had to limit their judicial actions to that described by the published law. In theory at least, the mystery of unlimited judicial discretion would be replaced by the emerging pieties of defined justice. Such a process, as Foucault would come to argue, was a central feature of European modernity: "For penal semiotics to cover the whole field of illegalities that one wishes to eliminate, all offences must be defined; they must be classified and collected into species from which none of them can escape."[56] To define the particularities of the law's possible exercise as "justice" is to define as such the human person organized within, and so as an expression of, that very discourse. What is more, the rationalization of the law defined the field of possible criminality more precisely. This kind of law forced the invisible life of crime into the visible order of jurisprudence. As applied just a decade later to the Quakers, colonial law transformed the religious agency of the Quakers into a defined form of transgression punishable by a rationalized penology defined by men. The law, we might say, became "less religious" as religion became more "legal."

THE ORIGINS OF HUMAN RIGHTS

The "Quaker Invasion" prompted renewed efforts of religious, political, and cultural consolidation in seventeenth-century colonial New England. A polemic written as if Roger Williams's famous "Bloody Tenent of Persecution" had itself never been written, John Norton's defense of the New England treatment of Quakers maintained that the punishments meted out to the Quakers "may be understood either of a Capital punishment Juridically dispensed, or of any other smart punishment piercing though not Capital. As God hath armed the Magistrate with Civil power for the defence of Religion, so hath he animated him unto the regular and seasonable exercise thereof."[57] They were no more "persecuting" the Quakers

---

56. Michel Foucault, *Discipline and Punish: The Birth of the Prison*, trans. Alan Sheridan (New York: Vintage, 1979), 98.

57. John Norton, *The Heart of New England Rent at the Blasphemies of the Present Generation* (Cambridge, MA: Samuel Green, 1659), 49.

than a judge imposing a fine could be considered to be "persecuting" a duly convicted petty thief. Because one persecutes a religious minority and executes a murderer, Norton furthers an increasingly secularist perspective on the problem posed by religious radicalism. His argument maintains the vitality of religious Otherness within the epistemological framework of a still religiously identified civil regime. Quakerism's refusal to concede effectively created the need for even more Puritanism.

Early Quakers differentiated themselves from state-identified religion and juridical culture by focusing on their shared experience of bodily pain. Quaker narratives of suffering frequently indulged a hyperbolic language of outrage borrowed from the lexical treasury of both Protestant anti-Catholicism and sectarianism. One such narrative, or rather collection of narratives, was Francis Howgill's 1659 *The Popish Inquisition Newly Erected in New England*. In all likelihood published in response to the dismemberments of John Copeland, Chris Holder, and John Rouse as well as the "cruel and merciless sufferings of William Brend" (*PI* 28), Howgill's text begins with a lengthy preface that typologically casts the New England persecution of the Quakers as Cain's killing of Abel. Howgill's hagiographical license retells the initial Edenic crisis: Adam's "loss" of the image of God at the hands of the "Prince of Air, who was a Murderer from the beginning" (*PI* 2). In Howgill's version, Cain "was of that wicked one that went out of the Truth, and . . . rose up in envy and slew Abel the just, who was of the Seed." New England's envious persecution of the Quaker "seed" thus extends biblical history into Quaker eschatology, as Howgill appropriates New England's "errand into the wilderness" as one properly belonging to the "Lamb [that] hath been slain . . . throughout all ages and times, throughout all nations, Kindreds, Tongues, Regions, Countreys and Kingdoms" (*PI* 3). Old Testament typology authorizes Quaker martyrology. Although no Quaker has yet been executed, Howgill's polemic assumes a continuum of meaningful suffering that is both historical and theological, from the 1657 imprisonment and whipping of Robert Hodshon in New Holland (the first portrait of suffering in the *Popish Inquisition*) to the dismemberments of Copeland, Holder, and Rouse in Boston later that year. The lives of the Saints given to the Truth "will stand a witness against your Doctrines and cursed practices for evermore" (*PI* 3), and after noting memorable persecutors of God's seed in the Old and New Testament ("Cain, Herod, Murderer and Men of blood"), Howgill goes on to tell New

England that "you are worse then [sic] they" (*PI* 3). Howgill invokes an exceptional logic to sustain his polemic, which is to say that the enormity of the Puritan persecutions merits a special kind of commentary, the particular witness of the saints against "the greatest persecutors" of the Lamb yet witnessed, whose "wickedness, and cruelty, and hard heartedness the Papists, the Turks, the Heathens" cannot match because New England exceeds these traditional foes "in rage, cruelty, and madness" (*PI* 4).

George Bishop's two-part martyrological narrative, *New England Judged*, extends the hyperbolic range of Howgill's text to several jurisdictions and by several hundred pages of mocking disbelief written entirely in an accusatory second-person style. No longer confined to the primary den of "cruel professors" (i.e., Boston), the persecuting spirit "soon followed after you" to New Haven and Plymouth patents, if not "as to Banishment upon pain of Death, Death and Ears, Yet other Cruelties as to Fines, Whippings, Imprisonments, etc. And New haven [sic] will Exceed in Crueltie, all the former."[58] It would be impossible to detail the rhetorical aggression of Bishop's remonstrance, so one of the text's several subtitles will have to suffice in conveying the tone and the sheer verbiage of his attack on New England:

> The *Cruel Whippings* and *Scourgings*, *Bonds* and *Imprisonments*, *Beatings* and *Chainings*, *Starvings* and *Hangings*, *Fines* and *Confiscation of Estates*, *Burning* in the *Hand* and *Cutting of Ears*, *Orders of Sale* for *Bond-men*, and *Bond-women*, *Banishment* upon pain of *Death*, and *Putting to Death of those People*, are *Shortly* touched; With a *Relation* of the *Manner*, and *Some* of the *Other most Material Proceedings*; and a *Judgement* thereupon.[59]

The "judgement" promised here attaches itself rhetorically to every incident the narrative details. The incident and the excessive rhetoric of its presentation are in fact largely indistinguishable, which is to say the persecutions, under the handling of Quaker martyrologists like Bishop, take on something like a life of their own. The prolix detail of the punitive Puritans effaces the ostensible spiritual cause for these worldly effects, replacing the spiritual life of Quakerism with the precise penology of its state-sanctioned

---

58. George Bishop, *New England Judged*, 122.
59. Ibid.

punishments. Justifiably angry Quaker bromide adopts what we might call a secular relation to its own religious commitment.

Anti–New England Quaker polemic and hagiography typically and even exhaustively detailed the corporal punishments endured by Quakers. The Quaker archive is, to borrow Saidiya Hartman's analysis of the archive of nineteenth-century slavery, "a death sentence, a tomb, a display of the violated body."[60] In one of his letters to Margaret Fell in 1658, John Rouse reports:

> We were examined and committed to the prison, and the 7th day in the evening they whipt us with 10 stripes a piece with a threefold whip to conclude a wicked weeke's worke which was this: on the 2nd day of the weeke they whipt 6 friends, on the 3rd days of the weeke the jailor laid with William Brend (a friend that came from London) neck and heels as they call it in irons as he confessed for 16 hours, and on the fourth day the jailor gave William Brend 117 strokes with a pitched rope, on the 5th day they imprisoned us and on the 7th day we suffered; the beating of WB did much work in the towne and for a time much liberty was granted, for severall people came to us in the prison seeing the forwardness and love in the people towards us, he plotted, and a warrant was given forth that if we would not worke, we should be whipt once in every three daies, and the first time have 15 stripes, and the 2nd time 18, and 3rd time 21, so on the second day was a 7 night after our first whipping, 4 of us received 15 stripes a piece, the which we did so worke with the people yet on the 4th day after we were released, soe we returned to Rhode Island, and continued there awhile.[61]

The description precisely identifies the dates, times, frequency, kind, distribution, and severity of the beatings. As much as Rouse and other Quakers sought to bear witness to the miracles of their Father, here and elsewhere they bore equal witness to human-commissioned crimes against actual persons. Humphrey Norton details his and Rouse's beating

---

60. Saidiya Hartman, "Venus in Two Acts," *Small Axe* 12, no. 2 (2008): 2. I should note here that my own analysis intentionally replicates the violence of this archive in order to represent and to commemorate the Quaker attempt to publicize their suffering. The story of the "Quaker invasion" still remains something of an invisible domain in early American studies.

61. John Rouse to Margaret Fell, 1658, Swarthmore Collection, Friends House Library, London, 1/82.

in Plymouth—"the Executioner coming to put off our Clothes, was bid to have patience, and he should see that we could give our backs to the smiter, which being done he laid upon us thirty eight stripes"—and then offers an interpretive account of the experience—"After this was done . . . we returned in the glory of true suffering, kept far from transgression, but in truth."[62] They complained against punishments irrationally determined and severely delivered. William Brend describes, in agonizing detail, the experience of being put in irons:

> Then he [the Boston jailer] began to threaten us what he would do to us and said he would put me in Irons that night, so the next day he came with his Irons, and put one Iron on each thigh and another about my neck and he locked them together with a Horse-Lock, that there was no more liberty between the Irons then [sic] the Lock allowed (so that my body was crumbled together, my head close to my thighs) those Irons was upon me from about the fifth hour in the morning, till after the ninth hour at night (which was sixteen hours) And when I lay in the Irons, I was strengthened in the power of the Lord. (PI 31)

The concluding cadence—that the Lord uplifts either in spite or more probably because of extreme abjection—is naturally to be expected here, but the spiritual lesson receives virtually no exposition compared with the lengthy description of an improvised neck-violin and Brend's experience of close-confinement torture. Friends believed God called on them to spread the Truth as revealed directly to them as and through the "Light," but as the persecutions in New England continued, they shifted their attention increasingly to witnessing against—by describing in excruciating detail—the work of the devil let loose on the earth.

Were these Quaker persecution narratives evangelical—that is, driven by the need to carry the Gospel ever outward—or were they at this point serving some other purpose? The title page of Edward Burrough's *Declaration of the Sad and Great Persecution and Martyrdom of the People of God, Called Quakers, in New-England, for the Worshipping of God*, cannot be said to augur "the good news":

---

62. Humphrey Norton, *New England's Ensigne: It Being the Account of Cruelty, the Professors Pride, and the Articles of Their Faith* (London: G. Calvert, 1659), 35–36.

Wherof {
22 have been Banished upon pain of Death.
03 have been MARTYRED.
03 have had their Right-Ears cut.
01 hath been burned in the Hand with the letter H
31 Persons have received 650 Stripes.
01 was beat while his Body was like a jelly.
Several were beat with Pitched Ropes.
Five Appeals made by them to *England*, were denied by the Rulers of *Boston*.
One thousand forty four pounds worth of Goods hath been taken from them (being poor men) for meeting together in the fear of the Lord, and for keeping the Commands of Christ.
One now lyeth in Iron-fetters, condemned to dye.
}

FIGURE 1. Edward Burrough, *Declaration of the Sad and Great Persecution and Martyrdom of the People of God* (London: Robert Wilson, 1661).

Burrough attempts to quantify the inner life of persecution, to summarize injustice as a mathematical calculus, to describe the abstraction of religious persecution as a verifiable catalogue of earthly injustices. As a direct petition to Charles II, the text goes on to describe in detail the injustices just enumerated. Given that Burrough is not evangelizing the King, it is clear that the text seeks political rather than spiritual effects. His narrative of suffering insists less on the theological arguments than on the worldly consequences of those arguments, drawing repeated attention to every singular act of perceived injustice with the seventeenth-century typographical equivalent of a shout:

> My occasion is this, Because of a Paper presented to thee, called *The humble Petition and Adresses of the General Court* at Boston in New-England: In which is contained **divers Calumnies**, unjust **Reproaches**, palpable **untruths**, and malicious **slanders**, against an Innocent People, whom they scornfully call **Quakers**; whom, for the name of Christs sake, are made Reproach through the world, and by these Petitioners, have been persecuted unto **Banishment**, and **Death**; it is hard to relate the **Cruelties** committed against these People, and acted upon them by **these Petitioners**; they have *spoyled* their Goods, *imprisoned* many of their Persons, **whipped**

them, **cut off their Ears, burned** them, yea, **banished** and **murdered them**; and all this *I aver* and *affirm* before thee, O King, wholly *unjustly* and *unrighteously*, and without the Breach of any Just Law of God or Man; but only for and because of *Difference in Judgment* and *Practice* concerning *Spiritual things*, & without any transgression of the Law of God, or their own Laws; Saying that they made Laws against them, on purpose *to spoil* **their Goods**, imprison **their Persons**, cut off *their Ears*, yea and *kill them*, which Laws were made by them, without any Power truly derived.[63]

As with *Bishop's New England Judged*, the emboldened and blackened words provide indices of legal, ethical, and political outrage, a typography of scandal he sustains over the course of the narrative before appending a summary "Declaration of some part of the Sufferings" endured by these people of God "Only for the Exercise of their Consciences to the Lord." His text moves between the symptoms of the disease—the enumeration, in nineteen summary points, of the "Inhumanity and Cruelty" committed by the New England "professors"—and the cause of these inhuman effects: the exercise of religious conscience.[64] What Burrough's and other texts connote, in other words, is the political life of religious being: the translation of religious experience into the modern political terms of the state's power to punish the individual as a secular subject, however motivated by the unseen life of religion. Where the essentially mystical and unrepresentable experience of Quakerism's faith frustrated a ministry charged with monitoring and "educating" the life of Christianity, the juridical intervention of the state effectively transcribed the invisible mystery of Quaker Truth into the discernible marks of the state's mandate to punish. The corporal punishment of the Quakers thereby conceded the irrelevance of the spirit to the functioning of the state, effectively "feminizing" religion itself with respect to its increasingly "invisible" status within the judicial view. Broadly speaking, the marginalization of religious life under the anti-Quaker penal regime of Puritan authority was a subordination to which Quaker belief was theologically prepared to consent.

The beaten bodies of the Quakers realized the spiritual "nothing" of Anne Hutchinson, but in doing so they implied the existence of differing, if not competing, orders of human suffering. One order, what we might

---

63. Burrough, *Declaration*, 3.
64. Ibid., 17, 19.

think of as the "historical" way of pain, linked bodily abjection to spiritual uplift and further grounded religious community in the experiential life of suffering. The second we might, following Talal Asad, designate a linking of suffering to judicial and political understandings of bodily pain. "Penalties," he writes, "whether emerging as incapacity from within the living body's functions, or imposed as punishment on the body externally, are regarded as a necessary part of learning how to act appropriately." In this second order of pain—the one which counts the number of lashes and determines that moment where experience becomes "too much"—the spiritual significance of suffering emerges with less clarity that it did in biblical and postbiblical typologies of suffering, for example, historical identifications with Psalm 119: "It is good for me that I have been afflicted that I might learn your statutes." Conceived as an epistemic shift, the relation of the first to the second order of pain might be well described as a tension between "eschatology and sociology."[65] Where we might expect seventeenth-century Quakerism to be a staunch defender of the first order, we find that the religiously motivated protest against state-sponsored injustice promoted the interests of secularist understandings of suffering—that it had become "scandal" rather than anointment, an assault on body rather than on spirit.

From within the discursive life of the struggle, Quakers framed their spiritual agency within a proliferating rhetoric of human cruelty and outrage which continued throughout the later seventeenth century. Consider the following poem, "Innocency's Complaint," a broadside attributed to "George Joy, Mariner," in 1677:

> Twelve Innocents, without e'er Guilt or Crime,
> With cruel Whips were scourged at one time;
> And six Days after, fifteen more by Force,

---

65. Talal Asad, *Formations of the Secular: Christianity, Islam, Modernity* (Stanford, CA: Stanford University Press, 2003), 91. See also his discussion of torture, in which he claims "the secular Christian must now abjure passion and choose action. Pain is not merely negativeness. It is, literally, a scandal" (107). For the important, and contrasting, view of pain and its relation to human expression, see Elaine Scarry, *The Body in Pain: The Making and Unmaking of the World* (New York: Oxford University Press, 1985), which argues that pain is fundamentally private and serves simultaneously as the condition for certainty and for doubt. For a historical Christian account of suffering, see Judith Perkins, *The Suffering Self: Pain and Narrative Representation in the Early Christian Era* (New York: Routledge, 1995), 200–214; and Geoffrey Harpham, *Ascetic Imperative in Culture and Criticism*, 19–44.

>Were like the first twelve, beaten without Remorse.
>Seven tender Women, young and old, were stript,
>All naked to the Waist, and cruelly whipt.
>Immodest Action! Greatest Wrong with Shame,
>Which never will be clear of Guilt or Blame:
>And twenty Men, well bred, of good Descent,
>Fit for Assistants to their Government,
>Each of such good Report and high Repute,
>Their Goes could not accuse them, but were mute,
>Only a Law unjust forbid their meeting
>To serve the Lord, and Whips must be their Greeting.[66]

Outrageous as such latter-day typology may have been, the enumeration of the punishments, the "immodest" treatment of women, and the brutalization of upstanding men are calculated to make as great a rhetorical impact as the equally outrageous implication that twelve Quakers have achieved apostolic status. The vocabulary of Protestant religious polemic—hypocrisy and popery chief among them—stands alongside what we might call an ascendant vocabulary of ecumenical inhumanity. The poem convenes a rhetoric of injustice, savagery, torture, and blood around the body of the beaten Quakers that sketches plans for a new kind of tribunal that would speak a language of worldly justice. For the purposes of the poem's polemic, Quaker spirituality seems almost beside the point.

As the beatings continued before giving way to the dismemberments and, eventually, capital punishments, Quaker witness took on a nearly forensic quality. The value of Quaker testimony lay as much in bearing witness against unjust secular authority as in witnessing for the power of the Truth. The severity of the New England persecutions distracted these Children of the Light from their sacred calling, gradually replacing the evangelical purity of their mission with increasingly desperate appeals to "reasonable men" to treat the Quakers humanely. After the dismemberments of Chris Holder, John Copeland, and John Rouse, Humphrey Norton wrote a letter from the Boston Prison. This letter, probably written in the early fall of 1658, is one of the most rhetorically violent anti-Puritan

---

66. George Joy, "Innocency's Complaint against Tyrannical Court Faction in Newengland [sic]" (Boston, 1677).

polemics written in seventeenth-century New England. As such, it is worth reproducing here in whole:

> Accursed are thy rulers thy towne of Boston, for they are become the high priests servants and hath cut the Saintes right Eares,—Accursed are thy teachers for they are of the Troop of Robbers which murder in the highway by consent. Accursed are the people who votes up, and consents unto these Actions of bloodshed, murder and cruelty.—Accursed is that Counsel that sits to shed the blood of the Innocent as hath bin done in thee.—Accursed is thy Governor who passed the Sentence against his own Soul, be being forewarned of it in express words from me, Cursed is that hangman that did it (as he is called) So is his name, he is a Servant to the Devil, one of his familiar spies, his Name in the Hebrew tongue is Abaddon, his master which first cast him into Prison, and now hath caused him to cut off there [sic] Ears, must be his Name there shall rot, and his posterity shall perish, his Government is accursed. He rules in unrighteous power and sheds blood for reward, Cursed are his upholders in this very Thing, His days upon Earth is heaviness, Leprosy his life, They cry of blood pursues him day and Night and that Issue can never be cured in house. Let his days be as Sodom and be burned in his blood as Gomorrha, and they that consent and partake with him as the inhabitants of the same land. Where that monstrous beast, Woe be unto him, cursed be the tongue that takes pity on him, for he pitied not his own Soul, neither shewed he mercy to the Saints of the most high. Double give him to drink for what he has done. The righteous Soul loathes his life, yea and the righteous Spirit cries for vengeance to be taken on him Seven fold. Let not the earth be suffered to drink up his blood. Let not it rot in his breast as an untimely birth,—Vengeance for Evermore is thy reward thou manslayer. The irresistible curse swallows thee up for Evermore. Pity is past away from thee, Mercy and remission tho canst not have, for the Sentence of the irresistible vengeance is gone out against thee in this very day, Witnessed unto by his servant who is they Judge—H. N.
>
> The Curse of God rest upon thee John Endicott for my brethren and companions sake, the curse of God rest upon thee. Thy deeds shall tho answer for, as sure as Ever thou consentest unto that deed (thou Son of a Murder) Lucifer thou cursed bird, who dares attempt to say thou Spokest from heaven, Get thee down into the lowest lake, thou liar, for within the gates of hell is thy habitation.

Let this Letter be delivered with care to John Endicott, Governor of Boston, so called.[67]

Between Howgill's *Popish Inquisition* and Norton's "Letter from the Boston Prison," we see the emergence of spectacular evil in the face of the elected Governor of Boston. On one view, the exceptional evil of the Puritans is the inverse mirror of the exceptional grace of the Quakers, but Norton's intent here is at least as theological as it is political. A few of his imprecations rely on familiar biblical curses—Sodom and Gomorrah, for example—but rather more of them do not. The "priests" and leaders of New England have become common thieves, political dupes or opportunists, merciless heathens, blood cannibals, and "manslayers." Norton abandons strict typology in favor of a more vernacular account of present-day evil. He even tosses a generic monstrous birth into the mix before associating the ministers and leaders of Boston with the divine pretense of the great liar himself. Norton is not looking for converts; he is identifying and denouncing worldly evils using a language of imprecation that might circulate in the world independently of any specifically Biblicist or even generally religious hermeneutic. In short, evangelism passes into accusation just as surely as meaningful martyrdom begins looking like senseless violence.

Outraged Quaker polemic struggles against its own religious hermeneutic, threatening to eclipse its commitment to a divinely ordered world. From the Quaker perspective, the Puritan persecution can only proceed through the license of God himself, an idea which, of course, buttresses the Quaker commitment to suffering in God's name which these Friends knowingly assumed and, as we saw in Henry Fell's disclosure that his "bowells ached" to visit New England, for which they actively prayed. Seventeenth-century Quakers affirmed the idea of meaningful suffering, which assumed that the agency of evil played an instrumental role within God's providentially ordered plot for his elect. Their belief that affliction was in the first place divinely ordered and, in the second, that their antagonists were no less part of the story of bringing Truth to the world than were the "Children of the Light," enabled Quaker persecusants to meet their fates with equanimity and, on one surprising occasion, with poetry:

---

67. Humphrey Norton, "Accursed Are Thy Rulers," 1658[?], Swarthmore Collection, Friends House Library, 6/22.

> Your goales (gaols) we fear not, no nor banishment
> Terrors nor threats can ere make us lament
> For such we are as fear the living God
> Not being vexed by persecutions rod
> Away hipocrisie, adew false fear
> Immortal life's the crown which we doe bear
> Which can not be removed from us away
> That makes us scorn your threatenings every day
> These are our prayers and thus our souls do cry
> Let justice live and all oppression die.[68]

Howgill's affirmation of meaningful suffering was shared by all Quakers in New England and England alike (and would be a central feature of Mary Rowlandson's narrative, as we shall see in the next chapter). But between Humphrey Norton's surprisingly secular denunciation of New England's ruling elite, on the one hand, and Howgill's serenely triumphalist lyric, on the other, the hitherto neatly braided relation of saintly suffering to divine intentionality starts to unravel.

In his 1658 letter to Margaret Fell written on the eve of his right ear's removal, John Rouse drew attention to a curious fit between the New England law ("according to their law") and God's will for his Elect ("we are kept in the dominion of God"). New England's anti-Quaker laws, while unjust, were still part of an omnipotent God's plan. Quakers held that the saint's submission to the will of God—even one staged by New English persecutors and their "hireling priests"—only shortened the path to eternal glory. On the eve of his execution in Boston in October 1659, William Robinson wrote:

> For of a truth the Lord God of the whole Earth commanded me by his Spirit, and spoke unto me by his Son, whom he hath made Heir of all things, and in his Life I live, and in it I shall depart this earthy tabernacle, if unmerciful men be suffered to take it from me; and herein I rejoyce the Lord is with me, the Ancient of dayes, the life of the suffering Seed, for which I am freely given up, and singly do I stand in the will of God, for me to live is Christ, but to die is gain.[69]

---

68. Francis Howgill, "The Cogitations of My Heart . . . ," 1662, A. R. B. Collection, Friends House Library, London.
69. William Robinson and William Leddra, *Several Epistles Giv'n Forth by Two of the Lord's Faithful Servants Whom He Sent to New England* (London, 1669).

The Quaker God determines the action of saint and sinner alike, a recurrent thematic in Quaker martyrology, which held that the "suffering Seed" sprouted truth so long as they continued to "stand in the will of God." In another missive from New England, Rouse reported that "Some time after C. H. [Christopher Holder] and J. C. [John Copeland] were put in prison, I John Rouse was commanded of the Lord to go to Boston also" (*PI* 21); both the suffering at the hands of the Bostonians and the effectual calling of the Seed elsewhere occur within the same "dominion of God." In his 1658 narrative of suffering (which included a lengthy imprisonment and one of the more severe applications of corporal punishment in the 1650s), William Brend relates that he "spoke a few words against their bloody Law (which lay upon me to witness against) by which we suffered." In a letter to Margaret Fell written after his release from a lengthy imprisonment in Boston in the summer of 1660, Joseph Nicholson reported that God "hath delivered us out of the hands of bloodthirsty men. We put our lives in his hands for the honor of the truth and through the power of God we have them as yet." One account of Mary Dyer's final return to Boston claims that in June of 1660, Dyer "had Movings from the Lord, to go to Boston." Imprisoned and resentenced to be executed, Dyer tells the court: "I came in Obedience to the Will of God the last General Court, desiring you to Repeal your unrighteous Lawes of Banishment upon pain of Death." Questioned further by John Endicott if she, like Anne Hutchinson before her, "was a Prophet," Dyer "spake the words that the Lord spake in her; and now the thing is come to pass."[70]

All of these accounts, Quaker and Puritan alike, advance two perspectives: the first, that worldly agency is only ever a consequence of divine command; and the second, that the world is little more than a divinely staged theatre for the playing out of God's commands, otherwise known as Providence. The Puritans, for their part, believed the same thing: the Quakers were little more than a divinely licensed test of his Elect, which is to say that Quaker and Puritan believer alike subscribed to the doctrine of saintly affliction. Thus the Bostonians believed themselves to have been acting on behalf of God's special ordering of things in New England, while the Quakers—and in particular Mary Dyer—were acting on God's command to protest the banishment law. The braiding of divine order

---

70. Joseph Nicholson to Margaret Fell, August 10, 1660, Swarthmore Collection, Friends House Library, London, Trans. 2, 927–30; Burrough, *Declaration*, 28.

with profane enactment provided the fundamental logic of both Quaker martyrdom and Puritan discipline. Although Quaker martyrs bowed their head to a God who ultimately permitted Puritan injustice, they also—and nearly to a person so far as the surviving records indicate—believed the increasingly severe anti-Quaker laws and the men behind their passage to be the instruments either of Satan himself or even of a wholly inhuman manufacture. If suffering Quakers indeed feared not the scourge of "persecutions rod," then the angry and indeed rhetorically violent language of a Humphrey Norton seems somewhat misplaced. Even Howgill's concluding epigram sponsors a view of "justice" and the end of "oppression" that does not easily reduce to the afflictive hermeneutic which would hold that hypocrisy, oppression, and threats are God's own instruments for creating the conditions whereby a saint might wear the crown of "Immortal Life." Somehow, what the secular authorities were doing to the Quakers crossed a line whose transgression the promised rewards of Quaker sainthood could neither manage nor forgive.

There was something so particularly terrible about New England's persecution of the Children of the Light that the persecution of those saints became something that Protestant hermeneutics could neither easily nor completely explain. The whippings, dismemberments, and executions prompted a response in the Quakers which, while not always approaching existential despair, indicated an unwillingness to accept without some sort of resistance the enormity of the Puritan persecutions. The Puritan response to the Quaker invasion sponsored in the Lambs a form of outrage that could not easily be contained within submissive martyrology. In their protest against extraordinary suffering, the Quakers emerge less as religious martyrs than as victims of unjust state practices.

Such a vocabulary of unholy suffering is familiar to us today in the discourse of modern human rights, a regime of legal and political knowledge that doesn't so much rewrite the unholy as the unspeakable as it redesignates the sacred as the "protected."[71] In the twenty-first century, they

---

71. For differing approaches to this idea of sacrality as a form of separation, see Georgio Agamben, *Profanations*, trans. Jeff Fort (New York: Zone Books, 2007), 74: "Religion can be defined as that which removes things, places, animals, or people from common use and transfers them to a separate sphere." Agamben's formulation follows from an earlier position in religious anthropology taken by Mary Douglas, who observes that "holiness" in the first instances means "to set apart." See Douglas, *Purity and Danger*, 49. For more recent discussion of religious speech as "protected," see Wendy Brown and Saba Mahmood, eds., *Is Critique Secular?*

would be applicants to Human Rights tribunals, subjects around which a discourse of the universal human would cohere. Indeed, the Universal Human Rights Accord adopted by most members of the United Nations in the late 1950s outlaws torture and protects religious practice, almost as if its twentieth-century proponents had heard the pathos and the anger of Humphrey Norton's curse. What is important is that a concept of "the religious" persists—even where it goes unnamed—in the discourses of modern human rights, and that, indeed, the idea of "universality" derives its secular power from the old idea of an omnipotent God overseeing the unfolding of creation in its entirety. Religion secures concepts of a modern humanity whose history remains beholden to narratives of emancipation from religious cosmologies of all kinds (enchantment, diabolism, shamanism, papism, and so forth). There is, within secularism, a value and meaning of religion, even when—perhaps especially when—its "separateness" from secular thought is what defines it as religion per se. The seventeenth-century Quaker resides, both historically and theoretically, in the house of Universal Human Rights, which is to say that a concept as profoundly indicative of modern secularism as a Universal Human Right is profoundly indebted to the radical spirit of the seventeenth century.

In the American context, this means revising somewhat a largely intact declension thesis, which continues to hold that the story of early America was the steady decline and dissipation of religion and coterminous rise and assertion of Enlightenment values that would eventually issue a revolutionary "spirit" (as it were); a protocapitalist work ethic derived from a spiritually specious Protestantism; and a political sacrality toward which the new adherents to liberal democracy might turn. To the extent that these ideas derived, in U.S. historiographies, from an American Puritanism in decline, we might now say additionally that seventeenth-century spiritual radicalism crucially contributed to the emergence of Puritanism's postsecular iterations as the modern nation's prehistory. The Quaker "inner light" was at once too bright and too immaterial for an emergent secular and judicial regime. Quakers' religious intensity, at once grounded in the body and independent of ecclesiastical curriculum, contributed to the sense of religion being irrelevant and marginal, which is to say feminine. Indeed, the Quakers made the case for a religious understanding of the public sphere: that rational debate between reasonable men could and should take place in a non-state-identified context, that is, the public sphere. Religion, in short, becomes the occasion for the exercise of public-sphere agency more generally. In this kind of story of the emergence of religious toleration, radical religion produces the conditions for American secularism's political life and the gendered orders of social and political relevance that came with it.

THREE

Mary Rowlandson *and the* Invention *of the* Secular

AT THE END of *The Sovereignty and Goodness of God* (1682), Mary Rowlandson tells us that after her return from captivity, she doesn't sleep well at night:

> I can remember the time when I used to sleep quietly without workings in my thoughts, whole nights together, but now it is other ways with me. When all are fast about me, and no eye open, but His who ever waketh, my thoughts are upon things past, upon the awful dispensation of the Lord towards us; upon His wonderful power and might, in carrying of us through so many difficulties, in returning us in safety, and suffering none to hurt us.[1]

It's a poignant moment of memory and loss: indeed, of memory as a kind of loss of self, as the Rowlandson writing in the "now" of the narrative's present tense records how the sleepless, memorial self is no longer the woman who used to exist "without workings in my thoughts." The work of memory, and its reconstruction as confessional and spiritual autobiography, has not yet released her from a traumatizing past that continues to grip her

---

1. Mary Rowlandson, *The Sovereignty and Goodness of God* (1682), in *So Dreadfull a Judgment: Puritan Responses to King Philip's War*, ed. Richard Slotkin and James Folsom (Middletown, CT: Wesleyan University Press, 1978), 365. All further references to this text are made parenthetically with the abbreviation MR.

present condition. "When Mary Rowlandson can't count sheep," observes Susan Howe, "she lets counter-memory out."[2] Howe is correct; Mary Rowlandson's memory counters rather than complements her present. We might say, in a modern sort of way, that she has not yet "processed" or "come to grips with" that memory. Whether or not Rowlandson intended this text to fulfill an expurgating imperative, or to reassert her part in English or female community—two distinctly modern understandings of life-writing that depart from the genre of "spiritual autobiography"—her desire to understand her captivity implies a corollary desire to contain that past, even as it is toward that traumatic history her troubled mind turns.[3] As a fragmentary mental portrait, the passage sketches an itinerant mind roving from the narrative present ("I can remember"), to the remote past of unconscious life ("used to sleep quietly"), back to a present radically different from the past ("but now it is other"), and back to a past identified as a haven from the turmoil of her sleepless present ("my thoughts are on things past"). It is in her past that her "redemption" took place; it is in her past that the "wonderful power and might" of God exerted itself on her and her culture's behalf; it is to that past her mind returns when left alone with a God who, like her, doesn't seem to sleep much.

This isn't the first time in the narrative that Rowlandson identifies mental turmoil with sleeplessness. Late in her captivity, her release imminent, Rowlandson reports:

> I think I can say, I did not sleep for three nights together. The night before the letter came from the council, I could not rest, I was so full of fears and troubles, God many times leaving us most in the dark, when deliverance is nearest: yea, at this time I could not rest night nor day. The next night I was overjoyed, Mr. Hoar being come, and that with such good tidings. The third night I was even swallowed up with the thoughts of things, *viz.* that ever I should go home again; and that I must go, leaving my children

---

2. Susan Howe, *The Birth-Mark: Unsettling the Wilderness in American Literary History* (Hanover, NH: Wesleyan University Press, 1993), 125.

3. For discussion of New English spiritual autobiography, see Daniel Shea, *Spiritual Autobiography in Early America* (Princeton, NJ: Princeton University Press, 1968). On female life-writing as therapeutic, see Suzette Henke, *Shattered Subjects: Trauma and Testimony in Women's Life-Writing* (New York: St. Martin's, 1998): "It is through the very process of rehearsing and reenacting a drama of mental survival that the trauma narrative effects psychological catharsis" (xix).

behind me in the wilderness; so that sleep was now almost departed from mine eyes. (MR 357–58)

Here, Rowlandson takes the trouble to delineate her seventy-two hours of wakefulness: on the first night, her worries keep her up; on the second, it's her joy at John Hoar's successful brokering for her release; and on the third, anxiety returns in the form of doubt and grief, returning her story to the narrative's deictic present ("sleep was now departed"), in which insomnia has become a constitutive feature of her postcaptivity existence. Rowlandson narrates her experiences of anxiety, joy, grief, and depression as cognates for her world of loss, captivity, and redemption. Alongside her religious self-understanding, one informed by her knowledge of God's apparently arbitrary and yet utterly intentional acts of divine affliction, Rowlandson sketches a mental experience that her religious epistemology seeks both to explain and to comfort. This chapter asks a simple question: does it?

In previous chapters we have seen aspects of American Puritanism developing in close relation to performances of female piety over the course of the first half of the seventeenth century. Hutchinson articulated and performed a spiritist critique of New England's inchoate ecclesiology, and was in turn transformed into a historiographical convenience for secular and revolutionary discourses of American national identity. Only a few decades later, the "Quaker Invasion" renewed aspects of Hutchinson's critique, particularly her interest in an experientially based religious spirituality whose victimization by entrenched authority served to amplify its worldly ambit. As representatives of Protestantism's "radical reformation," both Hutchinson and her inspired successors advanced the Calvinist agenda of English Protestantism, even as their performances made possible universalizable claims about eliminating human suffering and advancing concepts of state-recognized personal sovereignty that post-Enlightenment intellectual history would then claim as a consequence of the secular. In turning to Mary Rowlandson, we now consider another aspect of female piety's invention of Puritanism; this aspect I am provisionally calling a recognizably modern configuration of individual psychology, perhaps the beginnings even of what religious historian Jackson Lears has called a "therapeutic worldview."[4] Picking up on ideas articulated by

---

4. T. J. Jackson Lears, *No Place of Grace: Antimodernism and the Transformation of American Culture* (Chicago: University of Chicago Press, 1994). Although Lears's study focuses on

earlier performances of feminine piety in New England, Mary Rowlandson helps us see what it is like to have become "modern" in the later seventeenth century.

Rowlandson's text translates orthodox Protestant doctrine into psychological narrative animated by a spirit her text cannot perfectly record. Readers familiar with her text know that she wrote the narrative sometime after she returned to Boston. When she came to write it, her mind was not yet quiet, and that disquietude transferred to the pages of avowedly orthodox prose autobiography. So what is the noise that Mary Rowlandson cannot help but record in *The Sovereignty and Goodness of God?* As any insomniac knows, it is partly the knowledge that everybody else is asleep. The insomniac, in her definitive condition of wakefulness, registers her difference from unconscious community as a simple matter of Being-Awake. The need to resume her place within her English community remains to some extent unfulfilled, as the "restored" woman's involuntary nocturnal watch renders her extraordinary at precisely the moment when it is the ordinariness of life she craves; she remains self-consciously singular when unconscious community is the goal.[5] On this point alone, we might observe that Mary Rowlandson's "restoration" is incomplete, a notion the text suggests by juxtaposing her memory of "things past" on the one hand, to her knowledge of "God's awful dispensations" and "his wonderful power and might" in bringing her and others through "so many difficulties" on the other. Her ambivalence records the incompleteness of her redemption, testifying simultaneously to her desire to thank God for her rescue from captivity, and to her ongoing spiritual search for the assurance that God's wondrous power has indeed provided for her soul's salvation: that her worldly "redemption" in fact represents or re-enacts the spiritual election that remains the teleology of conversion narrative. While she can be sure that the sovereignty of God has seen to her rescue from the wilderness, she can't be sure of that rescue's significance in spiritual terms:

---

late-nineteenth-century *fin-de-siècle* American culture, it suggests that the turmoil of the period "led numerous troubled Americans to seek solace not from ministers but from mindcurists and mental hygienists whose cures for nervousness frequently lacked supernatural reference" (54–55). To be sure, these "cures" were driven by new modes of science and psychology that didn't emerge until the nineteenth century.

5. For a reading that finds Rowlandson's text resistant to its incorporation back into a monological Puritan culture, see Christopher Castiglia, *Bound and Determined: Captivity, Culture-Crossing, and White Womanhood from Mary Rowlandson to Patty Hearst* (Chicago: University of Chicago Press, 1996), 46.

her insomnia in this regard registers her redemption *out* of the conditions born of captive *extremis,* and *into* the normative conditions of a Puritan theology which restrained its adherents from fully enjoying the comforts of a lasting spiritual certainty: "Great Security is a sign that trouble is near," preached Increase Mather in 1674, rehearsing a central tenet of the Calvinist reformation on the eve of King Philip's War.[6] In 1682 New England, the voice of orthodoxy somewhat awkwardly belonged to a female convert expressing her faith within a complex confessional vernacular. By listening closely to that voice—perhaps even, as we shall see, to multiple voices inscribed within her text—we can both broaden and refine our understanding of the kinds of experiences both related and recalled by the term "American Puritanism."

From the perspective of mental health, Mary Rowlandson can only equivocally be said to be in much better shape after her captivity ends than while a prisoner to the Algonquin-Wampanoags.[7] When she refers, for example, to the eternally vigilant eye of God, she establishes a somewhat surprising parallel between her wakefulness and God's own. Mary Rowlandson is not suggesting, in any literal way, that the mind of God is too troubled to sleep quietly. She does, however, draw attention to a divinely witnessed and prompted agitation that would have been familiar to most New Englanders in the turbulent decades of the 1670s and '80s. How many times had they been told that the day of trouble was near, that God was provoked to wrathful notice of the sinful, unconverted, complacent, fornicating, Sabbath-shirking, ordinance-breaking, tavern-crawling, land-grubbing, and altogether backsliding swarms of hypocrites and atheists then overrunning New England? On the accounts provided in the Jeremiad's late-century proliferation, God's controversy with New England might lead even Him to stand nocturnal watch over the community whose ability to sleep peacefully in a time of such obvious transgression indicates the deservedness of their judgment. "And upon all these should sorrow come," preached Dedham minister William Adams in 1679.

---

6. Increase Mather, *The Day of Trouble Is Near* (Boston: Marmaduke Johnson, 1674), 8.

7. Here I am following the lead of Kathryn Zabelle Derounian's finding that Mary Rowlandson exhibits the clinically recognizable effects of the "Stockholm Syndrome," a condition experienced by many kidnap victims who come to identify with their captors; see Derounian, "Puritan Orthodoxy and the 'Survivor Syndrome' in Mary Rowlandson's Indian Captivity Narrative," *Early American Literature* 22, no. 1 (1987): 82–93. For a nuanced reading of the cultural politics of "brainwashing," see Castiglia, *Bound and Determined,* 98–99.

"Their troubles should spread among, and over them universally, and take away their mirth, and turn it into mourning."[8] In this reading, Rowlandson's wakefulness places her on the outside of the community to which she has finally returned, an excision that nonetheless aligns her ongoing inner turmoil with God's possibly unexpiated anger. Perhaps as much as any other Christian of more notorious fame, from Augustine to Bunyan to the martyred Quakers of New England's most recent intolerant phase, Mary Rowlandson tells us what it is like to be both redeemed and bereft, comforted and agitated, elevated to the special status reserved only for God's elect, yet deprived of the solace to be found in the ordinary life of worldly community. No wonder she cannot sleep.[9]

This chapter's point of departure is our recognition of insomnia as a shared condition of modernity.[10] Rowlandson's sleeplessness, as we have seen, observes only to blur the line separating her captive and postcaptive selves; her undesired wakefulness connects the experiences of captive imprisonment to comparative freedom, even as her text visibly struggles to insist on their fundamental difference. Rowlandson's representation of a traumatized self unable to escape her afflictive history not only records an ongoing religious crisis but reveals her experience and its representation as narrative to be products of a trauma that religious epistemology fails to render meaningful within a satisfying hermeneutic of salvation. At the end of her narrative, Rowlandson remarks, "It is then hard work to persuade myself, that ever I should be satisfied with bread again" (MR 365). In a doctrinal reading of the passage, we would observe that she is articulating a standard Christian skepticism toward the material world's ability to fulfill the soul. Her reliance on the term displays the Protestant inheritance of affliction's divinely purposive nature, but it also suggests a relentless search for satisfaction among worldly possibility: finding lost children, securing

---

8. William Adams, *The Necessity of the Pouring Out of the Spirit from On High upon a Sinning Apostatizing People* (Boston: John Foster, 1679), 2.

9. For reading of Rowlandson's insomnia that differs from this, see Dawn Henwood, "Mary Rowlandson and the Psalms: The Textuality of Survival," *Early American Literature* 32, no. 2 (1997): 175.

10. For a fascinating treatment of insomnia, see Eluned Summers-Bremner, *Insomnia: A Cultural History* (London: Reaktion Books, 2008), in particular her discussion in chapter 3 of how the "absence of unconsciousness" becomes a point of mediation between religious and postreligious understandings of temporality, individualism, and privacy. For Summers-Bremner and others, "anxiety" becomes a key condition of a worldview undergoing profound transition, a concept developed at length by William Bousma, *The Waning of the Renaissance, 1550–1640* (New Haven, CT: Yale University Press, 2000).

shelter at night, experiencing human contact, and eating food fit only for "beasts." Spirituality becomes less an agent of soteriology than part of a daily regime of self-comforting practices. Her quest for deliverance reads not as the Bunyan-esque pilgrimage of the saint's lifelong approach to heaven but as a daily quest for satiety and inner quietude. Mary Rowlandson wants to take a break from pain, to put it that way, and so gestures suggestively toward an understanding of suffering and trauma that modern "secular agency," as Talal Asad has put it, "seeks to eliminate universally."[11] In seeking her way back into the embrace of Protestant community, Rowlandson identifies a form of selfhood "at home" in both religious and postreligious regimes.

In the Protestant-Calvinist framework, affliction is meaningful within a rendering of saintly perseverance derived typologically from familiar Old Testament models, whereas modern secularity defines human suffering as the definitive challenge to the project of modern civilization and its cultivation of human possibility. Is Mary Rowlandson "sad" because her God remains distant and inscrutable, or is she so because she is coming to realize that God will not save her from her sadness? What happens when the management of emotional life becomes a human rather than divine problem? Under Rowlandson's narrative control, personal suffering stubbornly resists its translation into the Protestant allegory of divinely appointed affliction. As the salvational narrative of redemptive suffering stalls, the religious epistemology both defined and sustained by afflictive meaning begins looking like the more secular account of suffering in which pain's metaphysical ambitions falter and come to be replaced by therapeutic and legal discourses of modern self- and social management. Although her text displays important features of Protestant radicalism, *The Sovereignty and Goodness of God* presents Rowlandson's encounters with divinity through episodic and fragmented memorial: as a series of memories that function in her present as a legacy of her past. The text's divided status, its complicated identifications across ethnic racial, gendered, and memorial lines of demarcation, emerges also in regard to the text's negotiation of religious belief and modern forms of knowing. Her text allows us to experience her God as a distant collection of glimpses, fragments, traces, and echoes that her narrative attempts to organize, frame, and manage into a coherent historical and spiritual text. Rowlandson presents an important account of

---

11. Talal Asad, *Formations of the Secular*, 67.

what it will be like to understand God as an indicator of modernity's traumatic past, as a symptom of modern secularity's own beliefs about what it no longer believes. We experience, that is to say, the lost God of American Puritanism.

EXTRAORDINARY EXEMPLARITY: THE DOCTRINE OF AFFLICTION

So far we have been arguing that female piety in Puritan New England performed two broad functions. On the one hand, it became a primary location of vital religious experience and so a point around which the institutions of Puritanism gathered. On the other, radical female piety imaged a fundamentally anti-institutional disposition. Rowlandson's 1682 text inhabits both of these positions and adds something new to our story: a sense of religion as historical artifact. Written after she returns from captivity, the text recalls her experiences and memorializes them as a record of faith's exercise. As the text struggles to present and maintain a religious perspective that will fulfill the text's exemplaristic ambition, faith in affliction becomes an emblem inextricably associated with personal loss. Mary Rowlandson the *narrator*—sleepless, anxious, and troubled—seems to be looking elsewhere and elsewhen from the space and time from where she writes. In its very recollection, her experience remains in the past as a record of grief, doubt, trauma, and war, which the *narrated* Mary Rowlandson seeks always to interpret within a Protestant framework. Rowlandson's attempt to transform herself into an emblem of remembered religious experience only distances herself from the religious integrity she is trying to capture and encourage through her text. It is in this sense that her text construes and inhabits the secular.

Although often studied alone and long viewed as a "special" text of the seventeenth-century New England archive, *The Sovereignty and Goodness of God* was by no means the only later-seventeenth-century Puritan text to elevate the experiences of a saintly women to the status of special emblem. We might usefully view her text alongside an increasingly popular sermonic genre of the early eighteenth century: the funeral sermon. Charles Hambrick-Stowe and Harry Stout have argued that the funeral sermon gained importance in New England as the first generation of civil and religious leadership began dying off. The resulting devotional anxiety of the passing of the saints prompted succeeding ministers to commemorate their lives as a way to "engender mass religious feeling" and to urge "the rising generation to remember their predecessors and imitate their piety." Seen in this way, the later-seventeenth-century funeral sermon's celebration of the exemplary piety of departed saints was part of a wider culture of the colonial Jeremiad, in which the passing of the saints served as occasion to bewail the spiritual insufficiency of the surviving community.[12] To the extent that Rowlandson's narrative intends to deliver an exemplaristic message of faith and perseverance in the face of worldly calamity, the didactic aims of the funeral sermon align well with the "best intentions" design of Mary Rowlandson's text. Both the ascendant genre of the funeral sermon and Rowlandson's undertook to prompt and to manage the anxiety of redemption inherent in the Calvinist reformation.[13] What is more, both funeral sermon and Rowlandson's text regard the occasion of the message—be it the dead or captive saint—to be, in the end, largely beside the larger point of the undertaking. Neither the life nor the death of the individual serves as the takeaway point; to think otherwise would be to suggest that the very category of the person—whether living or dead—in some way eclipses the importance of her example and the entire purpose of her memorialization in print. But this is precisely the tension between living and historical (i.e., "dead") religion that the funeral sermon and Mary Rowlandson's narrative tighten.

As readers of Rowlandson know, the bodies start piling up quickly in *The Sovereignty and Goodness of God*, and right from the start it is not entirely clear what use we are to make of the projects of individual witness and cultural memory as they unfold here. One of the early scenes in Rowlandson's narrative depicts the death of her sister during the initial raid on Lancaster:

---

12. Charles Hambrick-Stowe, *The Practice of Piety: Puritan Devotional Practice in Seventeenth-Century New England* (Chapel Hill: University of North Carolina Press for the Omohundro Institute of Early America, 1982), 255; Harry S. Stout, *The New England Soul: Preaching and Religious Culture in Colonial New England* (New York: Oxford University Press, 1986), 123. For other commentary on the funeral sermon, see Emory Elliott, "The Development of the Puritan Funeral Sermon and Elegy, 1660–1750." Elliot notes, with Greven, *The Protestant Temperament*, that many of these funeral sermons focus on women.

13. On this point see David Stannard, *The Puritan Way of Death: A Study in Religion, Culture, and Social Change* (New York: Oxford University Press, 1977), 81–83. David Hall connects Rowlandson to the funeral sermon, in particular Cotton Mather's 1702 *A Token for the Children of New England*, suggesting that such practices "may have been more widely practiced after 1660 than before." See Hall, "New England, 1660–1730," in *The Cambridge Companion to Puritanism*, ed. John Coffey and Paul C. H. Lim (Cambridge: Cambridge University Press, 2008), 151.

> My eldest sister being yet in the house, and seeing those woeful sights, the infidels haling [sic] mothers one way, and children another, and some wallowing in their blood: and her elder son telling her that her son William was dead, and myself was wounded, she said, And Lord, let me die with them, which was no sooner said, but she was struck with a bullet, and fell down dead over the threshold. (MR 324)

By invoking the power of God to reward her faith by ending her life, the sister calls on an absent God in order to provoke her own escape from the world. The sister courts not merely the unforgiveable sin of suicide but the charge of excessive spiritual agency. Rowlandson writes, with what quickly becomes a mix of conviction and uncertainty, how she "hope[s] she is reaping the fruit of her good labors, being faithful to the service of the Lord in her place" before concluding the portrait by speaking of her sister's earlier

> trouble upon spiritual accounts, till it pleased God to make that precious scripture take hold of her heart, 2 Corinthians 12.9. *And he said unto me, my grace is sufficient for thee.* More than twenty years after I have heard her tell how sweet and comfortable that was to her. (MR 324)

We are left here in an even more doubtful understanding of the miraculous death of her sister. As she compresses her sister's spiritual history into a shorthand conversion narrative, the representation retreats into an imperfect nostalgia. She recalls her sister's spiritual struggle in order to reassure herself and her readers, even as the sister's divine murder emerges as an ambiguous emblem of the consequences of desperate faith. For Rowlandson, the recollection of the spiritual past—here connected to her sister's death—affords a disquieting form of comfort for her in the present.

Rowlandson's portrait of her sister paradoxically initiates the story as both spiritual autobiography and worldly survival: it sketches both soteriological and self-comforting narrative simultaneously. As other readers have pointed out, the text's recollection of her sister's death contrasts strikingly to her own subsequent narrative of survival.[14] But the passage

---

14. Jill Lepore observes that "the defining moment of her captivity" (Rowlandson's decision to accept captivity rather than death) "swells with ambiguity" as she vacillates between two different understandings of "captivation": that delivered by force on the captive, and that which charms the captive into compliance; see Lepore, *The Name of War: King Philip's War and the Origins of American Identity* (New York: Vintage, 1999), 128–29.

also cites Paul's Second Letter to the Corinthians, and specifically a verse in which Paul "boasts" of his mystical union with God through direct revelation, and discloses that God simultaneously afflicts him by a "sharp physical pain." The moment of mystical unity carries with it the experience of God's Otherness. If mysticism defines divine union in negative terms—that is, understands unity as a form of radical Otherness—then Rowlandson's reading of her sister signals divinity's presence and absence at the moment of her violent death. Thus the moment of divine reality—the sister's prayer being answered—signals the experience of the divine Other—that prayer not being answered at all. God's agency here is fundamentally incomprehensible, its meaning available only to the sister whose experience now serves only to baffle. Belief may belong to me, but its reality is always located in someone else. "The condition of belief," Jenny Franchot observes, "the attachment to invisible realities, is ours through not being ours."[15]

Rowlandson's text opens the possibility that the world of its author is religious only in terms of its pastness, as memorial, a condition the narrative thematizes structurally in the complex positioning of the author's memorial narrative and the text's exegetical scripting of those remembered fragments into the unified text of Puritanism. The ambiguous yet strangely powerful religious significance of the sister's death anchors the historical materiality of Mary Rowlandson's own spiritual autobiography, and affords a way to construe the text as a whole. The sister chooses to die within the embrace of a certain divinity, whereas Rowlandson chooses to live within a spiritual paradigm in no small part defined by divinity's uncertain presence. *The Sovereignty and Goodness of God* proceeds as recollection, memory, even souvenir: a fragment not merely of past experience but of a religion whose "pastness" Mary Rowlandson struggles over the course of her narrative to bring forward into a world God may have abandoned. As Susan Howe puts it: "Mary Rowlandson looks out at the absence of Authority and sees we are all alone." In holding this suspicion view of the *deus absconditus*, Mary is, for once, not alone.[16]

As we saw in the discussion of Anne Hutchinson's historiographical peregrinations, American intellectual authority has long figured America in relation to problematical femininity. Female piety, whether "spiritist" or

---

15. Jenny Franchot, "Unseemly Commemoration," 503.
16. Howe, *The Birth-Mark*, 94.

orthodox in its manifestation, became a significant experiential location of colonial Protestant spirituality. What some have designated "spiritist" faith proved a good "fit" for women, as the self-negations typically exercised in spiritist devotion mirrored the negations of feminine selfhood ordinarily prescribed within patriarchal culture.[17] Patriarchy, as one version of this argument goes, uniquely prepared women for the self-abasement required in the standard social and religious plots of New England. Protestant discipline could be said to be gendered feminine as well, insofar as successful self-renunciation was the goal of Protestant ascesis and devotional effort, an idea that mirrored the patriarchal ordering of women's place and role; ascetic and patriarchal discourse together created the conditions for socially abjected and spiritually vital female subjectivity. Asceticism thus provides a gloss on the idea of female exemplarity lodged at the heart not merely of Mary Rowlandson's captivity narrative but of the religious culture her narrative was designed to represent and reflect. As Geoffrey Harpham has argued, ascetic discourse shows "the way in which a human being can become imitable, how he can meet what are sometimes called the conditions of representation." The discourse of asceticism proceeds as a "bodily act that points beyond itself, expressing an intention that forms, and yet transcends and negates, the body." By denying the body/world in favor of imitable form, the ascetic can "anchor oneself in a community of imitation which both temporally and spatially exceeds the boundaries of the individual life . . . by situating the self in systems that exceed the self."[18] The ascetic body both represents community and, in its dissolution into perfect representation, gestures necessarily outside itself; the ascetic self, along with the mystic, is always in some sense selfless. As such, asceticism construes an array of cultural associations with feminine subjectivity in which, as we saw in the last chapter with the Quakers in New England, a punishing conception of the body might be considered one of the fundamental conditions of modern culture more generally. The female body

---

17. For a reading of the structural parallel between the theological and social orders of women, see Porterfield, *Female Piety in Puritan New England*, 3–13. Ivy Schweitzer observes that Puritan conversion "affirmed the existence of a new kind of interiority, of a private, unique, inner space—the space of self-consciousness, of subjectivity—only to demand its sacrifice, renunciation, and occupation by Another." See Schweitzer, *The Work of Self-Representation*, 23. For another account of the Puritan debasement of women, see Ann Kibbey, *The Interpretation of Material Shapes in Puritanism*.

18. Geoffrey Harpham, *The Ascetic Imperative in Culture and Criticism*, xiv–xv.

itself becomes a metaphor for the practices of self-denial and negation required of Protestant subjectivity more broadly.

Viewed this way, Mary Rowlandson becomes the basis for what Mitchell Breitwieser has called a "society of the example."[19] Breitwieser offers a powerful corrective to the blissfully orthodox exemplarity of Rowlandson and the "lucid essence" of a Puritanism which her text, for too many readers, unproblematically reflects. Observing that, "despite her best intentions" to fulfill the exemplaristic expectations that cultural authority demanded of her narrative, she "comes across significances that have teleologies leading, primarily, to mourning, rather than to faith as it was constructed by Mather and the other members of his cadre." For Breitwieser, the particular object reference of her mourning—her daughter's death—leads Rowlandson to open up an interrogation of Puritanism's "attempt to sublimate mourning, to block and then redirect its vigour to various social purposes."[20] The entire process of memorial and witness—the foundation of Rowlandson's narrative energy—thus carries her out of the timeless abstraction that the exemplary experience would reflect and promote, and into the rougher terrains of history, personal loss, memorial insufficiency, and all the libidinous particularities whose experience and loss the text simultaneously registers and mourns.

Breitwieser's crucial intervention opens another path to thinking about Rowlandson's experiences as both captive and memorialist: the extent to which her involuntary interpretive realignment forces her into becoming a reader of emotional trace, or what we might call the afterlife of affect. Rowlandson's recollected landscape is littered with the dead, the maimed, the terroristic, and the traumatized: her sister, her children, unnamed friends, even herself. These artifacts of loss distract her text from the demands of exemplary cultural hermeneutics, even as they become the substance of her most compelling narrative achievements. Early in her captivity she recounts the following horrific scene:

> Amongst them also was that poor woman before mentioned, who came to a sad end, as some of the company told me in my travel: she having

---

19. Mitchell Breitwieser, *American Puritanism and the Defense of Mourning: Religion, Grief, and Ethnology in Mary White Rowlandson's Captivity Narrative* (Madison: University of Wisconsin Press, 1991), 17.
20. Ibid., 8.

much grief upon her spirit about her miserable condition, being so near her time, she would be often asking the Indians to let her go home; they not being willing to that, and yet vexed with her importunity, gathered a great company together about her and stripped her naked, and set her in the midst of them, and when they had sung and danced about her (in their hellish manner) as long as they pleased they knocked her on head, and the child in her arms with her. When they had done that they made a fire and put them both into it, and told the other children that were with them that if they attempted to go home, they would serve them in like manner. The children said she did not shed one tear, but prayed all the while. (MR 331–32)

Rowlandson's portrait empathetically presents a figure of successful female piety, as the "poor woman," pregnant and holding one child in her arms, is burned alive as part of apparently grisly ritual. The woman refuses the language of emotional distress in favor of one consistent with the exemplary demands of the text's religious imperatives. But even as Rowlandson positions the murder as an ethnographically charged example of "Indian" evil, her text becomes caught in the detail of the event: the "poor woman" has already established herself as an object of human pity; she came, even with the supplicatory success of her prayer, to "a sad end" following experiences of "grief" and "miserable condition." Rowlandson is reading her own text closely, and in doing so asking the same of her reader, yet in the graphic detail of this episode, the invitation to close inspection may not result in the turn to spiritual introspection, or even hermeneutic suspicion. Perhaps it is closer to what Heather Love has called a form of reading that is "close, but not deep . . . a way of turning our attention to the flatness, objectivity and literalism" of an event and in doing so "registering the losses of history rather than repairing them."[21] In her Protestant mode, Rowlandson might say she is leaving the duty of reparation to God, but in her role as memorialist and witness, she is producing a descriptively precise realism whose effect may actually lead out of the exemplary demand and into one of Breitwieser's "alternate teleologies." It is not merely the case that it becomes unclear exactly what Mary Rowlandson is asking us to remember about her religious past; it is also the case that she is theorizing

---

21. Heather Love, "Close but Not Deep: Literary Ethics and the Descriptive Turn," *New Literary History* 41, no. 2 (2010): 375, 386.

the affective traces of traumatic history outside the prescribed interpretive space of orthodox hermeneutics.

Mary Rowlandson's presentation of her experiences at times threaten to exceed what we might call the Puritan doctrine of imitability, an idea displayed at the conclusion of Increase Mather's prefatorial introduction to Rowlandson's text in which he enjoins the reader to "Read, therefore, peruse, ponder, and from hence lay by something from the experience of another against thine own turn comes, that so thou also through patience and consolation of the scripture mayest have hope." Rowlandson's example is worthy because another might imitate her piety. And of course, what should more "peculiarly concern" her readers is the "wonderfully awful, wise, holy, powerful, and gracious providence of God towards that worthy and precious gentlewoman." The text is significant, ironically, for the ways in which it points away from her, and toward the invisible power of God. Although her text's narrative reveals the providentially motivated interventions on her and her community's behalf, those interventions are ultimately "about" God himself: about the manifestation of His will, "God's acts ... his wonderful Works," which her text communicates.[22] Mary Rowlandson's affliction, the piety displayed in her remarkable fortitude, and her deliverance from captivity, each and all witness the "strange and amazing dispensation" of God inasmuch as they tells us something about Mary Rowlandson. If Rowlandson's text leads away from timeless imitability and into the particular terrains of personal loss, then her own narrative, when read in the exemplaristic mode, could be said to dispense with her as its own object concern. The libidinal source of the text's mourning can be traced not only to Puritan theology's programmatic denial of the emotional significance of human sadness, but to the emotional residue of the person Mary Rowlandson, whose text has, in effect, dispensed with its author.

We are equally interested here, however, in the text's failures: in the ways in which *The Sovereignty and Goodness of God* stumbles around in the rough terrains of Mary Rowlandson's complex perspective and memory. As a captivity narrative, the text invokes the thematics of the self's abjection, or negation, by means of her theft into the quasi-slavery of compulsory servitude. It establishes a parallel between the erasure and assertion of

---

22. Increase Mather, *An Earnest Exhortation to the Inhabitants of New England* (1677), in Slotkin and Folsom, *So Dreadfull a Judgment*, 322, 320, 319, 321, and 319.

selfhood carried out by the process of human captivation, and also theorized by Puritanism's doctrine of exemplary affliction.[23] This parallel leads to an unforeseen consequence: the indirect rendering of a "humanity" unclearly related to any specifically religious or even ethnological origin. Consider, in this regard, her widely discussed conflict with Weetamoo, one of her "owner's squaws." The ethnological order of the text tends to exploit the differences between English and Native/Aboriginal cultures, with the latter being subject to a predictable colonial gaze. Highlighting the capricious, grasping, and manipulative character of her mistress, Rowlandson appears committed to a cultural politics predicated on the assumption of Anglo-Saxon racial superiority. In dwelling on the childish whimsy of Weetamoo while maintaining the civilized rationality of her responses, Rowlandson reverses the terms of her enslavement-captivity by showing the captor to be the barbaric villain and the victim the virtuous heroine. Such a thematic of degradation and endurance would become a key plot of the English novel, as Nancy Armstrong and Lennard Tennenhouse have argued.[24] Yet even the assertion of difference threatens to collapse into a more baffling identity, as for example when Rowlandson describes Weetamoo at her daily toilet: "a severe and proud dame she was, bestowing every day in dressing herself neat as much as any of the gentry of the land: powdering her hair, and painting her face, going with necklaces, with jewels in her ears, and bracelets upon her hands" (MR 351). Readers of English and colonial Puritanism wouldn't be surprised to encounter a Puritan man or woman criticizing excessive concern with fashion; even within the Puritan semiotic of visible character, the worldly "externals" of dress and finery had little bearing on the interior world of spirit, other than to disclose the hypocrisy of those who would flatter themselves with such vanities. But this is exactly the point at which Rowlandson's critique of Weetamoo not only fails to abject the Native before Anglo-Protestant racial privilege; it also quite dramatically suggests a similarity with the indigenous woman born, ironically, of Rowlandson's contemptuous regard: Weetamoo is too much *like* an English woman of fashion, or even a Cheapside prostitute,

---

23. Lisa Logan similarly argues that "Rowlandson's test is an inquiry into the position(s) of woman as subject in/of/to discourse; and 'captivity' is both the occasion for her writing and a telling metaphor for her position," See Logan, "Mary Rowlandson's Captivity and the 'Place' of the Woman Subject," *Early American Literature* 28, no. 3 (1993): 256.

24. See Armstrong and Tennenhouse, "The American Origins of the English Novel," *American Literary History* 4, no. 3 (1992): 386–410.

to be merely dismissed as some racially inferior "Other." Rather, in the condition of captivity to which she is reduced, Rowlandson feels herself to occupy a footing similar to that of her female mistress, which is to say that her experience of quasi-slavery redefines her understanding of what she previously was, rather than serving exclusively, as some have argued, as occasion to reaffirm English ethnological superiority in the face of her reluctant hybridization.[25]

At the very moment Rowlandson's text wants to assert radical difference, it betrays a stubborn identity along gender lines, and furthermore defines one of her "exemplary" moments of affliction in surprisingly personal terms. No remembered episode in the text more dramatically sustains the creation of the "personal" within the cross-ethnic identification with Weetamoo than when Rowlandson relates how she must "confess that I could not much condole with" the grief-stricken indigenous woman whose papoose has just died in the wilderness. Here, as elsewhere, Rowlandson's denial of any intimacy with Weetamoo draws undue attention to the terms of the refusal. A shared experience of loss and grief construes an occasion for identification between these two abject mothers. Notwithstanding Rowlandson's attempted repudiation of that identification, we can nonetheless suggest that her text sponsors an emotional agency they clearly share. Although avowedly repulsed by her mistress, Rowlandson repeatedly discloses such scenes of cross-ethnic inter-identification, as for example in the scene where she feeds her master and mistress, the latter of whom jealously rejects the Englishwoman's efforts to participate in the domestic and implicitly sexual economy of her owners. Within the patriarchalized terms of female jealousy and rivalry for male favor, what emerges is an account of the feminine that extends well beyond the localized ethnographic and religious confines of the moment. The terms of Rowlandson's "suffering" in these episodes indicate a condition of feminine identity more or less universal within patriarchal culture, which is to say that from the experience of this kind of affliction, the text sketches a more

---

25. Teresa Toulouse also notes the competitive dimension of the Weetamoo conflict in "'My Own Credit': Strategies of (E)valuation in Mary Rowlandson's Captivity Narrative," *American Literature* 64, no. 4 (1992): 657. Castiglia, *Bound and Determined*, finds that the text "destabilized the rigid hierarchies of Puritan orthodoxy, hierarchies based on firmly held binarisms (white/Indian, society/wilderness, male/female, divine/evil)" (48). Ralph Bauer, "Creole Identities in Colonial Space: The Narratives of Mary White Rowlandson and Francisco Nunez de Pineda y Bascunan," *American Literature* 69, no. 4 (1997), discusses the problem of hybridity and "the anxieties involved in the colonials' own sense of transculturation" (680).

generalized concept of human complexity that extends beyond both racial and hermeneutic fields. More broadly, the text stages a conflict between ethnology and theology, as the doctrinal reading of Rowlandson's afflictive narrative struggles to contain those "irruptions" of excessive indigenous personality and shared feminine identity into the ethnologically singular stasis required by the exemplaristic model of imitative piety. If Rowlandson finally remains unable to resist the necessity of even temporary creolization and enculturation, then she remains similarly unable or unwilling to suborn herself to the interpretive demands of her culture as well.

THE INVISIBLE HAND

Rowlandson's attempts to make sense of her affliction do not always explain the experiences she is having. Breitwieser's analysis of mourning's persistent tug on her narrative and interpretive awareness quite clearly demonstrates this point. In addition to detailing a mourning problematical because too personal, the text's complex construction reveals a potentially contradictory fit between experience and interpretation that only deepens the text's theological conflicts. While none, to my knowledge, have ever seriously questioned that Rowlandson was the primary author of *The Sovereignty and Goodness of God*, the text's divided structure has attracted some comment over the years.[26] While we should be careful, given the lack of a corroborative archive, to assert an account of the text's creation in which authorship is held to be shared by Rowlandson and Mather, I will exploit the tension between empirical and rhetorical narratives identified by Derounian and others to argue that some measure of the text's theological anxiety can be taken by considering more particularly the relation between Rowlandson's recorded experiences and the exegetical uses to which they are put in the text. As with the displaced ethnological conflict with Weetamoo, in which her depiction of the struggle departs from its exemplaristic function, Rowlandson's experiential narrative doesn't always fit neatly into its exegetical framework. Whether considered "spiritual" or "profane" as she makes her way through the memory of her captivity, her recorded experience at times imperfectly registers its attempted scriptural management. By drawing out some of these dissonances between

---

26. See Derounian, "Puritan Orthodoxy and the 'Survivor Syndrome,'" 83; and Logan, "Mary Rowlandson's Captivity," 264, 265.

experience and exegesis, we can better hear the sounds of a still deeper theological clash between a corporate model of exemplaristic representation and a more recognizably modern narrative of individual and collective rationalization haunted by its religious history.

Scholars have for a variety of reasons been reluctant to speculate on the extent of Increase Mather's participation in the crafting of *The Sovereignty and Goodness of God*. The most obvious reason, of course, is that there is no hard evidence that Mather wrote even the preface, although most assume with David Richards that Mather encouraged her to write the story shortly after her return from captivity, saw the text through publication in 1682, and supplied the infamous "ter amicum" preface, which appeared in all four of the 1682 editions that appeared in print.[27] Lacking any textual archive by which editorial emendations and collations might indicate a controlling or singular authorial hand, and assuming the biblical literacy and intelligence of Mary Rowlandson (to say nothing of not wanting to diminish her achievement or gender by questioning her text's composition), most have stayed away from precisely this sort of speculative skepticism.[28] We are less interested here in the gendered politics of authorship—although this is certainly an approach worth considering further—than in the complex interpretive spaces that might be opened by questioning, rather than assuming, a harmonious fit between what Mary Rowlandson recalls and how her text construes memory in its Biblicist inscriptions. While the sorts of dissonance to be heard in the text might imply a more intrusive Matherian presence in the composition of the text "proper" than scholarship has been thus far prepared or able to concede, the composite-authorship question can be more or less bracketed in favor of considering the cultural work performed by the text in terms of its mediation of doctrinal influences on practical piety.

Consider the following moment, recorded during the Fifth Remove, and describing the escape of Rowlandson's captors from the pursuing English army:

---

27. See Richards, *The Memorable Preservation: Narratives of Indian Captivity in the Literature and Politics of Colonial New England, 1675–1725* (Honors thesis, Yale College, 1967), 20–30.

28. There are a few exceptions to this. Teresa Toulouse discusses aspects of the dissonance between Rowlandson's narrative and the biblical references she employs. See Toulouse, "'My Own Credit,'" 661–62. Dawn Henwood, "Mary Rowlandson and the Psalms," argues that the scriptures supply Rowlandson "with a public liturgical language" that "empowers her to speak passionately of her own grief, confusion and anger" (171).

> For they went, as if they had gone for their lives, for some considerable way, and then they made a stop, and chose some of their stoutest men, and sent them back to hold the English army in play whilst the rest escaped: And then, like Jehu, they marched on furiously, with their old and with their young: some carried their old decrepit mothers, some carried one, and some another. Four of them carried a great Indian upon a bier; but going through a thick wood with him, they were hindered, and could make no haste, whereupon they took him upon their backs, and carried him, one at a time, till they came to Baquag river. (MR 332–33)

It's an important scene in several ways, not least because Rowlandson returns, toward the conclusion of her narrative, "to mention a few remarkable passages of providence, which I took special notice of in my afflicted time," including this moment of providentially authorized escape by the "enemy" when the English were close enough "to destroy them utterly." Yet, Rowlandson surmises, "God seemed to leave his people to themselves, and order all things for his holy ends" (MR 358). In what becomes a routine gesture of apparently self-authorizing lay typology, Rowlandson compares the "furious" march of the Indians to Jehu's driving of his army to the gates of Jezreel to overthrow the corrupt house of Ahab, worshippers of Baal. But exactly what sort of typology is being established here? Jehu's victory over the house of Ahab temporarily re-established the one God of Israel and an anointed king over Israel and Judah; he is, that is to say, one of the military heroes of the Old Testament, a scourge of polytheism, idolatry, and sin, whose inability to follow the law of God subsequently diminished his star considerably.[29] Jehu provides an ambiguous referent for typological thinking: on the one hand, he exemplifies the figure of the holy warrior by fulfilling the terms of his sacred anointment without question; on the other, he serves as a cautionary figure who, following his otherwise glorious triumph, fails to sustain his side of the covenant by allowing Israel to slide back into idolatry and religious malaise. In its reference to failed promise, the casual Jehu reference seems Jeremiadical. Given Increase Mather's desire to read the war as God's judgment on the failures of New England / Israel, we might construe the Jehu reference as a Matherian gesture, one designed to draw attention to New England's

---

29. 2 Kings 10:30, King James Version.

status as simultaneously anointed and sinful, the chosen remnant sliding ever further into a darkness more stygian because the promise of glory was once so bright. As Rowlandson's husband Joseph put it in his sermon on Jeremiah 23:33, "The point is to be understood of a people that are visibly and externally near and dear to him, and these may be totally and finally forsaken of God."[30] Whether or not Mather actually "wrote" the Jehu typology into the text, we can still understand the hermeneutic established by the gesture as they become characters of a Matherian-identified drama of the modern saint's choice: that New England will either make good on the failures of the Old Testament heroes by upholding their side of the gospel covenant, or it will go the sorry way of Old Israel, and return to an interrupted sequence of covenant-breakage and yet more sin.

This doctrinal reading of Jehu (and the text as a whole), however, doesn't account for another way of thinking about the typology established. The passage explicitly compares the flight of the Natives to Jehu's driving of his tattered army to the gates of Jezreel; the typology, as grammatically and logically constructed, compares the experiences of an (admittedly ambiguous) Old Testament military hero to those of a starving band of indigenous peoples trying to escape a pursuing Christian foe. To make the typology "work" would be to understand that both Jehu and the Wampanoags share a desperate nobility, an acceptable reading given the sacrificial heroism of the defending warriors, to say nothing of the text's frequent (if unintended or begrudging) depictions of Native endurance, compassion, and even heroism. A second, and more intriguing, reading beckons: the Natives, like Jehu, are the anointed scourge of the unbelieving Israelites. What emerges here is a surprising critique of the official "reading" of the war provided by the colony's religious and political leadership, including Increase Mather, who had been himself involved in various scrambles and intrigues with his peers to control the official interpretation of the war. In a sense, the divided typology and authorship of *The Sovereignty and Goodness of God* reflected the divided state of New England's leadership and conduct of the war. And even where most believed, with Mather and the ministers, that the war was a judgment on sinful New England, there was disagreement about which sins were at fault, and who was responsible

---

30. Joseph Rowlandson, *The Possibility of God's Forsaking a People That Have Once Been Visibly Near and Dear to Him* (Cambridge, MA: S. Green, 1682), 3.

for their commission. The Lord's smile shines upon any and all efforts to punish the sinful English for their ongoing crimes of personal unbelief, evangelical failures, doctrinal laxity, and national sin.[31]

This alternate reading is one which the collectively authored and self-divided *Sovereignty and Goodness of God* solicits, and, at key points, sustains. We might, for example, point to the marked similarity between the inscrutable, apparently arbitrary and even capricious mind of the Puritan God—"Thus all things come alike to all: none knows either love or hatred by all that is before him" (MR 319)—and the equally baffling, totally unpredictable behavior of Rowlandson's captors: "Sometimes I met with favor, and somethings with nothing but frowns" (MR 340). By advancing the possibility that God has decided to switch sides, that the eerie mimesis of divine and Native unintelligibility signals a new covenant with the Natives, the text's readers encounter the "savages" as something other than mere instruments of God's scourge. In the concluding movement of her text, Rowlandson remarks "the wonderful providence of God in preserving the heathen for further affliction to our poor country" (MR 358–59); and then again: "yet how to admiration did the Lord preserve them for his Holy ends, and the destruction of many still amongst the English"; and then again: "Though many times they would eat that, that a hog or a dog would hardly touch; yet by that God strengthened them to be a scourge to His people"; and then again: "I can but stand in admiration to see the wonderful power of God, in providing for such a vast number of our enemies." Although the text attempts to manage the ontology of the Natives back into Christianity's toolbox of divine instrumentality, the compulsive repetition produces its own counterorthodox resonance: "Strangely did the Lord provide for them," Rowlandson interjects, "that I did not see (all the time I was among them) one man, woman, or child, die with hunger." God "feeds and nourishes them up to be a scourge to the whole land" (MR 359), a claim which, on the face of it, asserts the instrumental claim, even as the rhetoric of Natives as divine affliction characterizes that relationship in terms of God's compassion for them. Jehu's anointment as scourge to the unbelieving house of Ahab does not limit him to merely instrumental status; in similar fashion, the typologizing of the Natives in relation to Jehu can be understood as part of a wider crisis of corporate covenant. Indeed,

---

31. For discussion of the complexities of the religious meanings of the war, see Lepore, *The Name of War*, 97–121.

the confusion around the typological significance of the Natives broadens the "anxiety" of the text from one affecting an individual woman to one affecting a broader cadre of religious and political leadership in New England.

In one significant way, then, these two readings of the Jehu typology (that either the English or the Algonquians are like Jehu) are similar: they both imply an insufficient English commitment to the terms of anointment and covenant, and regardless of whether Native or Englishwoman occupies the typological position, the perils of vitiated faith and incompleted Holy task are writ large. These two typologies are quite different, and advance decidedly opposed understandings of what cultural work the typology will perform in its reception by a New English audience. By positing several hermeneutical frameworks, the Jehu typology undercuts any monological regard of the text as being the singular teleological endpoint of a historical narrative begun in the Pentateuch, partially fulfilled in the New Testament, and carried through into the New Israel of the seventeenth century. Whether this textual polyvocality implies the presence of a multiple authorship or not misses the larger point here: that the text invites multiple readings, and that in doing so makes the case for an *individual reading practice* residing at the heart of any interpretive project in which a believer makes sense of her experience relative to scripture. Without overstating the case, we might at this point propose that the space for interpretive independence opened up by the text's typological multiplicity could be said less to invent than to reconfigure the radical interpretive agency assumed by Anne Hutchinson's Antinomianism and the Quaker's intimate mysticism. Rowlandson's is more subtle, to be sure, but its possible effect on orthodox community is by no means less "dangerous" than its more radical predecessors. Quite the opposite is the case. Whether in spite or because of Increase Mather's authorial contribution, Rowlandson's text folds its own divided hermeneutic into the exemplary text, thereby incorporating the pious woman's potentially wayward spiritual history into the memorial text ostensibly designed to further orthodoxy's ambitions.

Even where the text explicitly interpolates biblical excerpt, whether in historically typological or more generally theological modes, Rowlandson's recorded experience threatens to squirm out of the Mather-tailored straightjacket. In the Third Remove, when Mary's daughter dies and the mother is forced to leave her daughter's lifeless body in the wilderness, she describes her attempt to cure the wound she took during the Lancaster raid. "Then I took oaken leaves and laid to my wide, and with the blessing of God it cured me also; yet before the cure was wraught, I may say, as it is in Psalms 38:5–6. *My wounds stink and are corrupt, I am bowed down greatly, I go mourning all the day long*" (MR 328). Quoting from one of the so-called Lament psalms in which the psalmist's cry for divine comfort takes on a desperate and wholly unrequited edge ("Hasten to my help," the psalm concludes), Rowlandson appears to position her experience within the context of psalmic desperation, even as she reports receiving comfort from her oaken field-dressing. Indeed, her text registers the dissonance between medical and scripture comforts, as it acknowledges that the outcome of her "cure" is more than Psalm 38 would give her grounds to expect. Her experience of mourning—"I sat much alone with a poor wounded child in my lap" (328)—accords with the melancholy lament of the Psalm, even as the exemplaristic demands of the corporate model require her text to gesture toward a redemptive account of suffering. Her presentation of the psalm recasts her experience—"yet before the cure was wraught"—so as to accord with the exhortational mode of her piety. It's almost as if her authorship comes to restructure her very memory, as she recalls this moment of wilderness medicine only to deny its remembered efficacy. Despite its commitment to a corporate rendering of representative affliction, the text envelops Protestantism's individuation of faith into the bargain as well, potentially undercutting the federal impulse pressuring Rowlandson and her audience to read her experiences a certain way. Like Lot's Wife, she keeps looking back, and even as her text routinely attempts to press experience into a scriptural leaf, the backward glance lingers on, performing the complex psychological work of memory and mourning. The narrative could even be said to mourn the loss of Rowlandson herself; it registers her own transformation into the exemplary text that always points away from herself and toward invisible realities. She both is inimitable and must be imitated, which is to say that Rowlandson's text does not so much update Winthrop's "City on the Hill" as rewrite it as a personal drama. Mary Rowlandson's text manifests both the state-identified Puritanism it is expected to represent—*The Sovereignty and Goodness of God*—and an unsettling evasion of Puritanism's representational terms. We keep returning to the emotional confusion of her many losses, and in those returns—or "removes" as her text would put it—we keep encountering God from a distance.

SURVIVING FAITH

Perhaps no aspect of *The Sovereignty and Goodness of God* has prompted more interest in the student encounter with Rowlandson's text than her representation of the acquisition, circulation, and consumption of food.[32] Given the compelling cultural, ethnological, political, economic, military, and theological issues subtending the text, it is easy to forget that the "Narrative of Mrs Mary White Rowlandson" is a compelling story of survival, and I mean to invoke the term "survival" here in a very literal and material fashion, as have others.[33] Not only did her captivity take place during the bleakest months of an obdurately long New England winter when food stores would be at their lowest, but the military struggle between the Native alliance and the English colonists further diminished food-gathering capabilities where it did not more directly destroy increasingly precious food reserves. Starvation, both experienced and imminent, was a very real issue for captive and captor alike, and it should therefore come as little surprise that Rowlandson should write so movingly and so frequently about her eating habits during the captivity. Indeed, of the twenty "Removes" that divide her narrative into temporal periods within the eleven-week captivity, fifteen refer to food. Rowlandson scrounges, barters, and steals food, and when she does not, the Bible does more than just spiritually sustain her: "and now may I say with Jonathan," she writes in the seventeenth Remove, "'See, I pray you, how mine eyes have been enlightened, because I tasted a little of this honey' (1 Samuel 14:29). Now is my spirit revived again; though means be never so inconsiderable, yet if the Lord bestow his blessing upon them, they shall refresh both soul and body" (MR 349–50). Even in those few Removes where she does not

---

32. Carruth argues that Rowlandson's "representations of her disorderly eating and excess appetite" foreground an investment in the abject which forges a "counternarrative" against the official ministerial interpretation of the war. See "Between Abjection and Redemption: Mary Rowlandson's Subversive Corporeality," in *Feminist Interventions in Early American Studies*, ed. Mary Carruth (Tuscaloosa: University of Alabama Press, 2006), 70.

33. Slotkin and Folsom introduce their edition of Rowlandson's narrative by describing the story as "an examination of the price of survival, of what one must learn and of the compromises one must make merely to stay alive." See Folsom and Slotkin, introduction to *So Dreadfull a Judgment, Puritan Responses to King Philip's War, 1676–1677*, edited by Richard Slotkin and James Folsom (Middletown, CT: Wesleyan University Press, 1978), 309. Dawn Henwood, "Mary Rowlandson and the Psalms," also maintains that "Mary Rowlandson is, however, above all a survivor" (172).

describe the food problem literally, she invokes the comfort of scripture sustenance, as for example when the words of Jeremiah prove "a sweet cordial to me when I was ready to faint" (MR 332). If she does not in any literal way consume the Bible she finds in the wilderness, she certainly consumes its words with an appetite prompted at least in part by her experience of bodily deprivation.

The "simple" survival story cannot be told independently of the soul's proximity to hunger, feast, and famine, and in the survival narrative of *The Sovereignty and Goodness of God*, we can see the spiritual struggles of its primary author in perhaps their most dramatic terms.[34] In no small part due to Calvinism's diminishment of human effort in Protestant salvation theory, New England Puritan theologians had labored to work out spiritual effort's place within a general theory of agency. Thomas Shepard, for example, argued in his 1652 sermon cycle "Of Ineffectual Hearing of the Word" that God speaks to us in two voices, one "containing letters and syllables," and one that "secretly speaks to the heart."[35] External and internal languages define the agency of the listener as one that strives to hear the former and, in doing so, is prepared to receive the mysterious power of the latter and so move into a closer state of divine intimacy. As we saw in Hutchinson's spiritist rejection of the significance to be accorded the semiotics of sanctification, the doubled language residing within spiritual confessional work did not necessarily resolve the tension between human effort and holy agency. In its representation of the food relation, Rowlandson's text exhibits the double language of Shepard's preparationist theology, as she expends considerable effort (in the survival mode) to acquire nourishment and so continue the story of afflicted perseverance, while at the same time she understands the acquisition of food in terms of the language—illustrated by scripture—of divine closeness. Unlike

---

34. I am indebted here to Caroline Walker Bynum's study of food in medieval British women's religious lives. Bynum argues that the "extreme asceticism and literalism of women's spirituality were . . . efforts to gain power and give meaning" and that because female spirituality was centered on the consumption of the body or "flesh" of Christ, "this flesh is simultaneously pleasure and pain." See Bynum, *Holy Feast and Holy Fast*, 208 and 245. In making the case for food relations serving a symbolically significant role in the spiritual drama of the text, I am following Roland Barthes's observation that "one could say that an entire 'world' (social environment) is present in and signified by food." See Barthes, "Toward a Psychosociology of Contemporary Food Consumption," in *Food and Culture: A Reader*, ed. Carole Counihan and Penny Van Esterik (New York: Routledge, 1997), 23.

35. Thomas Shepard, *On Ineffectual Hearing of the Word*, in *The Works of Thomas Shepard*, vol. 3 (1652; repr., Boston: Boston Doctrinal Tract and Book Society, 1853), 365.

Hutchinson, Rowlandson appears willing to participate in the Puritan analysis of the material world's indirect indication of divine intention, and the food relation provides ample opportunity for her to play her role in the salvific drama so staged. Food becomes the occasion, and the means, to further the text's Puritanism.

Food—its acquisition, its refusal, its sharing, its withholding—takes on aspects of the Puritan understanding of divinity itself. She is, for example, blessed with food at unexpected moments. In the ninth Remove, she is forced to leave her putative owners' wigwam and seek shelter in another, whose owner gives her food and a fire's warmth. Recognizing divinity's uncanny proximity to and distance from Protestant spiritual desire, she remarks, "yet these were strangers to me that I never saw before" (MR 339). In the next Remove, she is denied food for no apparent reason: "I went home and found venison roasting that night, but they would not give me one bit of it" (MR 340). As with the occasionally inscrutable behavior of her captors, the unpredictability of nourishment provides occasion for both bafflement and understanding, which is to say that the food problem becomes another site for the penitent to grapple with the dilemma of uncertainty and assurance. Insofar as the wilderness location of the captivity places the food relation in close proximity to an English person's understanding of a precultural natural world, moreover, the exigencies of food bring the Puritan mind into closer inspection of the world-as-divine text. In her "reading" of the intentionality behind the seemingly arbitrary provision and withholding of food (whether by God or by his appointed instruments, the natives), Rowlandson characteristically holds the scripture-text up as a way to understand or explicate the meaning of the revealed world. The food narrative also coordinates the fit between World and Word, flesh and spirit, and so locates Rowlandson at the interpretive crux of that structure. The seemingly arbitrary logic of food acquisition and denial provides access to the spiritual struggles of Mary Rowlandson, which is to say that the text stages the spiritual drama of the hungry soul alongside the human survival tale. Indeed, these two stories are inseparable for most of the text.

There is even something of a conversion narrative told through the story food scarcity and unseemliness, although this narrative is somewhat disjointed, thereby drawing attention to a lack of fit between spiritual and profane realities. At the beginning of the captivity, she forces herself to eat the Native's "filthy trash," but by the end of her struggle she finds the same food "sweet and savory to my taste" (MR 333). To the extent that the food problem tells the story of the reluctant and starving sinner's conversion to accepting and joyous saint, we might profit by reading *The Sovereignty and Goodness of God* as a kind of vernacular theology in and of itself. The text offers a representation and a theory of spiritual agency not only without recourse to any specific liturgical demands, but does so in the "common" plainspeak of an ordinary Puritan gentlewoman talking about a domestic issue over which women could be said to have some authority. At the conclusion of her story, she reflects at length on the issue of food, emerging over the course of these remarks as something of a theorist of food's relation to spirituality. Indeed, food relations parallel and intersect with the text's religious commitments throughout her story, not only providing an orthodox gloss on the spiritual dimensions of bodily affliction, but providing a vista to a terrain of spiritual agency in which the exigencies of the self's place within the natural world start taking on a life of their own.

For in its depiction of human–food connections, the text at times diverges from its signifying relation to the immanent spirit the world is supposed at all times to register.[36] Right from the start of her dramatic captivity, Rowlandson invokes the food problem to represent the trauma of an experience whose spectacular violence insists on being read in simultaneously material and spiritual terms. After describing particular instances of Native-on-English violence, she comments: "Thus were we butchered by those merciless heathen, standing amazed, with the blood running down to our heels" (MR 324). The rending of human flesh images the specter of cannibalism, a figure that haunts the edges of Rowlandson's narrative in the figuration of the English as a "company of sheep torn by wolves" and the Natives as "ravenous beasts" (MR 325). While the bestial vocabulary derives from a familiar fund of ethnocentric linguistic capital, it is worth pointing out that the implied animalism of the human has nearly always organized itself around beastlike eating practices, including cannibalism, which the anthropologists tell us have served different functions in

---

36. For an anthropological view of the cosmology of food systems, see Mary Douglas, who observes that "when the classifications of any metaphysical scheme are imposed on nature, there are several points where it does not fit." Speaking specifically of the emergence of blood ritual in Mosaic law, she continues: "So long as the classifications remain in pure metaphysics and are not expected to bite into daily life in the form of rules of behavior, no problem arises. But if the unity of Godhead is to be related to the unity of Israel and made into a rule of life, the difficulties start." See Douglas, "Deciphering a Meal," in Counihan and Van Esterik, *Food and Culture: A Reader*, 51.

different societies, including acting as a "rite of vengeance or the celebration of victories in war, or even used to provision an army in the field."[37] The ascription of bestial appetite to the Native attackers presents them as violating a cultural dietary taboo, even as the bestial gives way to the cosmological: their cannibalistic savagery renders them "a company of hellhounds" (MR 325). Thus the Natives are at once beyond the human, yet also actors in the Christian drama of salvation. The braiding of the inhuman and the holy into the hybrid figure of the ferociously appetitive Indian enters the text before we even meet one of Mary Rowlandson's despised "Praying Indians." Unwittingly or not, the text scrambles the domains of the sacred and the profane even as its author strives to separate them.

The human ingestion of blood is, moreover, clearly a resonant term relative to the Christian Eucharist, to say nothing of being a significant ritualistic practice in religions across the world. In the Seventh Remove, she describes her consumption of an undercooked horse's liver which she greedily eats "with the blood about my mouth, and yet a savory bit it was to me" (MR 335). Later, in the Fourteenth Remove, she recounts the Native practice of boiling deer blood, but insists that she "could eat nothing of that, though they ate it sweetly" (MR 347). The ingestion and refusal of blood both weakens and enforces ethnic boundary relations between English and Native persons, a wavering practice of taboo observance and evasion that itself speaks to the larger issue of human–animal boundaries on which the text's ethnocentric critique of Native identity partially depends. Rowlandson, that is to say, attempts at times to refuse any possible identification with her captors through her performance of a food relation. At the same time, her participation in Native food-consumption habits is presented as being part of the traumatic nature of her experiences, as she frequently depicts her eating in terms of human agency *in extremis*. That she has been brought so low that eating raw horse liver—or the fetus of a deer—can be not only possible but "very good" (MR 347) serves as a measure of her extraordinary suffering, and also provides her with an ethnocentric alibi for her involuntary engagement in these "inhuman" eating practices. As survival narrative, her account of food represents a trauma that exceeds cultural dietary taboo and at least partially explains her divergence from a strict performance of English coloniality, but the

---

37. Margaret Mead, "The Changing Significance of Food," in Counihan and Van Esterik, *Food and Culture: A Reader*, 13.

traumatic origin-as-explanation of her appetitive savagery succeeds only to the extent that her relation to food remains at all times involuntary where not more explicitly the result of a coercion born of desperation.

Were Mary Rowlandson's understanding of the food problem defined exclusively in terms of an enforced acquiescence to cultural Otherness, its significance relative to her spiritual ambitions would remain an interpretive nonstarter. Such a coercion-alibi would extend to its readers as well. As with so many other aspects of this text, however, the retrospective construction of the experience as historical representation introduces the perspective of the post-experience author into the story. A certain authorial knowingness emerges at various points during the story, and this perspective makes it difficult to accept that Rowlandson was coerced into intimacies with her captors. One measure of the text's knowingness relative to the food issue might be taken with the following passage, which appears toward the end of the Fifth Remove:

> The first week of my being among them I hardly ate any thing; the second week I found my stomach grow very faint for want of something; and yet it was very hard to down their filthy trash; but the third week, though I could think how formerly my stomach would turn against this or that, and I could starve and die before I could eat such things, yet they were sweet and savory to my taste. (MR 333)

As one of several passages in *The Sovereignty and Goodness of God* that introjects a retrospective authorial comment, the text could be said to anticipate and thereby manage the impact of subsequent depictions of Rowlandson's increasingly questionable eating practices. In the Seventh Remove she eats the horse liver; in the Fourteenth the deer fetus; in the Seventeenth she eats a broth made of "horses feet" (MR 349), and in the Eighteenth she infamously steals a horse-hoof from a teething infant (MR 350). The inserted commentary itself follows a pattern loosely analogous to the standard Protestant conversion narrative; initially, she refuses food, whether on the grounds of taste or a deeper refusal to "commune" with her captors; in the week following, her hunger overcomes the nausea she feels for the Natives and their food; but in the third week she not only concedes to the demands of extremity but takes apparent pleasure in her eating among the Natives. Abjection gives way to a kind of cultural transcendence as she sheds her commitment to sanctioned eating practices and acquiesces to the pleasures—however meagre—afforded by her diet in the wilderness. To this parallel story of appetite's salvation, Rowlandson frequently appends scriptural comment, as for example when the blood drips from her mouth and she remarks the uncooked horse liver's savory taste, she adds, "For to the hungry soul every bitter thing is sweet" (335; Proverbs 27:7). She offers a scriptural gloss from Job 6:7 to the scene where she steals food from an infant: "The things that my soul refused to touch are as my sorrowful meat" (350). During her captivity, Rowlandson's changing understanding of her food consumption parallels the soul's changing relation to sin in salvation theory and conversion narrative. The abjection of self that is the soul's condition of original sin parallels the unfulfilled appetitive self of the starvation story. The struggling soul "awakened" to the need for conversion intersects with and describes the ravenous self who will accept anything to assuage her hunger, whether materially or spiritually satisfying. The arbitrary decisions of God find earthly expression in the seemingly random dispensations of scarcity and plenty. Read in this way, the food narrative sustains the Puritan epistemology of the world as the gradual revelation of God's invisible domain, as the various acts of scrounging, praying, hoarding, stealing, eating, and refusing correspond to acts of divine dispensation, succor, punishment, notice, mercy, and so forth. The intertwining of food's materiality and spirituality sustains the exemplary message of the text's orthodox intent and provides repeated occasion for Rowlandson to engage in either introspective analysis or outward perseverance.

The exemplarity of the text with respect to Rowlandson's negotiation of eating is not without its complications. In the Fifteenth Remove, she inserts another retrospective comment that invites us to consider how she feels about food in the present tense of the narrative's composition, some five years after her bartered release from captivity:

> I cannot but think what a wolvish appetite persons have in a starving condition; for many times when they gave me that which was hot, I was so greedy, that I should burn my mouth, that it would trouble me hours after, and yet I should quickly do the same again. And after I was thoroughly hungry, I was never again satisfied. For though sometimes it fell out, that I got enough, and did eat till I could eat no more, yet I was as unsatisfied as I was when I began. And now could I see that Scripture verified (there being many Scriptures which we do not take notice of, or understand till

we are afflicted) "Thou shalt eat and not be satisfied" (Micah 6.14). Now might I see more than ever before, the miseries that sin hath brought upon us. (MR 347–48)

The passage replays the "food conversion" we have already seen, as Rowlandson relates her ability to overcome her resistance to formerly unpalatable foods. Her consumption habits clearly metaphorize the spiritual struggle of the soul's resistance and acquiescence to sin, which she further develops by the scriptural reference to the prophet Micah's damning of the house of Hezekiah of Judah for its continued worship of Ba-al. Here as elsewhere in the text, Rowlandson implies that she and her fellow Puritans have earned their punishment, and are suffering the consequences of their sinful behavior in the form of King Philip's scourge. So far, in terms of the text's desire to manage the war into a cultural hermeneutic commensurate with ministerial orthodoxy, so good.[38] As retrospective narrative, however, the passage returns us to the present of Rowlandson's authorship of the narrative. "Now might I see more than ever before," she writes, that the merited punishment of herself and her people not only fulfilled the Old Testament's prophetic warnings but explain the hunger of her present condition as well. Her present perspective remains informed by her past experiences of sin, merited punishment, and ongoing dissatisfaction. It is the last condition that is of interest here. Rowlandson uses some pretty strong language to describe her unfulfilled appetite: "And after I was thoroughly hungry, I was never again satisfied." Certainly it would be easy to read this in a manner consistent with the exemplary logic of the orthodox purview: that she is referring to the idea of unslaked appetite during the captivity only, and that appetitive desire remains in any case a metaphor for the hungry soul. Read along with the Micah typology, however, the passage implies that Rowlandson's appetite continues in the present: that, only "now," some five years after her experience, can she relive the bodily needs of her captivity and therefore fully understand the significance of Micah's curse. At the very least, her memory of abject want is revitalized as the present-day rhetoric of her text's hortatory ambitions.

---

38. Carruth reads the passage similarly: "This is the prophet's denouncement of the Israelites for their sins, the prefigurement in Puritan typology of God's punishment of his chosen people and an aptly selected scripture to support Increase Mather's interpretation of Metacom's war." See Carruth, "Between Abjection and Redemption," 71.

Food mediates the ambiguous relationship between her present and historical selves throughout the narrative, including *The Sovereignty and Goodness of God*'s coda. Under point four of Rowlandson's remarkable summing up of those events "which I took special notice of in my afflicted time" (MR 358), she observes that "though many times they would eat that, that [sic] a hog or dog would hardly touch, yet by that God strengthened them to be a scourge to His people" (MR 359). Although she retains the instrumentalist view of the Natives being little more than tools in God's afflictive design for the chosen, the passage nonetheless implies that even the Natives are something other than the beasts with whom she has previously compared them. She goes on to provide a catalogue of what earlier she described as the "filthy trash" of the Native cornucopia: "*They* would eat horse's guts, and ears, and all sorts of wild birds which they could catch; also bear, venison, beaver, tortoise, frogs, squirrels, dogs, skunks, rattlesnakes; yea, the very bark of tress; besides all sorts of creatures, and provision which they plundered from the English" (MR 359; italics added). The particularization of the Native's desperate diet asserts only to withdraw the Native's shared humanity, a familiar enough move to readers of the story. But does the enumeration really advance the spiritual ambitions? Why the detail? As involuntary anthropologist, Rowlandson provides the results of her ethnographical research. As colonial author of a text written with the reading audience of London's metropole partially in mind, she provides a sensationalistic account of life in the extraordinary conditions of colonial experience. As spiritual autobiographer, she relates the extreme conditions— in this case, the menu—of her divinely sanctioned affliction, but where this last authorial role might otherwise serve to bundle the menu into regenerative paradigm of the text's exemplaristic desires, its focus is less on the English settler's pursuit of this extraordinary diet than it is on the Native Other's normative consumption of it. For the real point of the section is for Rowlandson to "but stand in admiration to see the wonderful power of God in providing for such a vast number of our enemies in the wilderness, where there was nothing to be seen, but from hand to mouth" (MR 359). The extreme unpalatability and Otherness of the Native food catalogue stands oddly disconnected from her wondrous admiration of God's provision to the Enemy. At the very moment of spiritual victory, the profanation of experience obstructs the clarity of her text's theological message.

Rather than assert a certain and thereby comforting narrative for comprehending the significance of the wilderness diet, Rowlandson offers the shocking particulars only to withdraw into contemplative wonderment and abstraction. While analysis of the particular events of the material world offers a glimpse of the divine intentionality in the back of it, the text's approach to this foundational account of Puritan semiology invokes only to scramble the relations between visible indices (the diet) and invisible agency (God). In the end, that is to say, the text never finally settles on identifying the wilderness diet as either "filthy trash" or "sweet and savory." The interpretive undecidability here certainly rehearses the standard Puritan dilemma between doubt ("filth") and assurance ("nectar"), and so could fairly be understood as another example of an essentially Puritan encounter with its theology's uncertainties. The problem, however, is that the doubt or uncertainty displayed in the food negotiation sustains itself throughout the narrative and continues to sound through the text's deeply personalized and individuated account of the traumatized self. The uncertainty never settles into comfort. The food narrative both concedes and resists the theological demands placed upon its primary author, providing both an opportunity to sustain a relationship with God and an invitation to imagine a life without Him.

RANDOM ACTS OF ABANDONING

Although an overdetermined concept in colonial New England studies, the "Jeremiad" remains a useful way to make sense of some of the dominant cultural and religious preoccupations of late-seventeenth-century New England. Perry Miller's famous thesis has become a way to describe America's ability to redescribe dissent as consent, the critique of America as its affirmation. Whether we read the Jeremiad as either "declension" or "affirmation," it is important in either case to consider one of the characteristic features of the genre: its suggestion that God has at least temporarily removed himself from the affairs of New England, even as the sinfulness of New England has attracted God's special and punitive notice. In the former move, God's abandonment of a sinful world to some extent rehearses the initial punishment of our crimes in Eden; we are, following the Fall, always and already separate from God. In the second move, God's affliction, even of his chosen ones, indicates that he continues to take an interest in the affairs of men, even the bad ones. The "ambiguity" that scholars have located in the structure of the Jeremiad has still deeper roots in the Calvinist theology behind it, specifically the problematical fit between the consequentialist account of sin and malediction developed in the Old Testament, and the anticonsequentialist account of the same developed in Calvin's New Testament theology. Thus God abandons us because we have earned his lasting displeasure, but then that abandonment itself establishes the miraculous hope represented in Christ. Hope is the fulfillment of despair, a condition Rowlandson interrogates throughout this text.

We can see the former concern that God has abandoned the world to its own iniquity, in the prefatory remarks to William Adams's *The Necessity of the Pouring Out of the Spirit from On High*, a Jeremiad preached in Dedham, Massachusetts, in 1678. Observing that God made a "promise of the donation, and effusion of the Spirit, and so a dispensation of saving grace," authors Samuel Torrey and Josiah Flint go on to observe that God "doth at present so far suspend the accomplishment of this promise, and so far with hold [sic] his Spirit and grace" from us.[39] As with many seventeenth-century New England ministers and leaders, Adams speaks in the idiom of corporate rather than individual salvation. The sermon develops both senses of God's displeasure, articulating a vindictive God "with an angry countenance" who "engages his Power and wrath against them." But even in the threatening proximity of a wrathful God, Adams implies a more troubling turning away: "The Lord in the way of his Providence exposes them to Judgement, sets them in the way of misery, sorrow and calamity lighting upon them, follows them with evil . . . he does as it were set them as a mark to shoot the Arrows of his displeasure at them."[40] In the "providential way" of teleological narrative, the people become the protagonists of their own undoing, less the victims of omnipotence than the agents of their own weakness. As a reading of King Philip's War, which this 1679 sermon undoubtedly was, the text sketches God's displeasure in a number of frames, from vengeful punisher to passive emplotter.

This idea of God's abandonment of the nation to its own iniquities receives careful attention in Joseph Rowlandson's 1682 *Possibility of God's Forsaking a People That Have Once Been Visibly Near and Dear to Him*. None other than Mary White Rowlandson's first husband (whom she would outlive by quite a few years), Joseph preached this sermon just a few weeks

---

39. Adams, *The Necessity of the Pouring Out of the Spirit from On High upon a Sinning Apostatizing People* (Boston: John Foster, 1679), i.
40. Ibid., 7.

before his death on November 24, 1678. The sermon wasn't published until 1682, when it appeared, in London, alongside his widow's "History of the Captivity of Mrs. Mary Rowlandson, a Minister's Wife in New-England," possibly one of the earliest husband–wife publication ventures in English print.[41] In the sermon, Joseph attempts to answer the question "What doth God's forsaking mean? What is intended thereby it?"[42] His answer, predictable in some regards, is that "God withdraws himself, as the prophet Hosea phraises [sic] it," but that this withdrawal must be qualified: "We must here distinguish betwixt God's general presence, and his precious presence." In the former sense, God "is not far from any of us, *for in him we live, and move, and have our being (Acts 17.27.28).*" In this ontological account of God, Joseph insists that we can no more hide from God than from ourselves; God's being is the case for our own. The missing God of the Jeremiad's pessimistic viewpoint, however, takes the form of an absent "special presence, his favourable and gracious presence," a forsaking which amounts to the removal of what he calls "Affection" and "Action."[43] The loss of God's affection signals the removal of "his love from a people," whereas the loss of His action takes the form of God vexing his people "with all manner of Adversity." In this second version of earned abandonment, we see the Jeremiad's tendency to glorify the benefits of saintly affliction even as it advances a potentially tragic theology of a God turned indifferent to the needs of his people. In asking its listeners to contemplate a world from which God has deliberatively withdrawn and left in the hands of human adversity—"not by taking away this, or that outward comfort from them, but by taking away himself from them"—the sermon asks that we understand menace in terms of abandonment.[44] The entirely merited punishment of the once chosen, we might say, not only leaves sinner and saint alike at the mercy of earthly torment and affliction, but implies the existential case for the conditions of unbelief itself. A world without a God is the fundamental argument of modern secularism, that is to say. The abandonment thesis is both a formation of the secular and a way to better read that formation from the perspective of persistent religious belief. Rowlandson's late-seventeenth-century text serves as a primer in this regard.

---

41. Edward Arber, ed., *The Term Catalogues*, 3 vols. (London: Edward Arber, 1903), 507.
42. Joseph Rowlandson, *Possibility of God's Forsaking a People That Have Once Been Visibly Near and Dear to Him* (Cambridge, MA: S. Green, 1682), 4.
43. Joseph Rowlandson, *Possibility*, 4–5.
44. Ibid., 7, 10.

Trauma theory tells us that Rowlandson's attempt to reconstruct her experiences will invariably result in two stories: one that communicates the trauma of the event itself, and a second that repeats the trauma of the survivor.[45] These two stories never coincide, even as their repetition speaks to the trauma-survivor's desire to expiate the experience by making the trauma and its survival somehow "fit." Resolution emerges as the ideal; Rowlandson discloses the desire for identification with her earlier self, only to reveal the painful recognition of her difference and distance from it. Rowlandson the writer can never merge with Rowlandson the captive, even as the repeated scenes of her "howling and lamenting" in the wilderness resonate with the anxious insomnia she experiences five years later. As the traumatized self, she is like her dead child: abandoned in the wilderness and unrecoverable from its embrace. Having been "redeemed" from captivity and transformed into the imitable text of the exemplary penitent, Rowlandson tells and retells her story only to stand with "but wonder and admiration," and then spend her nights recalling that story without apparent end. One could extend this insight into the domain of Puritan typology as well. Rowlandson's repeated identifications with Old Testament figures like Lot's Wife and Job speak to the Puritan desire to understand the self as a reiteration of earlier biblical types. The analogical identification—Rowlandson is "like" Lot's Wife but naturally would never presume to believe herself either the same or as significant—defers its own gesture both temporally and theologically. It works to establish the spiritually significant aspects of her story both to her writerly self and to her interpreters; Rowlandson offers the exemplary text and with it the means to spiritualize a world whose events have had the effect of victimizing her and removing the hope of spiritual vitality from her grasp. Whether we are conceding to the demands of the exemplary text, or pausing to mourn with a grief-stricken Mary Rowlandson, a single question may be asked: What does her suffering mean? More broadly: Does her suffering mean anything at all?

Increase Mather's infamous preface offers an answer when it bewails the "sad catastrophe!" of the Lancaster raid, and observes, "Thus all things come alike to all: none knows either love or hatred by all that is before him. It is no new thing for God's precious ones to drink as deep as others, of the cup of common calamity: take Lot (yet captivated) for instance

---

45. Cathy Caruth, *Unclaimed Experience: Trauma, Narrative, History* (Baltimore: Johns Hopkins University Press, 1996), 7.

beside others."⁴⁶ The interpretive frame Mather provides here pressures the exemplary reading, as the case for omnipotence derived from Lot's captivity and redemption—"all things come to all"—threatens to compromise the distinction between saint and sinner otherwise maintained in the Lot story. Blessed affliction, this is to say, carries with it the potential to be misunderstood not merely by the sufferer but also by the reader(s) in whose place the sufferer stands. The theology of affliction places a heavy demand on its interpretive community, not least because Christ's passion itself demonstrated the possible outcome of saintly suffering: the inculcation of unbelief at the very moment of divine proximity. The random acts of divine arbitration visited on Old Testament hero and Puritan captive alike, while undoubtedly contributing to the typological reading of the text, its author, and the society of chosen Christians for which she stands, nonetheless lodges interpretive ambivalence inside the text's case for the redemptive powers of divinely ordered human suffering. We might say that in order for affliction to be religiously successful, its meaning must be comprehensible to the sufferer. If divine suffering fails to indicate something other than the mental or physical experiences of pain—if suffering fails, in other words, to be something other than identical to itself—then the religious belief that divine affliction would inculcate is lost. Rather than functioning as a kind of self-extension into and as community identification, human suffering becomes a relentlessly individuated event. Elaine Scarry has suggested that physical pain "has no referential content" and so resists its "objectification in language." Physical pain and, at times, "a state of consciousness other than pain . . . deprived of its object" can shatter the self's relation to the object world, thereby producing the peculiar self-referentiality of suffering with which Rowlandson struggles.⁴⁷ Suffering becomes meaningless, in this reading, when it fails to indicate transcendence. Pain becomes, following Asad, a signpost of the secular itself. The removal or prevention of human suffering constitutes a central ethical imperative of an episteme no longer anchored in a comforting Divinity, but rather left—abandoned—floating in the cognitive spaces of human sense-making and frustrated analysis.

Consider the key moment in her text when she compares herself to Lot's famous Wife:

---

46. Increase Mather, *An Earnest Exhortation*, 319.
47. Elaine Scarry, *The Body in Pain*, 5.

> I went along that day mourning and lamenting, leaving farther my own country, and travelling into the vast and howling wilderness, and I understood something of Lot's Wife's temptation, when she looked back: we came that day to a great swamp, by the side of which we took up our lodging that night. When I came to the brow of the hill, that looked toward the swamp, I thought we had been come to a great Indian town (though there were none but our own company). The Indians were as thick as the trees: it seemed as if there had been a thousand hatchets going at once: if one looked before one there was nothing but Indians, and behind one, nothing but Indians, and so on either hand, I myself in the midst, and no Christian soul near me, and yet how hath the Lord preserved me in safety! Oh the experience that I have had of the goodness of God, to me and mine! (MR 334)

Rowlandson asks more of typology than her religious culture is prepared to grant. She proposes to understand her affliction not merely in terms of a doctrinal rendering of Old Testament prefiguration but also in terms of her interpretation of an object world whose missing components—children, houses, spouses—produce a narrative "promising minutely mimetic repair" rather than one subjoined to a corporate typology of salvation.[48] Alongside the abstractions of self demanded by her culture's exemplaristic Protestantism, she stacks the details of her experience. Like the bewildering proliferation of Indians—whose numerous ubiquity refuses to recede into the background—or like Anne Bradstreet's enumeration of material loss in the poem commemorating her house's burning, Mary Rowlandson's memories of captive experience resist their conversion from memory to monument, from wife of faith to pillar of salt.[49] Her memories become a site for continued introspection and contemplative disengagement from religious hermeneutics.

---

48. Breitwieser quite rightly makes much of this passage, observing that "Rowlandson's identification with models such as Job and Lot's Wife discovers subdogmatic complexities in the Bible, a plurivocality that echoes with the tensions of grief and thereby establishes an intertextual rather than a didactic typology." Breitwieser, *American Puritanism*, 104, 105.

49. Tara Fitzpatrick follows a similar line of argument, observing that Rowlandson's "experience of survival, accommodation, and enlightenment in the forest resist[s] ready translation into the Puritan spiritual rhetoric of submission and self-effacement within a congregational community." See Fitzpatrick, "The Figure of Captivity: The 'Cultural Work' of the Puritan Captivity Narrative," *American Literary History* 3, no. 1 (1991): 12.

Even considered as a doctrinal typology in which Rowlandson positions herself as a latter-day Israelite lost in the wilderness and longing to return to New England's fold, there is a remarkable critique of New England at play in this passage. For if Mary Rowlandson reads herself into Lot's narrative of divine affliction and reward (such as it is), then what kind of typological analogy emerges between the two communities here? Is her Lancaster, or New England more generally, a latter-day Sodom? If the temptation to look back implicates these women in the sin of unbelief, then the historical destruction of Sodom just as surely places New England under similar terms of well-deserved judgment. Such a critique of corporate failure would be in keeping with the reading of Rowlandson's text as Jeremiad. Even so, it is worth observing that the voice of this critique is a woman's. Moreover, her possible critique of New England as a latter-day Sodom from which she has been taken perforce separates her ensuing narrative of affliction and redemption from that of New England's own.[50] The problem of her text remains the alignment of corporate and individual acts of human suffering and divine response. Her implied criticism of New England establishes the sovereignty of Mary Rowlandson not just as an author-recorder of her own experiences, but as a person claiming a personal religious experience independent of New England's spiritual discipline. Rowlandson's anxious recording of God's possible abandonment of the world imagines the exercise of religious belief as radically separate from its cultural and communal inscriptions. To be religious, in short, is to be alone.

Consider Rowlandson's meditation on Deuteronomy, an important text of New English theological and political thought which narrates the renewal of God's covenant with his chosen people during their wilderness nomadism following the Exodus. In a few respects, *The Sovereignty and Goodness of God* as a whole reads as a gloss on Deuteronomy, particularly the pivotal chapter 28, which Rowlandson cites (MR 331), in which Moses concludes his giving of the Law, and offers the Israelites two quite different outcomes: that reserved for those "who obey the Lord your God" (Deut. 28:1) and the other for those who "do not obey the Lord your God"

---

50. Cf. Castiglia, *Bound and Determined*: "White women have consistently used accounts of captivity to transgress and transform the boundaries of genre in order to accomplish their own ends, even—perhaps especially—when they contradict the desires of their white countrymen" (4).

(Deut. 28:15).[51] The antiphonal structure of chapter 28, in which the consequences of obedience are reversed, point for point, verse by verse, in the outline of disobedience's maledictions, strongly implies a consequentialist account of the self's relation to divine authority in which gestures of obedience or disobedience entail logically appropriate outcomes. Rowlandson goes on to cite her comforting reading of Deuteronomy 30, in which corporate contrition earns back God's compassion, simultaneously restoring the Manichean ethic established in Deuteronomy 28 and introducing an ambiguous reading of the finality of divine malediction. That is, if the Israelites, and New England's Puritans, have failed to obey and have thereby earned the punishments Moses details in Deuteronomy 28, the delicious reprieve later granted implies that it's somewhat difficult to enter into an absolutely cursed condition. "It is true the Covenant effectually made, can never be really broke, yet externally it may."[52] So when Rowlandson finds "there was mercy promised again, if we would return to him by repentance" (MR 331), not only does hope spring eternal even for those under *temporary* judgment, but damnation becomes something that happens mostly to other people: "the Lord would gather us together, and turn all those curses upon our enemies" (MR 331). Of course, retributive justice more or less structures the Mosaic covenant's understanding of human act and divine response, and Rowlandson's application of that logic to her and her society's ethnological struggles with the Wampanoag league should come as no surprise. But considered as a problem within reformed theology, Rowlandson's management of affliction highlights the problem of human agency in a religious system famously suspicious of the instrumentality of human capacity in matters eternal. Rather than providing comfort in the context of affliction, Reformed theology's complication of Mosaic law's retributive system introduces uncertainty.

The Calvinist theology of seventeenth-century New England quite famously diverged from the quid pro quo arrangement of Mosaic law. In the complex relation between human work and divine grace elaborated most famously in the Antinomian crisis, the instrumentality of human

---

51. David Downing, "'Streams of Scripture Comfort': Mary Rowlandson's Typological Use of the Bible," *Early American Literature* 15, no. 3 (1980), notes Rowlandson's "heavy reliance on the Old Testament. Of her numerous Biblical references, fewer than one tenth are from the New Testament... This peculiar paucity of New Testament references is due primarily to the conscious identification of the New England Puritans with the Old Testament Hebrews" (255).

52. Quoted in Miller, *Errand into the Wilderness*, 22.

effort is minimal relative to the sovereignty of God's omnipotence. As we saw with Rowlandson's depiction of her sister's death, she remains unsure what to make of the visible effects of human decisions about spirit; indeed, her own "decision" to enter captivity rather than suffer death betrays this ambivalence:

> I had often said, that if the Indians should come, I should choose rather to be killed by them than be taken alive but when it came to the trial my mind changed; their glittering weapons so daunted my spirit, that I chose rather to go along with those (as I may say) ravenous beasts, than that moment to end my days. (MR 325)

Although exercising her will in the decision to remain with her Native captors, she remains mute on the possible consequence of that decision in terms of her salvation, which is to say that, in the decision itself, she recognizes the uncertainty of salvation offered by the Puritan theology of God's sovereign power. Better "go along with those . . . ravenous beasts" and prolong her finite existence, than risk an encounter with an uncertain eternity.

The ambivalent logic of Rowlandson's understanding of punishment and deliverance most clearly appears in the identification she makes with Lot's Wife. In breaking the injunction not to look back at the destruction of Sodom and Gomorrah, Lot's Wife becomes a pillar of salt, monumentalized, in the standard reading, into an icon of inappropriate regret and possible unbelief for the "crime" of turning back to witness the destruction of her home. Genesis 19:17 reads thus: "And it came to pass, when they had brought them forth abroad, that he said, Escape for thy life: look not behind thee, neither stay thou in all the plain; escape to the mountain, lest thou be consumed." Here the backward glance implies her unbelief, and that God selects her for a special punishment. Yet in Lot's Wife's salty end, it is only a retributive logic of punishment that might explain her transformation into the salt pillar, even as her somewhat innocent role in the "crime" invites the Calvinist reading which grants a certain arbitrary dimension to her extraordinary demise. Rowlandson's text exploits this tension in Lot's Wife's story. When she confesses her partial ("something of") understanding of Lot's Wife's desire—her refusal to accept her home's destruction without this nearly involuntary act of witness—she is also making a claim about divine retribution: that the punishment doled out doesn't fit the crime. What Rowlandson understands better is not merely the undeniable tug of grief but the divine obfuscation of the logic informing her loss. The potentially meaningless death of Lot's Wife and her monumentalization into exemplary lesson quite closely parallels Rowlandson's own experience as captive and as writer. This parallel implies that the meaning of Rowlandson's own predicament may remain remote from her understanding. In the uncomfortable typology, she recognizes the psychological discomfort prompted, rather than settled, by Puritanism's deferral of retributive justice by means of the New Testament's promise of free grace to the elect. Her earlier claim that she deserved her treatment becomes one of the less convincing moments in the text. In her words: "How careless I had been of God's holy time; how many Sabbaths I had lost and misspent, and how evilly I had walked in God's sight; which lay so close unto my spirit, that it was easy for me to see how righteous it was with God to cut off the thread of my life and cast me out of His presence forever" (328). Rowlandson would seem to subscribe here to the quid pro quo logic of the Mosaic covenant, in which sinful behavior merits malediction. In this case, however, her negligence of the Sabbath, an observance whose sacramental status was far from being a settled matter within reformation theology, earns her captivation by Natives, the death of her daughter, the burning of her house, and the loss of friends and neighbors, to say nothing of the mental anguish of her captivity.[53] As with Lot's Wife, the punishment seems to exceed the crime, which is to say that the Calvinist gloss on retributive justice only intensifies the uncertainty about the lesson of her experience. Rowlandson's vernacular theology proposes an alternate understanding of the doctrine of saintly affliction, in which the chosen's embattled status doesn't necessarily issue a narrative of redemptive suffering. The Puritan doctrine of affliction produces bafflement, wonder, admiration, trauma, clarity, and confusion. These are all states of the *person* as much as they are states of the soul. Rowlandson's text makes room for an account of suffering whose significance is intensely personal, and problematically so. It is when she is *most* Puritan that Mary Rowlandson becomes most recognizably modern.

---

53. Stephen Foster, *The Long Argument*, argues that in English Puritanism "the Sabbath became an unparalleled weapon for proclaiming and organizing the believer's participation in a Christian universe" and, citing the example of Winthrop, had "after a generation of Puritans . . . assumed a central position in Puritan devotion" (79).

THE PSYCHOLOGY OF AFFLICTION

It should be said that Mary Rowlandson was hardly the only "anxious Puritan" in seventeenth-century New England. One might take a comparative look at the career of the minister Michael Wigglesworth, whose poetry affirmed the righteousness of New England's continuing covenant with God just as surely as his confessional writing exposed his own protracted struggle to live up to the demands of his faith. Even without all of the "nocturnal emissions" and closeted sexual and social anxiety, Wigglesworth's *Diary* might fairly be described as part of a tradition of male-authored spiritual life-writing that extends back to Augustine and gestures forward to the personal ruminations of Jonathan Edwards. Cotton Mather, whom we consider more closely in the next chapter, also recorded an anxiety-filled personal life apparently at odds with his public career as an influential minister, and he paid the price, according to one of his best readers, for achieving the status of "representative personality."[54] Both of these men, and still others to be sure, negotiated some of the conflicts emerging within Rowlandson's text, which begs the question of why, in respect to the broader issues of religion, gender, and secularism, Rowlandson's example is in some way notably different from and historically more significant than theirs.

The shortest answer is that it isn't. All three of these redoubtable Puritans were part of the broader transformation in New England religious culture and belief in which feminine piety played a significant role. Although space prohibits a fuller discussion here, we might consider Wigglesworth briefly as an instance of the kind of unmanageable spirituality we have discussed so far as "feminine" piety. Noteworthy about Wigglesworth's struggles with sexuality is, rather precisely, the extent to which it could be said to crowd out and compete with his otherwise "spiritual" preoccupations. Nicholas Radel has suggested that the queer inflection of his text indicates a closeted sodomitical imagination, an observation I would extend by observing that one of the inheritances of the secular is the idea that sexuality and spirituality can be and often are metaphorically substituted for each other and are, what is more, regarded as being of equal importance to the life of the modern person. Just as Rowlandson substitutes food for the Eucharist, or personal loss for spiritual lesson, so does Wigglesworth's preoccupation

---

54. Mitchell Breitwieser, *Cotton Mather and Benjamin Franklin: The Price of Representative Personality* (Cambridge: Cambridge University Press, 1984).

with his sexual activity move to the forefront of the representational space authorized by his spiritual ambition. Spiritual desire doesn't "mask" his sexual nature; his sexual life authenticates and makes possible the drama of his own salvific narrative, which is to say that both gender and sexual practice inflect and inform his evolving religious beliefs in ways commensurate with those we are considering in relation to female piety. Wigglesworth is every bit a part of the culture of American Puritanism as Mary Rowlandson, and the complex way in which we remember and read him today is an example of the hermeneutics of modernity these complex texts helped usher in.[55]

That said, Mary Rowlandson is different in at least one fundamental respect: she evokes and sustains attention on the conflicts between religion and its evolving secularization on the same page, as part of one text or set of experiences. The slippage between credible faith and incredible doubt appears in a variety of Rowlandson's remembered experiences. Late in the Thirteenth Remove, one of the longer segments of the narrative, she recounts the following:

> My mistress's papoose was sick, and it died that night, and there was one benefit in it—that there was more room. I went to a wigwam, and they bade me come in, and gave me a skin to lie upon, and a mess of venison and ground nuts, which was a choice dish among them. On the morrow they buried the papoose, and afterward, both morning and evening, there came a company to mourn and howl with her: though I confess I could not much condole with them. Many sorrowful days I had in this place, often getting alone; *like a crane, or a swallow, so did I chatter: I did mourn as a dove, mine eyes ail with looking upward. Oh, Lord, I am oppressed; undertake for me*, Isaiah 38.14. (MR 346)

As with the earlier conflict with Weetamoo, under whose terms the two women occupy similar positions of rivalry within a patriarchal domestic and sexual economy, here the text registers another similarity between these two women: they have both lost a child *in extremis*. Yet just as the shared experience of gender failed in the earlier scene to generate female

---

55. For another view of the Wigglesworth diary and its representation of "sodomitical desire," see Alan Bray, "The Curious Case of Michael Wigglesworth," in *A Queer World: The Center for Lesbian and Gay Studies Reader*, ed. Martin Duberman (New York: New York University Press, 1997), 205–15.

camaraderie, so Weetamoo's sudden loss doesn't arouse any sympathy from the narrator. Far from it: the observation that with the baby's death she finds more physical comfort in the wigwam, however pragmatic, nonetheless seems excessively callous. When she goes on to "confess" her inability or refusal to "condole," the cool pragmatism becomes something else entirely, as Rowlandson rejects the invitation to participate in the communal scene of mourning, choosing instead to "pass many sorrowful days . . . often getting alone" (MR 346). In spite of her self-imposed, and no doubt ethnically motivated, separation from a social performance of mourning with her indigenous captors, Rowlandson's consequent recounting of "the sorrow that lay on my spirit" (MR 346) indicates quite clearly that the papoose's death has triggered a new bout of mournful distress and self-examination. Proceeding to read her sadness conventionally—she concedes her "careless" demeanor and excessive share of creature comforts—she concludes her sudden descent back into melancholy with a somewhat predictable flourish: "Yet that comfortable scripture would often come to my mind, *For a small moment have I forsaken thee, but with great mercies will I gather thee*" (MR 347). Curiously, the text doesn't identify the scripture here, possibly because it's so well known a verse from Isaiah 54, in which God reassures the faithful that Israel will be rebuilt. Even more tellingly, Isaiah 54 begins with an address to childless women: "Sing, O barren, thou that didst not bear: break forth into singing, and cry aloud, thou that didst not travail with child: for more are the children of the desolate than the children of the married wife, saith the Lord" (Isaiah 54:1). It's better never to have delivered a child than to have labored and delivered a sinner, and no doubt the Puritan elect would derive comfort from the passage's implication that few, indeed, are the saved. But even granting Rowlandson's genuine desire to read her experience within the appropriate theological framework, it would be difficult not to recognize the bitter irony Isaiah 54 makes available: that given the death of her daughter, she would prefer to be in the position of barren women who, never having to contemplate the loss of a child, are in a position to "break forth into singing and cry aloud."

As one of many moments in the narrative when recalled experience and scriptural figuration fail to cohere seamlessly, the epigrammatic interpolation of Isaiah 54 also opens a space for a radically personal understanding of suffering. Far from extending a Puritan tradition of female exemplarity and afflictive redemption into the latter half of the seventeenth century, *The Sovereignty and Goodness of God* in fact introduces a recognizably modern understanding of "personal life" into the religious culture of New England. In the penultimate paragraph of her narrative, Rowlandson writes: "I have seen the extreme vanity of this world: One hour I have been in health, and wealthy, wanting nothing. But the next hour in sickness and wounds, and death, having nothing but sorrow and affliction" (MR 365). Taken alone, Rowlandson's world-weary perspective recalls several of the text's theological preoccupations: the corruption of the world and its sinful participants; the apparently random visitations of blessing and curse upon a chosen yet still sinful people; and the challenge to faith—"having nothing but sorrow and affliction"—posed by her covenant with a wrathful God whose actions, while always justified and sovereign, are nonetheless baffling in terms of causality and merit. In the succinct recollection of these themes, the text appears poised to return to the doctrinal folds, inviting its readers to contemplate, with its chastised author, the difficult life of faith in a sinful world, and the need for the faithful to remain steadfast. Yet in the next, this time the final, paragraph of the text, she writes: "Before I knew what affliction meant, I was ready sometimes to wish for it" (MR 365). We might almost read this as a narrative introjection, in which Rowlandson calls attention to the text's construction as witness not merely to the past, but to the present condition of its first-person author. Now in the apparently sure possession of the ultimate meaning of affliction, she appears less ready to want more of it. Her old self, the pre-afflictive self, well-trained in the doctrinal understanding of divine affliction, wanted what she had never had in order to measure the strength of her covenant, and the likelihood of her ultimate salvation. To conclude that her narrative incoherently asserts the doctrine of saintly affliction would be to miss the more important point here: that Rowlandson claims to have figured out one of the more enduring mysteries of Christian religious faith and that, in doing so, she's not really sharing that knowledge with the rest of us. If one of the points of Puritanism's doctrine of saintly affliction is to offer a coherent epistemology of suffering not only to those experiencing the glorious scourge but also to those reading about it, then Rowlandson's text subverts that doctrine by relocating the understanding of suffering outside of a communal register and into one more intensely personal, if not, finally, opaque. Having struggled, Job-like, with the sorrows of divine challenge, she comes to terms with that experience by vitiating its communal meaning, by shrouding it, so to speak, behind the mask of representation. Unlike ministers like Michael Wigglesworth and Cotton Mather, who presented the face of a self successfully disciplined into abstraction, Rowlandson creates the idea of a private space of spiritual life resistant to her community's demands for "self-revelation."

Mary Rowlandson thus offers not merely a text but a theory about the place of feminine piety in an evolving culture of religious modernity. Against the imperative to exteriorize religious experience into the didactic utility of confessional prose, *The Sovereignty and Goodness of God* sponsors a competing, if simultaneous, project: to uphold the sanctity of faith by insisting on its nonrepresentational status. Such a theology anticipates, if it doesn't altogether structure, the gendered divisions of modernity's public sphere. Rowlandson's piety, powerful because individual, can be called "feminine" because "personal." Feminine personality exists simultaneously as the more "naturally religious" as well as the more "naturally private" case for subjectivity in the secular. As was the case with Anne Hutchinson a generation earlier, the mystery of private inspiration endures even when forced into representation. Moreover, the account of suffering that informs Rowlandson's feminine piety authorizes a narrative of human pain that is curiously self-referential. She has had "nothing but sorrow and affliction"; she has, in spite of the many signs of favor God has shown her, gone "up and down, mourning and lamenting" (MR 330, 334, 339); the final paragraph of her narrative refers to her "affliction" *five times*, and even as she writes in one sentence that she knows what meaning to attach to her suffering, in another she finesses this certainty into a more tentative rapprochement with her past: "I hope I can say in some measure, as David did, *It is good for me that I have been afflicted*" (MR 366). Puritans were, by default, seldom assured of much, but the concluding paragraph of the narrative elaborates a baffling logic of afflictive knowledge that takes the form of psychological extemporizing. She writes:

> The Lord hath showed me the vanity of these outward things. That they are the vanity of vanities, and vexation of spirit, that they are but a shadow, a blast, a bubble, and things of no continuance. That we must rely on God Himself, and our whole dependence must be upon Him. If trouble from smaller matters begin to arise in me, I have something at hand to check myself with, and say, why am I troubled? It was but the other day that if I had had the world, I would have given it for my freedom, or to have been a servant to a Christian. I have learned to look beyond present and smaller troubles, and to be quieted under them. (366)

Having not merely witnessed but experienced the "shadow . . . blast . . . [and] bubble" of the world's assault on the spirit, Rowlandson has learned to regard such particulars for the venalities they are. Eyes on the prize offered by "God himself," Rowlandson regards "smaller matters" with the skepticism of painfully acquired knowledge and understanding of the right ordering of things. Even so, it is through the vicissitudes of worldly experience that her capacity for transcendence is defined and by which her success is measured. Without the world's indexical relation to the invisible world it so imperfectly mirrors, the believer's induction of divine reality would be a difficult matter. In this sense, Rowlandson's refusal to "sweat the small stuff" implies a disconnect between the visible world's semiotic fit with its underlying invisible reality.

Her studied consideration of the value of the material world should reflect the religious understanding of that perceived world as a sum of particular details, any one of which might help her better understand the revelation of God's mind. However, her partial rejection of the vicissitudes of worldly life as having any significance to her spirituality means that she has taken up a worldview we might regard as "therapeutic." In the therapeutic perspective, the world functions less as a map to the mind of God than as the means for an individual to cultivate the conditions of mental stability and achieve a measure of human satisfaction in the mortal coil. The very idea of "sifting" through experience and choosing some parts of it as "significant" and discarding "the rest" as pointlessly irrelevant "vanities" implies the existence of a human mind using its own powers to comprehend the world on its own terms. A world unified by the promise of divine revelation is becoming one fractured by the distressed mind perceiving it. Her religiously ordered understanding of materiality coexists with one that is psychological: that is as concerned, so to speak, with spiritual as with mental health. Another way to put this is to observe that in the denial of life's "little" problems, the text proposes that some troubles have meanings that are, in the end, just that: pointless, indices even of waste and unmeaning. Indeed, they are merely "personal."

Rowlandson's existential accommodation of the reality and persistence of human affliction offers a gloss on suffering that evades orthodox or corporate religious explanation by locating its significance squarely within the remote psyche of the individual. Individual psychology becomes the cognate of spiritual experience the text sketches largely as memorial. The demands made on Rowlandson that she and her text assume representative status for New England derive as much from Increase Mather's orthodox supervision as from Puritanism's location of authority within the female self's relation to God. The orthodox persuasion depends on the powerful appeal of mystical commitment, here localized in the experiences of the feminine. In this sense, Rowlandson's elocutionary anticipation of modernity's coordination of a private female self in opposition to a masculine-identified public sphere might better be read as part of a longer historical narrative that becomes visible over the course of the seventeenth century. Female piety makes modern secularism possible in the same way that privacy anchors the new bourgeois public sphere. The privatization of religion, as José Casanova has summarized this phenomenon, implied that "the modern question for salvation and personal meaning had withdrawn to the private sphere of the self" and that terms like "'self-expression' and 'self realization' had become the 'invisible religion' of modernity."[56] Where the marginalization of religion to the domain of private contemplation constitutes part of the historical narrative of secularist thought, it simultaneously sponsors female religiosity as the ideal of spiritual authenticity within and, more importantly, *as* a crucial expression of the modern.

Since the Antinomian Controversy, the tension between individual belief's abstraction into representation and its sequestration into the mystery of private experience has defined the public history of New England female spiritual experience. All of these women offered and then declined aspects of a Puritan consensus that would ultimately dispense with them. Even as "doctrinal" a poet as Anne Bradstreet puts her finger on the problem, so to speak, when she recalls the experience of loss in her famous 1666 poem recounting the burning of her house. Bradstreet's lyrical recollection of material loss—"And here and there the places spy / Where oft I sat and long did lie: / Here stood that trunk, and there that chest, / There lay that store I counted best"—presents the object world of absent particulars as the "pelf" which slows her progress into "an house on high erect, / Framed by that mighty Architect."[57] Rowlandson's complex responses to the tugs of personal and material loss extend the paths staked earlier by these deeply religious and yet recognizably women. This path extends, the

---

56. José Casanova, *Public Religions in the Modern World*, 36.

57. Anne Bradstreet, "Lines Occasioned on the Burning of Our House," in Rich, *Works of Anne Bradstreet*, 292–93.

next chapter argues, into the thorny groves of the Salem Witchcraft trials, during which the peculiar status of female speech and personal religious witness became problematically entwined with civic regimes of knowledge production.

FOUR

Salem Witchcraft's Defense *of* Faith

MARY ROWLANDSON'S UNEASY REDEMPTION proposes two seemingly different readings of the cultural work of religion in later-seventeenth-century New England. On the one hand, Rowlandson's self-doubt and anxiety did not impede her commitment to furthering the communal project of practicing Puritan piety. On the other hand, as we have just seen, they did make it difficult for her to deliver. One way to move past this impasse is to propose that the contradiction between her communal and personal pieties becomes the testing ground for the saint's perseverance into redemption and modernity. Her continuing commitment to the personal dimensions of her own traumatic history might become, in the more orthodox reading, the new "self" whose very self-absorption needs to be overcome in order to prepare the soul for possible redemption. The larger point here, of course, is that the "new" account of the personal sketched in her narrative is quite specifically and emphatically not "postreligious." Mary Rowlandson has not "awakened" into the Enlightenment, thrown off the shackles of enchantment, and escaped the confines of a God-centered universe. She has instead awakened to—or, rather, has been unable to fall into blissful unconsciousness of—the nightmare of the insufficient consolations of belief. The Salem witch trials are nothing if not a nightmare of the consequence of female religious belief's continuing power in the secular.

As we have seen, Rowlandson asserted a flexible and adaptive interpretive scheme for making sense of her captivity. Although her individual practices may have opened up avenues for religiously inspired secular thinking to emerge, they also coincided with and followed from a significant effort undertaken by New England's religious leadership to adapt official religious culture to the changing realities of colonial settlement: the so-called Halfway Covenant accord, reached in 1662. The accord tried to correct for the problem of emptying churches and growing spiritual deadness by permitting the children of as-yet unconverted adults to attend church as "partial" members. By relaxing and modifying the discipline of the Congregational churches of New England, the clerical leadership of New England hoped to meet these potential saints "halfway" and thereby continue the mission of the reformation in New England. The Halfway Covenant was, among other things, a practical concession to the distractions of modernity.[1]

It was also a crisis for the colony's clerical leadership, one whose repercussions continued to reverberate over time and in various arenas of New England's religious life. While marauding "Indians" may have been the identified foes in *The Sovereignty and Goodness of God*, the encroachments of theological laxity and devotional indifference haunted the edges of the text's awareness, in no small part, we might surmise, because Increase Mather played a significant a role in the debates about the Halfway Covenant, and in the framing of Rowlandson's text some twenty years later. Mather's opposition to the Halfway settlement appears in the barely controlled outrage of the captivity narrative's preface, which exhorts New English Puritans to ever more-rigorous spiritual self-discipline and public piety as the correct responses to King Philip's War. Mather is not merely interested in controlling the meaning of the conflict some five to six years after the fact; he is interested in controlling the meaning of a Puritan spirituality that has been subjected to unwanted change, disciplinary loosening, and even, as we saw in the last chapter, to Mary Rowlandson. The war, after all, is over, at least that phase of it. For Mather, Rowlandson's assertion of a spiritually convincing interpretive independence is the problem still in need of solution. More broadly, in the wake of the Halfway Covenant and the war's disruptions, the actual practices of piety have become for Mather an as-yet undiscovered and thus threatening frontier

---

1. The fullest treatment of this phase of New England church history remains Robert G. Pope, *The Half-Way Covenant: Church Membership in Puritan New England* (Princeton, NJ: Princeton University Press, 1969). For a more recent general discussion and summary, see David Hall, "New England, 1660–1730," 145–50.

for managing Puritan spirituality. In the accusatory and confessional culture that emerged in Salem in 1692, Mary Rowlandson's private spiritual hermeneutic would find its most threatening expression.[2]

The Halfway Covenant made its guarded peace with the mysteries of the invisible world by encouraging New England's Puritans to become more attentive to the external, visible, and therefore verifiable signs of God's invisible world. Rather than holding to the idea that the unseen soul gives rise to manifestations of worldly character in the same way that the noumenal world of God gives rise to the phenomenal world, the Halfway Covenant implicitly conceded that this logic might, for pragmatic reasons if for no other, have to work the other way. That is, from the visible world we map and in some sense create an invisible one. The idea that one might derive conclusions about religious authenticity based primarily on "externals" like the accidents of birth, the observance of ritual, or the indications of public carriage not only implied the declension of the rigors of Puritan discipline.[3] It more broadly invited increased skepticism of the credibility of claims made on behalf of the invisible world. To be sure, the critical reception of what were called "conversion relations" had long been an accepted component of Puritan church discipline and a primary location for the clerical supervision of the laity's penitential experiences.[4] But the Halfway Covenant changed all that: it granted religious credibility without the need for public confession, and so untethered either the existence or the history of an individual's spirituality from their official status within the church community. Ritual and form, baptism and church attendance, rather than *sola scriptura* and the mysteries of God, became the official prerequisites for legitimate religious identity, to say nothing of the social and economic benefits that followed from it.[5] So on the one hand we

---

2. Benjamin C. Ray has recently pointed out that the Salem-Village church had not by 1692 accepted the Halfway Covenant, and that the minister Samuel Parris, an entrenched conservative, supported the trials as a way to combat the forces of liberalization behind its adoption. See Ray, "Satan's War Against the Covenant in Salem-Village Church, 1692," *The New England Quarterly* 80, no. 1 (2007): 69–95.

3. For this reading of the Halfway Covenant, see Sacvan Bercovitch, *The American Jeremiad*, 62–92.

4. For the foundational analysis of seventeenth-century Puritan conversion theory and history, see Edmund S. Morgan, *Visible Saints: The History of a Puritan Idea* (Ithaca, NY: Cornell University Press, 1963); and Patricia Caldwell, *The Puritan Conversion Narrative*. For a different approach that places individual and institutional understandings of conversion in collaborative rather than conflicted relation, see Michael Kaufmann, *Institutional Individualism*.

5. For discussion of the relations between religion, church membership, and economics, see Stephen Innes, *Creating the Commonwealth: The Economic Culture of Puritan New England*

have Mary Rowlandson quietly going about the business of asserting the credibility of private faith, while on the other, we have the Halfway Covenant granting religious status to people for no good reason other than their parentage and their good public behavior. Where Rowlandson expresses modernity's doubt and anxiety about the ultimate meaning of her suffering and redemption, her late-century Puritan culture seemed committed to obviating the need to dwell in such spaces altogether. Rowlandson's struggle, therefore, is not merely about a private encounter with her God; it is a struggle within a culture intent on rendering her intense piety irrelevant to the institutional arrangements of New England Puritanism. The marginalization of female piety was a chief concern of the Salem episode, as it would be for secular culture as well.

The idea that female piety both enabled and threatened Puritanism finds its most paradoxical and dire articulation in relation to the Salem witch controversy of 1692. It is neither coincidence nor mistake that religious belief found forceful and even aggressive articulation as the century waned and the colonies of New England appeared poised to move beyond the insular regime of the Puritan "experiment" and into the fuller discovery of the knowable world. Perhaps at no other time in the seventeenth century was the power of God more visible, and more suspicious, more insistent on the invisible life of spirit, and more compromised in its expression, by the exigencies of secularizing regimes of knowledge and community. It is precisely the assertion of this aggressive voice of religious belief within an emerging regime of knowledge premised on the deauthorization of religious claims that this chapter investigates more fully. Within an emerging secular culture of spiritual indifference, the Salem witch crisis erupted, and radicalized feminine piety asserted its spiritual power again in a dramatically staged religious insurgency.

HALFWAY TO HELL: THE PURITAN CONFESSIONAL

What is striking to many scholars about the testimonial culture of the Salem trials is the unwarranted elocutionary power assumed by witnesses notable for their lack of authority within seventeenth-century English

---

(New York: Norton, 1995). For a more recent analysis of the economics of colonial New England selfhood, see Michelle Burnham, *Folded Selves: Colonial New England Writing in the World System* (Hanover, NH: University Press of New England, 2007).

society. Mary Beth Norton has observed that "the role of the afflicted in communicating with the invisible world had assumed such centrality in the legal proceedings that it was even encroaching on the magistrate's function within the public space of the courtroom."[6] The accusatory voices—mostly those of adolescent women, many of whom were not even full members of the Salem-Village church—drove the juggernaut of the trials, ably assisted by the corroborative claims of the ever-increasing cadre of the so-called confessing witches. Their uncanny ability to peer into the otherwise hidden world of God's invisible domain superseded their ostensibly powerless position within the patriarchal organization of the visible world. This loudly articulated power re-radicalized the "feminization of piety," and brought that power into the public spaces of religious and civil experience.[7]

"Invisible" subjects of the fallen world, these women claimed a position of transcendent knowingness. They came to legitimize and at the same time compete with the authority of the male magistrates, trial judges, prosecutors, and divines. The collusion of female testimony and male judicial authority is precisely the problem here: with their vocal obstreperousness (the accusing girls routinely interrupted examiners, judges, and prosecutors), and their spectacular bodily performances (ranging from fainting spells to traumatic self-injury), the accusing women recalled and thereby continued the tradition of seventeenth-century outspoken female piety in New England first staged by Anne Hutchinson in 1637. Salem witchcraft was thus another of Anne Hutchinson's monstrous births.

Viewed this way, the accusers and confessants were "enthusiasts" of the highest order: precisely the wild-eyed fanatics and social incendiaries feared by folks like John Winthrop and Thomas Shepard earlier in the seventeenth century. The Quaker invasion, as we have seen, attracted robust critique for its excessive embodiment. Recall Thomas Jenner's 1670 *Quakerism Anatomiz'd*, a portrait of the quaking witness that might easily have come off the pages of the Salem examinations and trials:

> He [the devil] hath frequently appeared, and actually possessed them, bruising, tearing, tossing them up and down the prison, and tormenting

---

6. Mary Beth Norton, *In the Devil's Snare: The Salem Witchcraft Crisis of 1692* (New York: Knopf, 2002), 183.

7. For discussion of the growing participation and dominance of women in the seventeenth-century churches, see Amanda Porterfield, *Female Piety in Puritan New England*.

them with strange fits, convulsions, quakings, shakings in all their joynts, and swelling in their whole bodies, their skins ready to break, which made them cry out with great horror, as eye-witnesses of Quality can attest to it.[8]

What seems unusual to us today about the cultural authority assumed by the so-called accusing girls and confessing witches of Salem was perhaps not so unusual in the seventeenth century. The "fraud" Jenner is denouncing here is not the same "fraud" our modern eyes detect when reading the archive of the trials. Jenner's suggestion that the Quakers are actually witches is no less "religious" or even "radical" a claim than the "Truth" these quaking Christians believe themselves to be communicating, or the "truth" that invisible specters are harassing the people of Salem; everybody is still talking religion here. What makes the role played by the religious performances in 1692 Salem different, however, is that where in some of the earlier cases legal and religious authority together *denied* the legitimacy of the claims made by female religious performance, in 1692 the judges of Salem's Court of Oyer and Terminer validated them. Quaker "fraud," to put the matter differently, seems to have found an unlikely latter-day ally in the credibility-granting civil court presiding over the witchcraft crisis. The elocutionary space of the secular tribunal granted authority to the "wonders of the invisible world."

So where were the ministers—a group that had, as we have seen, steadfastly opposed all such lay prophecy and revelation for a century—in all of this? To answer that question, we need to back up a bit. Even before King Philip's War, the Boston ministry had faced formidable challenges to its cultural authority.[9] By most accounts, its power had for a variety of reasons been diminishing for some time, even before the advent of the "Jeremiad" in the early 1670s. Most of the elite clergy tended to blame the influx of post-Protectorate immigrants, along with the sins of the wretched "rising"

---

8. Thomas Jenner, *Quakerism Anatomiz'd and Confuted*, 161.
9. William McLoughlin makes the thorough case for the continual pressure exerted on the Congregational consensus by dissenting Protestants like the Quakers and, particularly, the Baptists; see McLoughlin, *New England Dissent, 1630–1833*. Harry S. Stout provides a more succinct account of this in *The New England Soul*, 76–82. On the reformist impulse and its frequent exercise, particularly in the wake of the Halfway Covenant, see Richard Gildrie, *The Profane, the Civil, and the Godly: The Reformation of Manners in Orthodox New England* (University Park: Pennsylvania State University Press, 1994), 2–18. The most thorough discussion of the complex interaction of religious, geographical, and imperial politics in relation to the war belongs to Jill Lepore, *The Name of War*.

generations, for having produced that lamentable worldliness which New England divines had, from the very beginning, alternately decried and courted. Among those material causes most readily cited in the historiography of the war and its aftermath were increased trade and contact with the Natives and the French, including skirmishes over the fur trade; the controversial and provocative missionary work of John Elliot Norton; expanded settlements in the hinterlands, many undertaken without the expressed consent of Boston's ruling cadre; and a preoccupation with the political affairs of England, as the Crown began asserting greater political control over the New England Confederation following the Restoration of the Stuart monarchy.[10] So when, some two years before the initial attacks on the English settlements, Increase Mather put pen to paper in 1674 to enumerate and bewail the sins of the gathered churches and anticipate that "a day of trouble is near," his prediction of a dire future depended not merely on a typological reading of New England's reproduction of the sins of Israel, but on the ministry's sense that "the signs of the times" were abundantly clear.[11] Whether or not Mather's assertion of a unitary clerical authority was little more than symptomatic of that authority's illusory status, his effort to read New England's woes in terms of an orthodox hermeneutic attempted to restore the immanence of Protestant religion to New England's local sociopolitical condition. So where had religion "gone" that it suddenly needed Mather's intervention?

According to some—including, at least initially, Increase Mather himself—it had gone to hell by means of a road paved with the good intentions of the Halfway Covenant. The agreement reached in the 1662 Synod, under whose terms the children of uncovenanted church members would be recognized as part of the Covenant and baptized, was a local solution to Congregationalist diffidence in a time of geographical and population expansion. Such diffidence, as Increase Mather would later complain at length in his 1677 *Earnest Exhortation to the Inhabitants of New England*, "will so highly provoke and incense the displeasure of God" that "what sins have in former ages brought the punishment of the *Sword* upon a professing people" will "if those very sins are prevailing among us" guarantee that similar "Judgment is come upon us."[12] Mather assigns

---

10. For a discussion of Halfway as a pragmatic measure in response to all of this, see Harry S. Stout, *The New England Soul*, 96–99.
11. Increase Mather, *The Day of Trouble Is Near*, 7.
12. Increase Mather, *An Earnest Exhortation to the Inhabitants of New England*, 175, 174.

the uncovenanted and unrepentant equal share in the responsibility for bringing God's wrath upon the land in the form of "King Philip's War," observing, in nearly perfect terms the structure of the Halfway Covenant, how "the *first Generation* which was in this Land, had much of the power of Godliness, but the present *Generation* hath the form, and as to the *body of the Generation*, but little of the power of Religion." For Mather, who had in 1674 bemoaned the "great decay as to the power of Godliness among us," the compromised church polity established in the 1662 Synod was both solution and failure.[13] It offered a solution to the problem of falling church attendance rates and a decline of "visible Godliness," while at the same time it relaxed strict church admission requirements and rested the terms of membership on good behavior and works. Before the 1662 accord, "The children of Church-members with us though baptized in their infancy" neither received the Eucharist nor enjoyed voting rights "till they c[a]me to profess their faith and repentance, and to lay hold of the Covenant of their Parents before the Church."[14] The Halfway Covenant represented a distinct break from earlier Congregational church discipline, as non-professing churchgoers were extended many of the privileges of professing church members without having to make a public confession of their Christian experiences and have that confession undergo congregational scrutiny. The Halfway Covenant minimized the significance of personal testimony and self-witness to the validation of authentic religious faith.[15]

Let us not forget the Quaker invasion here: it is no mere historical coincidence that New England Congregationalism reached its zenith of persecution at exactly the same time that its ministers would formalize the most profound relaxation of church discipline since the Great Migration. New England Quakerism, as we have seen, unleashed religious representation from its tether to institutional interlocution. While spiritual diffidence and worldly licentiousness were woefully on the rise, the proliferation of words about God's absence was as well. The increase in "publication," be it the extemporaneous variety pursued by the Quakers or the printed kind favored by people like Increase Mather, was symptomatic of the decline

---

13. Increase Mather, *Earnest Exhortation*, 179, and *Day of Trouble*, 21–23.
14. General Court of Boston, *Propositions Concerning the Subject of Baptism and Consociation of Churches* (Boston, 1662), vii.
15. For discussion of the public rendering of "conversion narrative," see Meredith Neuman, "Beyond Narrative: The Conversion Plot of John Dane's *A Declaration of Remarkable Providences*," *Early American Literature* 40, no. 2 (2005): 251–77.

of Godly culture. Where the Quakers demanded ever more narratives of "convincement," the Halfway Covenant diminished the significance of public confession to church standing. Against the impulse to noisy spiritual self-display, the minister wanted to quiet the room. While it would seem that these two positions advanced opposed agendas for colonial Protestantism, in fact they start and end in the same place: the individual's personal and private relationship with God. The Quakers (and Mary Rowlandson) insisted on its expression; the Halfway Covenant merely assumed it as the case. The Halfway accord would contain the excessive confessional agency of Quakerism on the one hand, while opening the door to piety's ongoing management on the other.

In solving one set of problems, however, the Halfway Covenant created still others. In 1677 the Congregational church of Dorchester, which had for fifteen years bitterly opposed the Halfway provisions, accepted 106 new members into halfway fellowship, requiring only that they "take their profession to heart and act sincerely," that is, without requiring them to make a profession of faith and conversion relation.[16] Sanctification, to the extent it denoted worldly observance of moral, civic, and church law, became the key condition for even provisional church participation and good standing, not least because it strengthened local community inter-identification at a time when both political and religious leaders fretted over the matter of a Catholic restoration and what a new Royal Governorship would mean for New England. The representational imperative of individual confession—of making the case of justification before Christ—thus became, under the terms of the Halfway settlement, a secondary aspect of Puritan devotional and congregational life. Not only was a growing population taking less interest in the religious mission of the colony, but Congregationalism itself had surrendered the requirement that Christians testify to God's ability to move the heart and confer grace before assuming the rights of "visible sainthood." The always fractious church in Salem, as Stephen Foster has found, offered the Halfway Covenant to four different classes of Christians, persons from any one of which might join in the Communion provided they were not "openly scandalous or ignorant."[17] The "power of Godliness" had become an increasingly invisible component of the orthodox examination of practicing Christianity, whose observance of outward

---

16. Robert Pope, *The Half-Way Covenant*, 188.
17. Stephen Foster, *The Long Argument*, 237.

forms became the more privileged because visible measure of authentic Christian experience. The condition of one's soul became, as we have seen in the example of Mary Rowlandson, an increasingly private concern no longer requiring one's "publickly professing," so much as demanding the observance of church and civic forms of virtue and piety. By relaxing the need for public confession, Halfway further privatized religious life.[18]

While he didn't say so, Mather would no doubt have correctly perceived this outcome as one Anne Hutchinson herself would have embraced. During the 1670s, the practice of "covenant renewal" became a way to counter this tendency to leave individual faith alone. As such, covenant renewal became an increasingly popular ritual in these years, one that reasserted the divine contract between individuals, congregations, and their God. This was no empty liturgical form; the ritual hoped to promote the re-experiencing of conversion: as Increase Mather puts it in a 1677 exhortation, "the need of going over the work of Conversion again."[19] Against objections to covenant renewal which held that such ceremony would lead to a church populated by "infidels" making a "meer external profession," Mather asserts that while neither covenant renewal nor baptism "constitute a member of the church," either contributes to the practical life of the church, an "agreement of Saints to walk with God, and one another, according to the Order of the Gospel." To reject covenant renewal would be to reject all ordinances of public devotional life, including Fast-Days, Humiliations, and Election Day sermons. In any case, the need for reformation is so great that the introduction of such a "lawful" ordinance will "prevent outward Judgements" on a publically covenanted people. Covenant renewal would restore a disciplined confessional body to church affairs, a body whose testimonial agency the Halfway Covenant had diminished.

Although nearly thirty years had elapsed between the 1662 Synod and the first arrest warrant issued in Salem on the suspicion of witchcraft (February 29, 1692), the Halfway Covenant had remained a contentious issue within individual churches during this period. Indeed, a sufficient number of prominent members of Cotton Mather's own First Church of Boston remained opposed to the dispensations of the agreement, even after Mather spent the winter of 1691–92 persuading members of his congregation to

---

18. General Court of Boston, "Propositions Concerning the Subject of Baptism," 19.
19. Increase Mather, *Renewal of Covenant the Great Duty Incumbent on Decaying or Distressed Churches* (Boston: Henry Phillips, 1677), 5–7.

accept its terms. In late 1692, after Royal Governor William Phips had suspended the Salem trials, Mather wrote a letter to John Richards, a wealthy merchant and longtime foe of the Halfway accord. In this letter, Mather explicitly connected the Halfway Covenant's conferral of baptism on the children of the unregenerate to the recent witchcraft episode:

> But when I have seen that the devils have been baptizing so many of our miserable neighbors in that horrible witchcraft . . . I must confess it has increased my uneasiness under that sin of omission wherein I reckon myself to live. I cannot be well at ease until the nursery of initiated believers, out of which this garden of God is from time to time to be supplied with the trees of righteousness, be duly watered with the baptism, as well as with the teachings of the Lord. I would mark as many as I should, that the destroying angels may have less claim unto them.[20]

Mather's "sin of omission" was his failure to secure congregational consent for the Halfway Covenant, one direct result being the diabolically parodic baptism of persons by the devil's minions. Although a compromise of church doctrine, the Halfway Covenant could, in this retrospective reading, have provided Mather and other ministers with something like a preemptive strike against the machinations of Satan. Even a "halfway" form of church membership was better than its diabolical subversion. There is more than a touch of historical irony that Cotton Mather's own flock overcame its resistance to the Halfway compromise and became part of the Halfway Synod polity just one year after the Salem trials were over.[21] The trials and much of their contemporary commentary foregrounded the issue of individual confession and specifically lay witness in relation to the manifestation of God's power in the visible world. The testimonial

---

20. Cotton Mather, *The Selected Letters of Cotton Mather*, ed. Kenneth Silverman (Baton Rouge: Louisiana State University Press, 1971), 48–49.

21. Mather records his successful persuasion of the 2nd church to accept the Halfway accord in *The Diary of Cotton Mather*, vol. 1, *1681–1709* (New York: Ungar, 1957), 161–62. This entry follows immediately on his first 1693 entry, which described the "many wonderful Entertainments . . . from the *Invisible World* [italics original]," a reference to the diabolical possession of Mercy Short, discussed below. David Levin also notes Cotton Mather's explicit connection of the need to accept the Halfway compromise to the incursions of Satan in 1691; see Levin, *Cotton Mather: The Young Life of the Lord's Remembrancer, 1663–1703* (Cambridge, MA: Harvard University Press, 1978), 194–95. Robert Pope, *The Half-Way Covenant*, discusses Mather's connection of Salem witchcraft to the Halfway accord as well (194).

component of Christian piety minimized by the Halfway accord would, with extraordinary force and violence, re-emerge in 1692 Salem, taking the forms of the accusatory performances of the "victims," and the self-serving speech of the so-called confessing witches. If the Halfway accord diminished the role of confessional speech in narratives of conversion as a necessary gesture of religious compromise, the Salem trials, at least temporarily, restored the significance of individual confessional speech to the credibility and the witness of faith. Whatever else might be said about the motivations behind the actions of the accusers and confessants at Salem, those actions implied where they did not insist on the material impact of the invisible on the visible, and on the spiritual power that had accrued to privately realized religious experience.

Some of the best scholarship on Salem has identified the related issues of speech and power as central problems for our understanding of the trials. Nancy Ruttenburg has traced the emergence of a preliberal "democratic personality" to the aggressive uncontainability of the Salem accusers, whose power eerily mimicked and eclipsed the authoritative utterances of clerical orthodoxy. Sandra Gustafson has argued that the accusing and confessing "demoniacs" of 1692 Salem undermined "clerical authority through their stagings of verbal power." The Salem accusers and confessing witches employed the power of the spoken word in such a way that their clerical observers feared that "authentic spiritual knowledge was being denaturalized and recognized as a set of signs rather than a foundational truth." Ruttenburg's and Gustafson's account of the interplay of vocal and written speech speaks to the ambiguous role of speech in Puritan religious culture more generally.[22] This ambiguity might usefully be traced to the radical reformation's rejection of confession as a sacrament, as Puritan divines and parishioners alike denied the efficacy of ritualized confessional speech even as they regarded the individual's witness of the spirit as a necessary component of salvation. The witch trials re-enacted the problem of testimonial speech in the Reformed tradition. Central to this re-enactment, of course, is the prominent role assumed by women in the legal culture of spiritual representation wherein women affirmed God's continued relevance in human affairs. In 1692 Salem, the voice of radical religion's resurgence belonged almost entirely to women, and in that voice

---

22. Nancy Ruttenburg, *Democratic Personality*, 31–82; Sandra Gustafson, *Eloquence Is Power*, 42, 43.

the mysteries of privately realized belief assumed a new prominence in the affairs of a secularizing world.

"WE MUST NOT BELIEVE ALL THAT THESE DISTRACTED CHILDREN SAY"

One problem with female speech at Salem was the fact that its theological persuasiveness exceeded prescribed gender roles. The vocal power of female accusers and confessors alike released religious speech from its interpretive subordination to clerical authority or to the space of religious privacy. As in the earlier cases of Hutchinson and the Quakers, Protestant theology's authorization of the laity to seek God in accordance with scripture and faith established what seemed a natural path connecting private spiritual experience to its public representation. At Salem in 1692, this path widened to include the witness of those claiming to see into the invisible world of God. Such claims were extreme in terms of seventeenth-century feminine deportment, as the aggressive speech and omnipotent perceptive power of the accusers were a far cry from the retiring piety extolled in Cotton Mather's "Daughters of Zion," a text published the same year. It was also radical in terms of religious epistemology. The supernatural witness and "inspired" speech which the Salem accusers claimed had also tended to be associated historically with the radical fringe of the transatlantic English reformation.[23] Yet an important characteristic of Salem's accusatory confessional culture was its literal application of three important teachings consistent with Reformed Protestant thought: first, that the workings of the invisible world are on occasion apprehensible to human perception; second, that individuals chosen by God to perceive the doings of the invisible world should bear witness to such events; and third, that such persons submit their experiences to scrutiny. If the Halfway Covenant adjourned the life of individual faith to public spaces of exterior protocols and liturgically managed ritual, then Salem witchcraft dramatically reconvened the trials of Puritanism's interior mysteries.

For this reason alone, to return to the question of the ministers, it is not difficult to see why the Mathers supported the trials, even if that support was, at times, equivocal where not altogether cautionary with regard to

---

23. For the classic historical argument, see Christopher Hill, *The World Turned Upside Down*.

the use of spectral evidence. Their views, moreover, were consistent with established witchcraft English jurisprudence. According to William Perkins' *A Discourse of the Damned Art of Witchcraft* (1608) and Richard Bernard's *A Guide to Grand-Jury-Men* (1627), there were only two reliable evidentiary bases for conviction. The first, and most reliable, was the witch's confession of malefice: in Perkins' formulation ". . . the free and voluntarie confession of the crime, made by the partie suspected and accused after the crime."[24] The second was testimony from at least two witnesses, either other witches, or, less problematically, others who had heard an accused witch confess to known acts of malefice. This second type of evidence, however, was less persuasive than the accused's own confession, which was, according to Bernard, the most "sound" form of evidence by which "they may bee found guiltie, and justly condemned, and put to death."[25] Both Increase and Cotton Mather repeatedly urged the *Oyer* and *Terminer* court to exercise caution with respect to spectral evidence claims, observing "that persons who have too much indulged themselves in malignant, envious, malicious ebullitions of their souls may unhappily expose themselves to the judgment of being represented by devils," such imaginary sinners deserve the benefit of juridical caution, lest "upon bare supposal of a poor creature's being represented by a spectre . . . it may be that a door may be thereby opened for the devils to obtain from the courts in the invisible world a license to proceed unto most hideous desolations . . ." Cotton Mather further cautioned the magistrates and judges against accepting the evidence of "diabolical representations" independently of a "credible confession"; only the latter would serve as "good, plain, legal evidence that the demons which molest our poor neighbors do indeed represent such and such people to the sufferers."[26] Already and for good reason concerned that the magistrates were altogether too credulous in their acceptance of spectral evidence—what Perkins and Bernard had earlier and Increase Mather and Samuel Willard would later describe as "the devil's testimony"—the younger Mather recognized that the freely made confession was not merely legally but, perhaps more significantly for an ordained minister, *theologically* credible.[27]

---

24. William Perkins, *A Discourse of the Damned Art of Witchcraft* (Cambridge, 1608), 211.
25. Richard Bernard, *A Guide to Grand-Jury Men* (London, 1627), 225.
26. Mather, *Letters of Cotton Mather*, 36.
27. Samuel Willard, *Some Miscellany Observations on Our Present Debates Surrounding Witchcraft* (Philadelphia: William Bradford, 1692), 10–12; and Increase Mather, *Cases of Conscience Concerning Evil Spirits* (Boston, 1693), 49.

The Mathers' insistence on the credibility of confession, however, was not without its own problems, not least because of the Protestant reformation's rejection of the sacramental status of confession, more formally known in the Catholic church as the sacrament of Reconciliation. This isn't to say that the individual's confession of sinful agency held no meaning for a Puritan; the conversion relation at the heart of Congregational church membership admission ritual was a form of extended narrative confession. Where Reformed Protestants drew the line was at the point where the act of confession would in some way cause or bring about a change in the soul's estate, or would provide a priest with the power to absolve the confessant of their sins. For Calvinists, such positions were altogether factitious. New England Congregationalism nonetheless understood the confessant's speech to be a necessary part of the church membership ritual, but such speech was demonstrative rather than hortatory. Janice Knight, among others, describes the testimonial culture of the Church admission protocols established by John Cotton at Boston's First Congregational Church as one intended less to "police" the confessant than "to draw the community together." There is, moreover, a performative quality to the public conversion relation: "The narrative ritual reenacts the moment of transformative grace, weaving the auditors into a single body," one in which "the saints were gathered together in congregations to experience the pleasure and beauty of union."[28] Although the convert's narrative might have proceeded as a retrospective account of the miracle of the individual's experience of grace, it performatively re-enacted that experience in the collaborative event of the relation itself. According to John Cotton: "Faith giveth a man fellowship in the invisible church, and in all the inward spiritual blessings of the church. But it is the profession of faith, that giveth a men fellowship in the visible church."[29] Speech externalizes the inner life of faith and thereby produces the conditions for that being a shared experience of a visible Christian community.

It would be difficult to overestimate the importance of what we might call Congregationalism's publication of faith to the enactment of early New England Protestant culture. At the same time, as we have now repeatedly

---

28. Janice Knight, *Orthodoxies in Massachusetts*, 152, 153.
29. John Cotton, *The Way of Congregational Churches Cleared* (1648), in *John Cotton on the Churches of New England*, ed. Larzer Ziff (Cambridge, MA: Belknap Press of Harvard University Press, 1968), 357. For further discussion of the role of the conversion relation in New England Congregationalism, see again Janice Knight, *Orthodoxies*, 152–54; and Patricia Caldwell, *The Puritan Conversion Narrative*, 135–63.

seen, individual and particularly feminine religious speech did interfere with the clerical and civic management of Puritan spiritual and civil community. The Halfway Covenant and consequent covenant renewal movement restored a communal, congregationally based order of religious expression. Taken together—pious voice and clerical frame—the quieting of New England Puritanism set the stage for the eruption of religious voice in 1692, when something like the repressed returned in the form of spectral evidence, which was a form of radicalized religious speech before it was anything else. Although clearly not identical to the conversion relation or to sanctioned forms of spiritual expression, spectral evidence indicated God's continued authorship of and presence in the world so authored. In the examination of Martha Carrier, to cite one of literally hundreds such examples, Susannah Sheldon "cryed out in a Trance I wonder what could you murder 13 persons" before subsequently falling into "the most intollerable out-cries & agonies."[30] Sheldon's speech both recollects and performs evidence from the invisible world. Her performance unites her individual experience of the invisible world with the courtroom's belief in that world's phenomenological reality.

The accusers' speech linked the invisible world of divinely licensed representation to the evidentiary order of the legal world. This interactive collaboration of the accused with the court also paralleled the relation of the penitent to the minister and/or congregation at the moment of formal church covenant. Nathaniel Morton's 1669 *New-Englands Memoriall*, for example, describes at length the dialogical interplay of confession and covenant by which the first church in Salem (not Salem-Village) was established. Having agreed on

> the 6th of *August* for their entring into a solemn Covenant with God, and one another . . . it was kept as a day of Fasting and Prayer, in which after the Sermons and Prayers of . . . two Ministers, in the end of the day, the foresaid *Confession of Faith* and *Covenant* being solemnly read, the forenamed persons did solemnly profess their Consent thereunto . . . Hence it was, that some were admitted [into full church membership] by expressing their Consent to that written Confession of Faith and Covenant; others did answer to questions about the Principles of Religion that were

---

30. Paul Boyer and Stephen Nissenbaum, eds., *The Salem Witchcraft Papers* (New York: Da Capo, 1977), 1:185. Further references to the examination and trials from this source are made parenthetically with the abbreviation *SWP*.

publickly propounded to them; some did present their Confession in writing, which was read for them, and some that were able and willing, did make their Confession in their own words and way.[31]

In a strange imitation of the pastor's relation to the penitent, the judges of Salem could be said to have "shepherded" the testimony of their flock. More disturbingly, contemporary observers noted the uncanny resemblance between diabolic and divine covenant. Cotton Mather, among several, observes in *Wonders of the Invisible World* that "The Devil which then thus imitated what was in the Church of the Old Testament, now among Us would Imitate the Affayrs of the Church in the New. The Witches do say, that they form themselves much after the manner of Congregational Churches; and that they have a Baptism and a Supper, and Officers among them, abominably Resembling those of our Lord."[32] In both accusations and confessions of witchcraft, the sacramental rites of baptism and Eucharist repeatedly emerge in narratives of diabolic imitation and parody, from blood drinking "black eucharists" to rebaptism of new converts, to the famous signings of the "black book," clearly a ritualistic enactment of the discourse of covenant so important to New England Congregationalism. Similarly, the ordinances of church discipline—the rituals of profession, confession, and covenant that had structured Congregational polity and practice for several decades—become the theological content of spectral accusation and narrative, which is to say that the covenant theology of New England Puritanism underwrote and, indeed, provided credibility, to the juridical inquiry into witchcraft. Religion authorized the Court of Oyer and Terminer, but the Court, in its turn, then proceeded to make claims entirely at odds with orthodox theology.

---

31. Nathaniel Morton, *New-Englands Memoriall* (Cambridge, MA, 1669), 75–76.
32. Cotton Mather, *The Wonders of the Invisible World* (1692), in *Narratives of the Witchcraft Crisis*, ed. George Lincoln Burr (New York: Scribner's, 1914), 245–46. For another contemporary take on the similarities between divine and diabolic covenant ritual, see Deodat Lawson's sermon "Christ's Fidelity the Only Shield," preached at Salem-Village on March 24, 1692: "It is a matter of terror, amazement, and astonishment, to all such wretched souls ... who by covenant, explicit or implicit, have bound themselves to be his slaves and drudges, consenting to be instruments in whose shapes he may torment and afflict their fellow-creatures ... if any that have sat down and eat at Christ's Table, should so lift up their heel against him as to have fellowship at the table of devils, and (as it hath been represented to some of the afflicted) eat of the bread and drink of the wine that Satan hath mingled." Lawson, "Christ's Fidelity the Only Shield Again Satan's Malignity," in *Salem-Village Witchcraft*, ed. Paul Boyer and Stephen Nissenbaum (Belmont, CA: Wadsworth, 1972), 126.

During the Salem investigations, confession became the privileged form of speech. Such confessions were defined as legally salient because they answered specific indictments issued by the *Oyer* and *Terminer* court. At the same time, however, they were examples of religious speech: they disclosed supernatural relations between the confessant and an invisible world. Take the July 21, 1692, confession of Mary Lacey Jr. as one of many such examples. Having confessed to witchcraft early in her examination, Lacey is then "absolved" of her crimes by Mary Warren: "After this confession Mary Warrin Came and took her by the hand & was no way hurt & she viz. Mary Lacy did Ernestly ask Mary Warren Forgiveness for afflicting of her and both fell a weeping Together etc." Having absolved Lacey, Warren invites her to become a new accuser, which Lacey Jr. obliges by immediately accusing her mother and grandmother of having made her a witch (*SWP* 3, 524). The older women then both confess, and name several others (Martha Carrier, Andrew Carrier and Mary Bradbury) as accomplices.

Because the Salem confessants were acting as religious savants and cultural insiders, the confessions were thus simultaneously instances of religious and profane speech. As religious utterance, they imitated the Catholic confessional; the confessing witches disclosed their sins to an interlocutive authority, in the case above, the accuser Mary Warren, who appears to have become endowed with the priestly authority to absolve and forgive a sinner. Not only did reformed Protestantism reject utterly the idea of confession having sacramental value, it also tended to take a dim view (as the Quakers learned) of women taking on any kind of religious authority. In this performance, Mary Warren enacts an imitation of Christian forgiveness and absolution on a legal stage. Her courtroom performance, to put it another way, parodies the structure of sin's public confession and communal forgiveness in a church, and crime's indictment and exoneration by a court. William Barker, one of the "Andover witches" examined on August 28, 1692, concluded his lengthy and detailed confession (in which he identified the already executed George Burroughs and Elizabeth How as witches) with the following:

> He saith he is heartily sorry for what he has done and for hurting the afflicted persones his accusers, prayes their forgiveness, desyres pray'rs for himself, promises to renounce the devil and all his works, And then he could take them all by the hand without any harme by his eye or any otherwise. (*SWP* I, 65–66)

The final gesture here—the accusers accepting both touch and gaze of a confessant—had by this point in the late summer of 1692 become a typical part of the confessing witch's courtroom performance. By this late phase of the trials, the Judges, accusers, and confessants had elaborated a formulaic ritual of surrender, penitence, hope, and, finally, forgiveness by communal embrace. The courtroom ritual is thus not categorically distinguishable from religiously structured ritual, including the Puritan conversion relation. The Salem trials replayed the invention of Puritanism as the court's framing of accusation and confession as the fundamental condition of its own credibility, and Puritanism's animating voice in this instance largely belongs to the radically energized voices of women.

Something was indeed very wrong in Salem, and not just because there were witches spectrally assaulting people, riding brooms, talking to animals, proffering black books, and killing cows. The confessional culture of the trials provided a complex expressive arena in which accusation and confession of witchcraft achieved meaning as both legal and religious speech. The examinations and trials themselves served as forums for religious faith to be both articulated and denied, performed as real and revealed as counterfeit. Persons noteworthy for their lack of social and political power suddenly assumed a power derived in no small part from their imitation of accepted religious convention. Now there were young women, several of questionable character, accusing their peers and superiors of religious crimes and then, depending on their response, either making possible their condemnation or absolving them of their sin. confessants similarly blended legal and religious discourse, adding their own fantastic narratives to those supplied by the accusers and therefore claiming privileged (if usually coerced) witness to an invisible world that enabled them to make claims about truths in the visible world. We might say that it is less the case that witches were destroying what was left of New England Puritanism than it was that New England Puritanism was being rearticulated in new narrative terrains defined by the religiously powerful women who dominated the legal culture of the trials.

TITUBA'S ELOCUTIONARY GAMBIT

With the exception of Cotton Mather and possibly George Burroughs, no other figure from the episode has generated as much scholarly and popular controversy as the Reverend Samuel Parris's enslaved female servant,

Tituba. Given her marginal position in New England society, the power she accrued and wielded has generated much puzzled head-scratching, as well as celebratory critical and artistic overstatement. Such divergence of opinion might be explained by the famously incomplete and vague archival record of her origins which, together with her role in the trials, has contributed to her possibly overdetermined place in the episode. Whether a "dark Eve" who tapped into long-held and never-resolved English racial beliefs and fears, or the actual high priestess of a Voodun spirituality smuggled from the Caribbean into Salem, she has emerged in both academic and popular representations as, at the very least, either the "spark" that ignited the flames, or, at the other end of the spectrum, the race-avenging rebel.[33]

In some ways, Tituba's is a pressingly "American" tale. Her known history triangulates an emerging regime of seventeenth-century knowledge in which religion, race, and the expanding sugar/slave economies intersected. Whether or not claims about Tituba's "actual" relation to the occult or her political autodidacticism are true, it is clear enough from the surviving record that Tituba's story brought recognizable features of popular magic into a messy dialogue with the "invisible world" of Reformed Protestantism. David D. Hall has claimed that this unexpected alliance of supernaturals "empowered" its users and allowed them to "overturn . . . the authority of mediating clergy."[34] We might broaden this insight and observe that the mingling of sacred and profane forces took on special form in the story of Tituba. First, Tituba can be read as the "Dark Eve" of seventeenth-century New England: "the dark woman, the alien, who enters the Puritan world and lunges it into chaos."[35] Second, Tituba's contribution to the epistemol-

---

33. Marion Starkey, *The Devil in Massachusetts: A Modern Inquiry into the Salem Witch Trials* (New York: Knopf, 1950), 10–11. For a useful review of the incoherent historiography that has attached itself to Tituba's racial status and role in the trials, see Chadwick Hansen, "The Metamorphosis of Tituba, or Why American Intellectuals Can't Tell an Indian Witch from a Negro," *The New England Quarterly* 47, no. 1 (1974): 3–12. Scholars and popularizers of Salem have offered a variety of interpretations, from the somewhat orientialist claim that Tituba really was an adherent of Voodun and other non-Christian occult traditions to the more radical exceptionalist claim that Tituba deliberately manipulated the epistemology of her gullible slaveholding Protestants in order to attack and destabilize the racist culture responsible for her perpetual chattel servitude. See, e.g., Elaine Breslaw, *Tituba, Reluctant Witch of Salem: Devilish Indians and Puritan Fantasies* (New York: New York University Press, 1996), 115, 132.

34. David D. Hall, *Worlds of Wonder, Days of Judgment: Popular Religious Belief in Early New England* (Cambridge, MA: Harvard University Press, 1989), 100.

35. Bernard Rosenthal, *Salem Story: Reading the Witch Trials of 1692* (Cambridge: Cambridge University Press, 1993), 13.

ogy of witchcraft and, by extension, New England Puritanism, is significant as much in terms of its racially marked invasive "Otherness" as in terms of its *consistency* with earlier episodes of radical female religious speech in New England. Particularly in its unexpectedly collaborative relation with both clerical and civil authority, her performance during the trials writes another chapter in the longer narrative of radical female piety as the unacknowledged core of American Puritanism.

We see this interactive relationship right from the start. The "story" of Salem witchcraft popularly begins with Tituba's role in the initial afflictions of Elizabeth (Betty) Parris, Abigail Williams, Anne Putnam, and Elizabeth Hubbard. Called on to nurse and cure the suddenly ill children in her care, Tituba "took some of the afflicted persons urine, and mixing it with meal had made a cake, and baked it, to find out the Witch, as they said." Tituba and her husband "John Indian" did then confess to Parris that she had learned of such things from her "mistress in her own country [who was] a witch," although Tituba maintains here that "she be no witch."[36] Under the direction of Mary Sibley, a white, church-covenanted, and professing Christian, Tituba baked the "witchcake" intended to identify the young women's tormentors. Exactly who then first accused Tituba is unclear, but upon consuming the cake the afflicted immediately "cryed out of the Indian Woman."[37] Possibly coerced and certainly instructed by a white woman to employ a popular magical remedy, Tituba found her efforts rewarded by an indictment for the very crime her efforts had intended to discover. At the "origin" of the Salem witch crisis, we find (with some digging) an episode that braids the inequalities of race and gender into a narrative of a privileged white woman's victimization of an enslaved colored woman. Coercion enters the story of Salem witchcraft via the politics of involuntary servitude.

And Tituba, it should be added, wasn't the only woman of color implicated in the practice of witchcraft who gambled on confession as the best defense against the gallows. Complained against by John and Thomas Putnam on July 1, 1692, a woman identified only as "Candy" faced examination by Bartholomew Gadney and John Hathorne on July 4, 1692. A "Negro Woman" belonging to or working for "Margaret Hawkes

---

36. John Hale, *A Modest Enquiry into the Nature of Witchcraft* (1697; repr., Boston: Kneeland, 1771), 22, 23.

37. Ibid., 24.

Late of Barbadoes" (*SWP* 2:385), Candy confesses to having been made a witch by her mistress, who "bring book and pen and ink, make Candy write in it" (*SWP* 1:179), and further reveals in a dramatic bit of courtroom demonstration how she and her mistress tortured the accusers using puppets or rags. Candy opens her confession by denying that she was a witch in Barbados—"Candy no witch in her country" (*SWP* 1:179)—thus reiterating the formula of white culture's production of black witchcraft represented in Tituba's witchcake episode. In Tituba's and Candy's transformation from instructed (and probably coerced) servant into occult high priestess, what emerges is a recognizably colonial thematic of white knowledge production about its ethnic others. Tituba's and Candy's "consent" to participate in the witchcake episode becomes even more obscure and problematical, as both credibly indicate they were only following orders, and doing so only to protect themselves from a credible threat of violence in failing to do so.[38]

The "confession-denial" we see here would become an important elocutionary model for the trials. Although Sarah Good is to be credited with being the first accused witch to indict another, Tituba is the first accused witch to confess. First examined on March 1, 1692, alongside two other women the afflicted women of the Parris household had identified, Tituba initially denied the charge of consorting with the devil:

JOHN HATHORNE: Titibe what evil spirit have you familiarity with
TITUBA: none
HATHORNE: why do you hurt these children
TITUBA: I do not hurt them
HATHORNE: who is it then
TITUBA: the devil for ought I know

(*SWP* 3:747)

It takes little time for Tituba to back away from total denial of any knowledge of diabolism, to denying any familiarity with evil spirits, to conceding that "the devil came to me and bid me serve him," and then offering that she saw "4 women . . . hurt the children." Finally capitulating to Hathorne's persistent questioning, Tituba "confesses" that she did, in fact,

---

38. For a reading of Candy's confession that identifies "the success of Tituba's and Candy's confessions in saving their lives," see Breslaw, *Tituba*, 152.

"hurt the children" because the four women she had seen told her "if I will not hurt the children they will hurt me" (SWP 3:747). In her confession, Tituba introduced the idea of nonconsensual malefice: that her participation in witchcraft was the result of coercion rather than voluntary consent, which is to say, as was with the earlier witchcake episode, that it was no form of "participation" at all. Tituba's role in the "origin" story of Salem witchcraft could in a sense be described as "spectral." As a human whose personhood was erased by a colonizing racialist culture, if not the legal economy of chattel slavery itself, Tituba participated in the trials as a kind of quasi-agent. Although legally disenfranchised and subjected to the dehumanization we associate with the history of American chattel slavery, Tituba not only acted the role of sociocultural agent but understood herself to be recognized as such even within the bounded terms of her servitude. The power granted to her accusatory confession allowed her temporarily to inhabit a visible position of authority. To put the matter differently, at this moment early in the larger narrative that would come to be the Salem witch trials, the most invisible woman in Salem became one of its most notorious and powerful agents. In the interactions of Mary Sibley and Tituba, we see the broader thematics of female piety writ large. Social and political subordination conditioned female religiosity and social experience. Feminine (and also ethnic) mystery enabled a more robust communion with the invisible world.

Simultaneously an agent of white "knowledge" about its ethnic others and a compromised person in a world ruled by white omnipotence, Tituba stands as a prototype for the invisible specters who would come to both represent and perform the agency of Salem witchcraft.[39] As the examinations and trials progressed throughout the early spring and summer of 1692, the question of the witch's consent to be represented spectrally would emerge as one of the most hotly debated and, tragically, unsettled issues of the trials' eventual outcomes. In Tituba's "instructed" consent to perform popular magic or "hurt the children" invisibly, we see a rudimentary version of the nonconsensual participation in diabolism that would become the defining elocutionary and narrative model of confession in

---

39. Gustafson, *Eloquence Is Power*, notes that "crucial aspects of the trials were determined by Tituba's testimony" particularly in the way in which her "coerced confession . . . introduced at a defining moment the figure of 'savage' orality behind a Puritan facade" (40). For my discussion of Tituba's coloniality and the similarity between enslavement and nonconsensual representation, I am indebted to Breslaw, *Tituba*, 122–26, and 188–97.

the examinations and trials. Little wonder, then, that Tituba became the first confessing witch to invoke the defense of coerced consent; she had, as an enslaved woman, been a socially invisible and involuntary agent well before her accusers claimed their victimization at her invisible hands. Her colonized identity, that is to say, could be described as an unbroken series of coerced performances. Involuntary spiritual witness and performance has been racialized, and with that racialization the anatomy of early modern religiosity grafts onto the bodies of slaves and other quasi-persons (old women, for example). Religious mystery becomes in this instance the mystery of blackness and of race-slavery.

The self victimized by either seen or unseen assailants, by the forces of slavery or Satan, becomes a self readable in both religious and secular terms. At the heart of the discursive life of Salem were claims that persons were being physically attacked and placed in states of extreme pain. The body in pain references a wounding God who is both the cause and the cure of trauma. As Asad puts it in a discussion of the role of pain in the modern period, pain "enables the secular idea that 'history-making' and 'self-empowerment' can progressively replace pain by pleasure—or at any rate by the search for what pleases one."[40] Diabolism and race-slavery parodically imitate God's ability to inflict pain on his creation. Coerced servitude and confession, backed by the threat and reality of violence and pain-infliction, found expression in a religious discourse that authorized a critique of the culture doing that very violence. Modernity's management of that power, its ambition to remove human suffering from the equation, thus mirrors religious authority's own attempts to eradicate the threat of witchcraft through the production of knowledge about it. The excesses of religious belief become an enabling condition for a regime of knowledge professedly uninterested in religion.

WITNESSING THE SPIRIT: THE SALEM ACCUSERS

Much—according to Bernard Rosenthal, perhaps too much—has been written on the dramatic testimony of "the girls" of Salem witchcraft. The role of these witnesses in the tragic events of 1692 continues to preoccupy modern and popular investigations of the Salem witchcraft crisis, in no small part because we moderns understand and "know" that they were, to a person, the

---

40. Asad, *Formations of the Secular*, 68.

most desperate frauds. On the eve of her own execution, Mary Easty famously requested that the judges "be pleased to examine these Afflicted Persons strictly and keepe them apart some time" (*SWP* 1:304). Nineteenth-century historiography more or less agreed with Easty's challenge to the accusers' credibility, holding, in the words of Charles Upham, that "the audacious lying of the witnesses" whose accusations were "utterly and wickedly false," was the product of a "cunning art which, on all occasions characterized their proceedings." W. S. Nevins would neatly summarize the fraud thesis by observing that "the terrible witchcraft delusion in Salem in 1692 was caused almost entirely by children."[41] *The Crucible*, Arthur Miller's cold war theatricalization of the trials, has probably done more cultural work in this regard than any other single historical recollection of Puritan Salem. Our continued outrage over the probably fraudulent content of the Salem accusers says as much about our own secular arrogance as anything else, but it remains true today that there was something outrageous about the accusers, if not about the apparently witless credulity of the judges and ministers.

Problems abound with the fraud thesis, of course, not least its inability to explain why "the girls" would have initiated such a hoax in the first place, either individually or as a group, to say nothing of accounting for why they sustained the fraud when the consequences of their behavior became, quite literally, murderous.[42] One problem with the fraud thesis is that it grants the accusers more power than they actually wielded, which is an understandable overestimation. For a period, however, lasting about nine months, this group of young women accrued and wielded an extraordinary elocutionary power, one far in excess of their gender and social station.[43] Indeed, they spoke with an authority that no other person in New

---

41. Charles Wentworth Upham, *Salem Witchcraft* (New York: F. Ungar, 1959), 2:105–6; W. S. Nevins, *Salem Observer*, August 30, 1890.

42. Many readers have, therefore, sought to understand the accusers in psychological terms, noting, among other things, neurotic behavior related to female adolescence in a severely patriarchal culture, and even holding that the accusers were classic victims/agents of pathological hysteria. In addition to such psychological explanations, there is evidence that some of the accusers told their stories on account of their social and domestic vulnerability. Then there is the ergot poisoning argument. For these different readings, see successively: Chadwick Hansen, *Witchcraft at Salem* (New York: Braziller, 1969), x; Linnda Caporael, "Ergotism: The Satan Loosed in Salem?" *Science* 192, no. 4234 (1976): 21–26; and Carol Karlsen, *The Devil in the Shape of a Woman: Witchcraft in Colonial New England* (New York: Vintage, 1987). Rosenthal, *Salem Story* (chapter 1), provides an excellent summary of various positions taken over the years.

43. The accusers were neither a fixed nor a finite number, although there was a "core" group that appears in most of the records; they were Ann Putnam Jr. (age 12), Abigail Williams (11), Mary Walcott (18), Elizabeth Hubbard (17), and Mary Warren (20). Warren has

England could reasonably be said to possess, and that authority derived in large part from the cultural perception that they were innocent victims of assault by unseen agents only they could perceive. Their victimized testimony was horrific at times, and clearly persuasive enough. Taken alone, the accusers' testimonial power is a strange spectacle indeed: without any real evidence whatsoever, the fanciful narratives of a group of women assumed power over the lives of their superiors, parents, employers, and rivals. Their accusatory power, impressive as it was, paled in comparison with what we might call their greatest elocutionary achievement: the ability to generate apparently widespread belief in their narrative renditions of a still deeply enchanted invisible world.

The persuasive logic of the accusers' speech for the most part depended on the compromised agency of the coerced self. At the May 28 Examination of Wilmott Reed (executed September 22, 1692), Elizabeth (Betty) Hubbard "said this Examinant had brought the book to her, & told her she would knock her in the head, if she would not write"; a second accuser, Ann Putnam, then "said she brought the Book to her just now" (*SWP* 3:713). It's a fairly typical moment in the testimony, with one accuser claiming a prior act of bedevilment, and a second "corroborating" the claim by testifying that the Accused was at that very moment doing it again. A third accuser, this time Susannah Sheldon, "was ordered to go to the examinant but was knock [sic] down before she came to her, & being so carryed to said Reed in a fit, was made well after said Reed had graspt her home" (*SWP* 3:713). Coerced into fits, directed to approach the alleged source of her torment, "made well" through a suspect's diabolical parody of Christ's healing touch, Sheldon conforms to a familiar script of female helplessness which she could not be said to have "invented" or authored. The fanciful details of their accusatory narratives indicated a certain creative free-play on the part of the accusers, as they drew on familiarly available images and folklore to flesh out their testimony.[44]

Involuntary female agency, whether that of accuser or confessor, produced authoritative spectral narrative. Over the course of the May 18, 1692, examination of John Willard, several of the accusers claimed

---

been credited with changing the course of the trials and deliberately introducing fraud into the testimonial behavior of the accusers.

44. For discussion of the contributions of folklore and magic, see, e.g., David Hall, *Worlds of Wonder*.

Willard's invisible specter was assaulting them. "Mary Warren cryed out, oh! He bites me . . . Ann Putnam cryed out much of him . . . John Indian cryed out he cuts me . . . Mary Warren in a great fit carryed to him, & he clapping his hand upon her arm, she was well presently" (SWP 3:823–24). In her performance of the assaulted self, Warren moves from the extravagant "testimony" of the body in pain to the testimony of the quiescent body rendered immobile by the visible touch. Warren's testimony perforce tells the story of the female body coerced by unseen assault, rendered helpless by an aggressive male whose actions are hidden from others, and then released from an orchestrated crucible of male-on-female violence by a seemingly humane act of nonsexualized touch. Religious narrative underwrote these stylized presentations of female victimization.

The specter of domestic abuse appeared in the tragic stories of John and Elizabeth Proctor. Famously popularized in Arthur Miller's cold war allegory *The Crucible*, the relationship between John Proctor and his indentured servant, Mary Warren, appears to have driven his legal prosecution. Proctor's examination record contains the deposition of Samuel Sibley, who recounted Proctor telling him "he was going to fetch home his jade" because if she (and others) "were let alone so we should all be Devils and witches quickly they should rather be had to the Whipping post but he would fetch his jade Home & thresh the Devil out of her" (SWP 2:683). This encounter took place the day after the examination of the doomed Rebecca Nurse, and Proctor clearly viewed his errand not merely as a preventative measure but as a follow-up to an earlier attempt to suppress Mary Warren's role in the unfolding drama of the trials: Proctor "also added that when she was first taken with fits he kept her close to the Wheel & threatened to thresh her, & when she had no more fits till the next day he was gone forth, & then she must have her fits again forsooth & . . ." (SWP 2:683–84). It is unclear from this record whether or not John Proctor or his spectral representation offered such violence to his servant. Mary Warren's deposition against her master referred to his threats of "tortures if she would not signe [the ubiquitous book] & since . . . have of times afflicted & tormented her" (SWP 2:684–85). If the sociolegal arrangements of the master–servant relationship normalized potential physical abuse, Mary Warren's accusations proved powerful enough to render such normal distributions of power not merely abnormal, but incriminating. In nearly perfect similarity, the accusers' narrative of incriminating hearsay replays the encounter between Proctor and John Sibley (whose wife,

Mary, as we have seen, was so instrumental in the witchcake episode), as the mere threat of physical violence gets retold as the accomplished act in the invisible world. Theorized violence becomes "real" in spectral narrative, arguably more potent as spectral than as historical text. To put the matter slightly differently: the story of potential domestic violence in the Proctor household becomes the reality of the Salem courtroom. As spectral narrative, a naturalized social relation becomes one perversely mirrored in the invisible world.

Both theologically and legally considered, this issue of a person's consent to representation lay at the heart of the court's struggle to establish or disprove a person's innocence. And while it is clear from the archive that the Puritan ministers advocated caution in the matter of spectral evidence's probative value, it is equally clear that their caution failed to manage the court's overly enthusiastic embrace of spectral narrative's evidentiary authority. As members of a religious culture that assumed the existence of an "invisible domain" with certainty, lay, legal, and clerical participants in the trials were prepared to receive such narratives with the same skeptical credulity with which they both offered and received narratives of religious conversion. The courtroom drama of 1692 Salem, in other words, enacted the confessional and interpretive drama of Protestant struggle in the civil domain of jurisprudence, and did so in riveting narratives that revealed the existence of secret conspiracies, supernatural wonders, and the continued participation of God in human affairs. The witchcraft crisis brought the issue of consent—a feature of the problem of agency within Protestantism more broadly—into the visible foreground of community and social relations at a time when issues like consent and choice were being redefined as central features of secularism, particularly in relation to women.

VICTIMS REAL AND IMAGINED

Following the June 10, 1692, execution of Bridget Bishop (the first witch convicted and sentenced to death), confession to *involuntarily* covenanted acts of diabolism would become the most consistently employed testimonial defense. These confessions became increasingly formulaic and conventional as the summer progressed, particularly after it became clear that confessing witches were not being brought to trial. The pattern had the following elements: often an initial denial of the charge; testimony about the first appearance of the devil; some sort of temporal information as to when the initial appearances of the devil occurred; claims about the devil's typically bestial appearance; revelations about the means of devilish temptation or the coercive force of his appeal; the infamous proffering and signing of "the book"; recollections of specific acts of malefice undertaken with the aid of the devil; the names of those afflicted (usually those testifying against the accused witch at the examination); and, finally and most tragically, the names of other witches with whom the now confessing witch had formerly claimed allegiance but from whose league, by virtue of the testimony itself, the confessor was now withdrawing. These confessions adhered with some variation to Tituba's March 1, 1692, confession.

Within this general scheme, a further distinction might provisionally be drawn: that between confessions in which the accused claimed to have been coerced into covenant, and those in which the accused claimed to have been lured or tempted into diabolic league. Ann Foster, who died in prison, confessed on July 16 "that it was Goody Carier that made her a witch that she came to her in person about Six yeares agoe & told her if she would not awitch the divill should tare her in peices" (*SWP* 2:343). In late August 1692 Mary Barker, one of the so-called Andover witches, confessed "after severall questions propounded and negative answ'rs Returned she at last acknowledged that Goody Johnson made her a witch, And sometime last sumer she made a red mark in the devils book with the fore finger of her Left hand . . . That Goody Johnson and Goody falkner appeared at the same tyme and threatened to teare her in peeces if she did not doo what she then did" (*SWP* 1:59). In another late-August confession, Mary Marston, also of Andover, testified that while her initial covenant was made under coercive terms, another witch (Martha Sprague) told her "she had confessed too much already and therefore would not Let her speak any more" (*SWP* 2:546). Over twenty confessing witches maintained some version of nonconsenting covenant, malefice, or speech as part of their defense, asserting a form of involuntary agency to explain their part in the diabolic conspiracy.

Such coerced confessors articulated a recognizable vernacular theology within the domain of the court. In the spectacle of the involuntary witch, that is, we see a version of the helpless sinner. A cornerstone of Calvinism's theory of inherited human corruption, the sinner (or even, as we saw with Mary Rowlandson, the uncertain saint) was always unable to keep herself from committing crimes against divine law. Original sin all too easily assumed the role of the human, and so played a starring role in the Calvinist story of never-certain redemption. Coerced confessors not only brought the spectacle of involuntary sin into the public domain of the courtroom confessional, but also premised their confession of guilt on the idea of their innocent intentions: that they were ultimately forced into diabolical covenant and acts of malefice against their will and their best intentions. The second variation of the confession defense claimed its "victims" to have been lured into diabolic covenant through promises of clothes, money, and/or power. Abigail Hobbs confessed to such temptation in her April 19 examination, revealing that the devil promised her "fine things, if I did what he would have me" (SWP 2:407). Hannah Post reported on August 25 that the devil came to her in the shape of a bird and "promised her new Cloths if She would Serve & worship him" (SWP 2:643). At the same board of examination, William Barker Sr. recalled that the devil "was willing to pay all his debts and he should live comfortably" (SWP 1:65). About the same number (eighteen) of confessing witches claimed enticement rather than coercion as their primary defense. Of this number, fifteen used the temptation model. Theologically considered, these confessants invoked the familiar theme of earthly temptation to explain these acts of covenant. Being lured into sin through Satan's guile, of course, is the founding sin of the Judeo-Christian tradition, and in this regard we should recognize the temptation defense as a latter-day imitation of Adam's fall—to be sure, and more precisely, as Eve's temptation. Biblical typology, whether intended or not and however cynically or ineptly invoked, served as the basis of self-defense in the criminal proceeding. Hermeneutics framed the terms of their reception by legal authority.

Earthly temptation was part of the daily life of Christian pilgrimage, which is to say that the snares of Satan, even those as extreme as the temptation to diabolical covenant, were easily understood and accepted events of typical Christian experience. Whether coerced or tempted, moreover, they were "feminine" in their performance: in the former case, the uneven and gendered distribution of social and physical force provided the alibi of involuntary consent, whereas in the latter the "venal" temptations of frivolous materiality appealed to conventional stereotypes about women. Although initially denying the accusations and being condemned to die on September 22, 1692, Dorcas Hoar made a jailhouse confession to a group of ministers, who subsequently petitioned Governor William Phips on her behalf. Observing that "the Lord we hope in mercy to the soule of

Dorcas Hoar" has led her "to open her out of distress of conscience . . . and confess her selfe guilty of the heynous crime of witchcraft," the petition asks that the condemned be permitted "a little longer time of life to realize & perfect her repentance for the salvation of her soule." Her legal confession thus functioned as a spiritual performance as well: "And this wee conceive if the Lord sanctify it may tend to save a soule, & to give opportunity for her making some discovery of these mystery of iniquity, & be providentiall to the encouraging of others to confess & give glory to God" (SWP 2:403–4). Dorcas Hoar's witchcraft, confession, and repentance thus fold seamlessly into the everyday drama of Christian conversion. The structure of her last-minute legal defense prompts a religious set of events and thereby brings her into the vanguard of Christian workers laboring to further the spiritual virtue and struggle of others. As a penitential discourse, Hoar's confession locates her within a long tradition of sin, its disavowal, and eventual recovenanting. From diabolical agent to practicing Christian, she provides a model of piety more imitable, even, than Mary Rowlandson's.

The legal, worldly concerns of Dorcas Hoar stage a powerful spiritual renewal and rededication to the covenant, which is to say that the secular (legal) and the sacred (spiritual) served as mutually reinforcing terms in the understanding of the late-century colonial New England Puritan's self. Whether coerced or lured into diabolism, the confessing witches avoided the gallows by telling stories that translated their diabolism into a more familiar idiom of spiritual struggle. Of course, the confessing witches of both tempted and coerced variety probably perjured themselves (both religiously and legally) in order to save their own skins. One exception would be Samuel Wardwell, who, on September 1, 1692, made a template confession of the temptation variety that contained the usual details of the late-summer confessional narratives (talking animals, the black book, and the names of other witches already indicted or confessed). Twelve days later, he recanted—"the above written: Confession: was; taken: from his mouth and that he had said it: but: he s'd he belyed: himselfe: he also s'd it was alone one: he: knew he should dye for it: whether: he ownd it or no" (SWP 3:784)—and a little over a week later he was one of eight victims hanging dead at Salem gallows. Eight denials of witchcraft resulted in eight corpses: little wonder that so many perjured themselves to escape such a fate. Another recantation, that of Mary and Hannah Tyler of Andover, specifically refers to Wardwell's experience to explain their own fearful willingness to lie: "Some time after, when we were better composed, they telling us what we had confessed, we did profess that we were innocent and ignorant of such things; and we hearing that Samuel Wardwell had renounced his confession, and was quickly after condemned and executed, some of us were told we were going after Wardwell."[45] The historical irony of the confessional culture of Salem was that cynical and calculated self-interest sustained a religiously meaningful culture. Skepticism, cynicism, irony, fiction, and even satire were crucially present in 1692 Salem, that time and place of extreme religious Otherness, as we moderns like to tell the story today.

MATHER'S FINAL INTERVENTION

"A Brand Pluck'd out of the Burning," Cotton Mather's unpublished narrative account of the diabolical afflictions of seventeen-year-old Mercy Short, was the second of several Mather-authored codas to the Salem witchcraft trials. In this account, Mather focused on the "trials" of Mercy Short, a young woman subjected to bites, pinches, scratches, and other physical attacks from unseen assailants. Mercy Short's experiences recalled in obvious ways the dramatic testimony of the 1692 accusers. Mather's report on the unseen assaults on the young woman's body, on their diabolical invitations to enter into covenant, and on their war with God not only recalled but summarized the collective spectral narratives of the confessional culture of the earlier examinations and trials. One important difference between the testimony of the Salem accusers and confessants, and that of Mercy Short, is that where the former famously revealed the names of their alleged spectral oppressors, the latter suppressed—or, rather, Cotton Mather saw to the suppression of—the identities of those afflicting her: "Had wee not studiously suppressed all Clamours and Rumours that might have touched the Reputacion of people exhibited in this Witchcraft, there might have ensued most uncomfortable Uproars."[46] In his narrative of witchcraft, the "wonders of the invisible world" erupt into the affairs of the visible; witchcraft blurs the line between invisible and visible domains.

---

45. Charles Wentworth Upham, *Salem Witchcraft*, 2:404.
46. Cotton Mather, *A Brand Pluck'd Out of the Burning* (1693), in *Narratives of the Witchcraft Cases, 1648–1706*, ed. George Lincoln Burr (New York: Scribner's, 1914), 276. Further references to this text are made parenthetically with the abbreviation *BP*.

Mather's suppression of Mercy Short's naming of witches amounted to a consignment of public representation to the private domain of the sickbed. This editorial act paralleled his theological desire to manage more assiduously the division between sacred and profane blurred in Mercy Short's affliction, and, as we have seen, in the examinations and trials themselves.

By re-establishing this division between legal and religious domains, visible and invisible terrains, Mather also asserted a division between public and private representation. The religious claims asserted over the course of the trials, and in the various Mather-authored narratives of those trials, amounted to a form of vernacular theology: a theorization of religious experience made and practiced by untrained members of the laity. Because Salem witchcraft threatened to relocate the power of the invisible world into the domain of theologically suspect arenas like the court, a ministry led by Cotton and Increase Mather belatedly attempted to restore the division between visible and invisible worlds collapsed by the language of Salem witchcraft. Mather accepted the religious authority of the (mostly) women making claims about the activities of the invisible world, yet only up to the point that such claims remained under the purview of orthodoxy. At the moment where lay religious utterance bled into civil and other nonreligious domains, Mather delimited female vernacular theology by assuming its power as his own. Female piety thereby became the marrow of Mather's public divinity. Even as his narrative would publicize her interior religious life, it would record religious experience as privately experienced and as privately meaningful. The alignment of private religious experience with the feminine, and wider discussion of such events as the "clamor" and "uproar" of the public sphere's reputational politics, would, of course, become a familiar discursive structure in the eighteenth century. Ironically, by retrospectively asserting religion's fundamental difference from the civic sphere of the trials, Mather's attempted framing of religious speech as different from other sorts of expression only served to further an evolving modernity that Mather and other Protestant theologians would otherwise want to deny. Mather's religious conservatism, to put it differently, indirectly furthered the discursive and secularizing modernity he has for so long been regarded as waging a lifelong and ultimately losing battle against.

A Brand Pluck'd is an example of Mather's characteristically cautious approach to spectral narrative, even though the text has been received as yet another Mather-authored defense of the Salem trials.⁴⁷ In this reading, the text is remarkable chiefly as evidence of Mather's support for the trials and their outcomes, which he defended not because they were legally or theologically compelling but because he opportunistically used the trials to reassert religious hegemony in a time of encroaching secularism and international war. The tale of cynical Puritan scare-mongering has since become a sort of bedtime story for modernity's triumph over the Mathers and what they represent to us now: everlasting "proof" that the Enlightenment ultimately vanquished the superstitious forces of the religious ignorance he exemplified. Even in the more stately view of American religious and intellectual history, Salem witchcraft shines as a spectacular and thankfully brief interruption of the seventeenth-century Puritan mind's growth into eighteenth-century religious rationalism, a progressive narrative that comforts by confirming secularism's belief in its total emancipation from the primitive grip of religion.⁴⁸

In this regard, the ministry's ambivalent relation to the trials stemmed not from the inherent *unbelievability* of spectral testimony but rather from its inherent persuasiveness *as* specifically religious speech. Take for example the extended interpolated passage in A Brand Pluck'd, in which Mather "records" Mercy Short's hostile encounters with her invisible tormentors: "You shall be no Christ to me," Short tells her spectral assailants. "When You have become a Man, and have suffered a cruel Death on a Cross for me; and when you have Reconciled me to God, and been some Ages in heaven powerfully Interceding for my Salvation from the Divel— Then come to mee again" (BP 268). Somewhere between child's catechism and minister's sermon, Short's diatribe asserts the theology of the Incarnation and Christ's Intercession in a spectral narrative of invisible bedevilment. It is telling that Mather quite literally frames the voice of

---

47. Richard Slotkin concludes his reading of A Brand Pluck'd as captivity narrative by remarking that the Mercy Short case offered "superb material for revival sermons attacking Puritan complacency" and that "this was the use Mather hoped to make of the account." Although he doesn't discuss the Mercy Short case, Larzer Ziff also maintains that the clergy supported the trials as a defense against "the still unacceptable declaration of the rationality of the universal frame." See Slotkin, *Regeneration Through Violence: The Mythology of the American Frontier, 1660–1860* (Middletown, CT: Wesleyan University Press, 1973), 139; and Ziff, *Puritanism in America: New Culture in a New World* (New York: Viking, 1973), 243.

48. Perhaps the most influential formulation of this opinion comes from Perry Miller, who claimed that the "intellectual history of New England up to 1720 can be written as though [the trials] never happened." See Miller, *The New England Mind: From Colony to Province* (Cambridge, MA: Harvard University Press, 1953; repr., Boston: Beacon, 1961), 191.

Mercy Short here, setting her lengthy speech off from the rest of the narrative to signal its subordination to Mather's authorizing narrative. Within an editorially framed vernacular narrative of diabolical affliction emerges a theory of Christian salvation, a congruence which, in asserting a similarity of demonic and divine agency, potentially compromised the theorization of pure divinity central to Christian religious life. Of course, Mather several times drew attention to the "diabolical" imitation of "Divine" rites undertaken by New England's parodic witches, whose "bloody Imitations, if the Confessions of the Witches are to be received," placed the diabolical and the divine in outrageous proximity to one another (BP 246). Under his ministerial and editorial care, Mercy Short's blurring of the difference between diabolical affliction and orthodox theology resolves back into a carefully managed integrity. Like so many of the Salem afflicted, Mercy Short is pricked with pins that "left Bloody Marks of them." Occasionally the invisible world would bleed into the visible, as "some of the Pins They [her invisible attackers] left in her, and those wee took out, with Wonderment." Conversely, actions taken in the visible world would have invisible effects, as Mather and his coadjutants would "with main Force" lift Short upright from the bed, causing the specters sitting on her chest to fall off (BP 264). As the story narrates the fluid interaction of invisible and visible domains, Mather's text works to separate them one from another by overlaying her text with his own, not unlike his father Increase's attempted management of Mary Rowlandson's text. *A Brand Pluck'd from the Burning* presents a fantasia of sorts: it draws on and furthers the religious power of its female informant whose management by the authoritative male cleric presents a vision of female piety's containment.

Mercy Short's theatrical agonies were, of course, reminiscent of the spectral performances seen during the examinations trials. But there is a crucial difference between Mercy's spectral performance and those of the Salem afflicted. If the latter's evidence achieved the status of authoritative speech during the trials, the former's testimony remains sequestered within Mather's narrative. "Reader," begins Mather in an extended address, "If thou hadst a Desire to have seen a Picture of Hell, it was visible in the doleful circumstances of Mercy Short." The affliction, somewhat predictably, becomes a case for repentance made in the language of the trials: "As for us wee have had not only the Damned coming to us from the Dead, in this Witchcraft, but the very state of the Damned itself represented most visibly before our eyes" (BP 267). Performing an exegetical examination of Mercy Short's example, Mather effectively suborns her experience and speech to his judicious interpretive agenda, an agenda that included, as scholarship has long noted, the careful suppression of the names of persons accused by Mercy Short of being her spectral attackers. The text also manages Mercy Short's frequent arguments with her unseen assailants, arguments which, if not employing the grammar of orthodox sermonic style, certainly advanced deeply orthodox views of things like the incarnation, the proper use of sacraments, and so forth. If Mather's October 1692 account of witchcraft took pains to reassert the integrity of the line separating invisible and visible domains, it also reasserted the primacy of Congregational theology over the arrogant legal intervention of a secular body like the Court of *Oyer* and *Terminer*.

The *Brand Pluck'd* suppressed the dangerous interpretive latitude authorized by the spectral blurring of evidentiary order during the 1692 Salem witchcraft trials. Unlike the judges at the Salem witchcraft trials, whose authorization of vernacular religious testimony led to injustice, Mather established an ordering of evidence in which female piety remained simultaneously central to and contained within an orthodox account of religious authority. In the presentation of Mercy Short as religiously exemplary, he locates divine intention in the tortured, probably anorectic, and assiduously edited body of a young women.[49] For Mercy Short refused to covenant with the devil, crying out "'Tho' you kill mee, I'l never do what you would have mee.—Do what you will, yett with the Help of Christ, I'l never touch your Book" (*BP* 267). Indeed, through Mather's management of her affliction, Mercy Short becomes a lay mouthpiece for his own religious ideals, rehearsing in an interpolated sequence of "her" narrative many of Mather's own most abidingly held religious principles. If Mary Rowlandson once wandered off the path of exemplary piety into the forest of private mystery, Mercy Short will receive no such interpretive latitude. Unlike the Salem afflicted, whose public confessions indicted the innocent, and the confessing witches, whose testimony helped convict them, Mercy Short's presentation lodges information from the invisible world firmly in the private realm of individual female experience.

---

49. Karlsen proposes an alternative reading of the afflicted young woman, arguing that Mercy Short and others like her "could rebel against the many restrictions placed upon her" by men like Cotton Mather and, "for the moment . . . be as powerful as he." See Karlsen, *Devil in the Shape of a Woman*, 247.

Mercy Short's otherworldly testimony, that is to say, inscribes religious witness as a fundamentally different order from the sort of testimony that matters in civic life, and yet that witnessing voice authorizes the agency of its secular successors. Mather's manuscript ultimately sequesters the religious from the civil, which perforce creates the conditions whereby the religious testimony of a Mercy Short is believable *only* as religious discourse, as a "special" rather than universal category of colonial discourse. Female piety enters eighteenth-century America as its religious other. In the coffee houses, as Mather resumes the narrative of a *Brand Pluck'd*, a different story is being told. Indeed, to the degree that "the Unjust and Absurd Reflections cast upon her by Rash People in the coffee-houses and elsewhere" (*BP* 271) appropriated her suffering as the subject of public conversation, the public order of civility could be said to both depend on and marginalize the religious preoccupations of the young woman and her shepherd. It is in this sense that we can conclude that Mather furthered the secular modernity he would deny by recasting religion into a gendered structure commensurate with a developing post-Puritan colonial order. Mercy Short's religious ravings no longer matter save as evidence of the rational public's fundamental difference from whatever she represents or recalls about a religious identity now lodged firmly in the secular spaces of modern memory.

The events of Salem continue to inspire and horrify us today. One of the techniques we employ to manage that relation is to position the Salem trials as a clear indicator of what the Puritans of New England really were or became. Hysterical girls, zealous ministers, penny-dreadful jealousies, and local rivalries populate a story that confirms our triumphalist vision of an Enlightenment that rescued us from "The Wonders of the Invisible World." The important point here is that secularism's disavowal of a Salem-identified Puritanism must also concede Salem's contribution to the creation of that very perspective, and, moreover, to the persistence of the gendered modes of religious identity that would become as characteristic of the modern, rationalized social relations of the eighteenth century as they had been in the previous. Perhaps then we might better understand American Puritanism not from the perspective of disavowal—that it is "ours" by not being ours—but rather from one of recognition.

AFTERWORD

Remembering American Puritanism

BROADLY SPEAKING, the single largest political divide at the national level of American political life is structured around a religiously identified "conservatism" and a religiously skeptical "liberalism." This isn't to say that self-identified liberal politicians do not themselves claim and even insist on having personal religious affiliations "in spite of" their political liberal agenda, nor even that all political conservatives proclaim their faith as a constitutive feature of their political motivations—although most do.[1] The point rather is that conservatives and liberals—generally speaking—tend to offer one or the other respectively, and many Americans expect their politicians to exhibit political tendencies based on creedal affiliation.[2] To be sure, much of this may just be media hype and political pandering, but the point still stands: in the twenty-first-century United States, religion drives the political agenda in ways that leave many observers scratching their heads and puzzling over how this could be so.[3] This book has sought to provide one sort of answer: America has never not been religious; it has

---

1. Religion may not always have been the job requirement it has become for the American presidency, as shown by Randall Balmer, *God in the White House: A History: How Faith Shaped the Presidency from John F. Kennedy to George W. Bush* (New York: Harper, 2008). Of course, prior to Kennedy, a Protestant Christian president was more or less always assumed, as was the idea that a president's religious life was his own.

2. William D'Antonio, "Religion and Political Affiliation," *National Catholic Reporter*, October 24, 2011.

3. Pew Research Global Attitudes Project, "Among Wealthy Nations: U.S. Stands Alone in Its Embrace of Religion," December 19, 2002.

never not been secular. Religion's location "within" secularism remains a salient feature of the U.S. national imaginary, all claims of successful secularization, and the "separation of church and state," to the contrary.

The most obvious example of this phenomenon may be seen in the continued debate about "prayer in schools." Secular-identified liberals have a hard time believing there even is a debate over a matter "clearly" settled by the First Amendment. Conservative politicians and media personalities argue that requiring schools to lead American children in a daily recitation of the Lord's Prayer is a fundamental part of learning to "be an American"; that America remains a Christian country because its Founders apparently were; and that being part of a tradition of belief and national destiny that extends back to the colonial period is an essential requirement for prosecuting the cause of America's successful future. Liberal opponents claim that the Lord's Prayer is an exclusively Christian devotion that only welcomes Christian-identified schoolchildren to participate; that those Founders, while they may have been Christian to a man, wrote a Constitution asserting that "Congress shall make no law respecting an establishment of religion, or prohibiting the free exercise thereof" and that the prayer-in-schools argument violates both of these prohibitions; and that, finally, schools, like all civil spaces, are public institutions defined as such by their secular neutrality. The terms of this debate depend on the idea that religious and secular perspectives are more or less mutually exclusive; that one perspective must be wholly right and the other wholly wrong; and that, morally speaking on behalf of the nation, choosing one or the other will result in nothing short of the end of America as we know it. This "all or nothing" approach resonates with the "all or nothing" secularization thesis of the modern West, as well as the corollary argument about American religion corralled securely because entirely "in the past," the gate shut and locked by the provisions of the First Amendment.

The "pro-religion" argument approvingly cites the nation's "origins" as a Protestant story of victimized religious freedom-seeking, and predicates the nation's present successes and woes, as well as its future achievements and failures, on remembering that story as America's ongoing narrative of special place and destiny among the world's nations, religions, cultures, and so forth.[4] Contrarily, "pro-secular" forces have long argued that the

---

4. For a development of this argument, see Seymour Lipset, *American Exceptionalism: A Double-Edged Sword* (New York: Norton, 1996).

nation's Protestant origins story is something of a false one, that it may not even be the really important one, and that whatever the history of the Puritan "experiment" may have been in the colonial period, that history is now just that—the past—and the more enduring legacies of that period, in any event, belong to a longer and broader histories of invasion, colonization, and race-based imperialism.[5] It is a curious feature of Americanist intellectual culture today that we are utterly willing to entertain the idea that select cultural and historical narratives of the United States have a measurable and necessary "historical afterlife" whose continuity with the past is assumed, whereas, when it comes to the nation's Christian past, at least until quite recently, no such continuity has been deemed salient. Whether we affirm or disavow the nation's religious-origins narrative ends up replicating the "religious" or "secular" division that still constitutes so much of U.S. political life, and is a symptom of a now pretty thoroughly discredited secularization narrative.

To the religiously affiliated conservative politician approvingly leading today's children in a daily recitation of the Lord's Prayer, we might remind him that Anne Hutchinson despised all such ritualistic incantations; that the Puritans banished her for saying loudly that she did; and that today she is remembered for standing up to precisely the sort of coercive state authority that twenty-first-century conservative and libertarian political thought claims as its own great cause. To claim the "Puritan Mind"—seventeenth-century Puritan culture more generally—as the decisive origin story of modern neoliberalism would be to seriously misread that mind's commitment to a theory and practice of state that was deeply instrumental, interfering, and controlling. To the secular liberal remembering Puritanism as precisely that assertion of a religiously intolerant state, we might offer that Hutchinson was, in fact, motivated by a set of religious beliefs far, far more important to her than the inappropriate interference of the state; that she wanted to be free of that control so that she could be left to follow her own conscience; and that the source of her "power" and the inspiration she drew from and bequeathed to us as our secularist arguments against the religious state was actually a sovereign and all-seeing god. To claim Anne Hutchinson, or the radical female piety of this book's archive, as the precursor to a godless secularism would be to seriously misread that history.

---

5. For a recent and extended critique of American exceptionalism, see Donald Pease, *The New American Exceptionalism*.

If anything, it was through the agency of their extraordinary piety that God still resides in the house of twenty-first-century American secularism.

We remember American Puritanism today as being either wholly "freedom-seeking" or repressing all such seeking—it was both at times, and so neither really. Our ability to view it as utterly theocratic depends on our belief that we are free from its influence. We read the Puritans as being completely enchanted by superstition by virtue of our being free of divine mystery. We note and critique Puritanism's patriarchal authority and commitment to the subordination and repression of women, while we expect religion today to remain safely contained within the secular cloisters of domesticity, private experience, or the physical spaces of churches. This way of remembering a religious past is, in the first instance, a symptom of secularist position-taking, and, in the second and perhaps more damagingly so, a way to sponsor deeply divisive, polarizing and troubling cultural and democratic politics authorized in the name of religion's complete control or absence. So politically conservative and religiously self-identified Americans claim their victimization at the hands of secular liberals, while politically liberal secularists are quick to identify instances where religion encroaches both incredibly and inappropriately into terrains of social and political life that should be free from the irrational nonsense of religion. Perhaps if we recognize and appreciate that, for example, the Puritan reception of Quaker belief enabled a discourse of "universal" human rights, then perhaps we might be able to think about some of these contemporary issues with a little more care than we do when choosing between a failed or fearful religion on the one hand and a terrible or triumphant secularity on the other.

These perspectives depend on a view of American Puritanism that this book has tried to complicate through a return to the archive that gave rise to it. But there is more at stake in this work than trying to say new things about old stories. The consolidation of Puritan authority around forms of radical female piety that it alternately enabled and suppressed may well offer a more nuanced and perhaps more satisfactory critique of this phase of American colonial history. Understood, however, within the reigning narratives of the secularization thesis—that once we were religious, and then we were not—such a cultural study, even a careful one, doesn't really make much sense. Of course, this is the broader point: that the archive of seventeenth-century New England, when read in this way, very much supports the "postsecular" perspective of contemporary religious and cultural studies, which generally seeks to invalidate the old secularization narrative by talking about how religion persists within the secular, and how secular concepts find expression within formations of the sacred as well. The invention of American Puritanism, as a distinct historiographical designation, has enabled the old secularization thesis to flourish in American culture and politics. The "forgetting" of women and femininity's distinctive contribution to Puritanism has been regarded too long as being coextensive with secularism's erasure of women and religion and their relocation to the margins of eighteenth-century bourgeois modernity and beyond. This forgetting of the feminine and religion in American culture is not only inaccurate, in ways we have seen; it is not only unsatisfying, in terms of the revision to the secularization thesis now more or less assumed in contemporary cultural critique. The modern forgetting of women and religion is also, finally, inadequate to the purpose of better understanding the continuing force and place of religion in contemporary American and global cultural politics today.

BIBLIOGRAPHY

Adams, Brooks. *The Emancipation of Massachusetts.* Boston: Houghton Mifflin, 1887.
Adams, Hannah. *A Summary History of New England.* Boston: H. Mann, 1799.
Adams, James Truslow. *The Founding of New England.* Boston: Atlantic Monthly, 1922.
Adams, William. *The Necessity of the Pouring Out of the Spirit from On High upon a Sinning Apostatizing People.* Boston: John Foster, 1679.
Agamben, Giorgio. *Profanations.* Translated by Jeff Fort. New York: Zone Books, 2007.
Ahmed, Sara. *The Cultural Politics of Emotion.* New York: Routledge, 2004.
Arber, Edward, ed. *The Term Catalogues.* 3 vols. London: Edward Arber, 1903.
Armstrong, Nancy. *Desire and Domestic Fiction: A Political History of the Novel.* New York: Oxford University Press, 1987.
Armstrong, Nancy, and Leonard Tennenhouse. "The American Origins of the English Novel." *American Literary History* 4, no. 3 (1992): 386–410.
Asad, Talal. *Formations of the Secular: Christianity, Islam, Modernity.* Stanford, CA: Stanford University Press, 2003.
Audland, Anne. *A True Declaration of the Suffering of the Innocent.* London, 1654.
Bailey, Richard. *New Light on George Fox and Early Quakerism: The Making and Unmaking of a God.* New York: Mellen, 1992.
Balmer, Randall. *God in the White House: A History: How Faith Shaped the Presidency from John F. Kennedy to George W. Bush.* New York: Harper, 2008.
Bancroft, George. *History of the Colonization of the United States.* Vol. 1. Boston: Little, Brown, 1844.
Barbour, Hugh. *The Quakers in Puritan England.* London: Friends United Press, 1985. First published 1964 by Yale University Press.
Barry, John M. *Roger Williams and the Creation of the American Soul.* New York: Viking, 2012.
Barthes, Roland. "Toward a Psychosociology of Contemporary Food Consumption." In Counihan and Van Esterik, *Food and Culture: A Reader,* 20–27.
Battis, Emery. *Saints and Sectaries: Anne Hutchinson and the Antinomian Controversy in the Massachusetts Bay Colony.* Chapel Hill: University of North Carolina Press, 1962.
Bauer, Ralph. "Creole Identities in Colonial Space: The Narratives of Mary White Rowlandson and Francisco Nunez de Pineda y Bascunan." *American Literature* 69, no. 4 (1997): 665–95.
———. *The Cultural Geography of Colonial American Literatures: Empire, Travel, Modernity.* New York: Cambridge University Press, 2003.
Baym, Nina. "Revisiting Hawthorne's Feminism." *Nathaniel Hawthorne Review* 30, no. 1 (2004): 32–55.

Bellah, Robert. *The Broken Covenant: American Civil Religion in Time of Trial.* 2nd ed. 1975. Reprint, Chicago: University of Chicago Press, 1992.
Bercovitch, Sacvan. *The American Jeremiad.* Madison: University of Wisconsin Press, 1978.
———. *The Puritan Origins of the American Self.* 1975. Reprint, New Haven, CT: Yale University Press, 2011.
Berg, Christina, and Philippa Berry. "'Spiritual Whoredom': An Essay on Female Prophets in the Seventeenth Century." In *1642: Literature and Power in the Seventeenth Century*, edited by Brancis Barker. Essex: University of Essex, 1981, 37–54.
Berkus, Catherine. *Strangers and Pilgrims: Female Preaching in America, 1740–1845.* Chapel Hill: University of North Carolina Press, 1998.
Bernard, Richard. *A Guide to Grand-Jury Men.* London, 1627.
Besse, Joseph. *Sufferings of Early Quakers: America.* 1753. Facsimile ed. York, England: Sessions Book Trust, 2001.
Bishop, George. *New England Judged, by the Spirit of the Lord, the First Part.* London: Robert Wilson, 1661.
Bousma, William. *The Waning of the Renaissance, 1550–1640.* New Haven, CT: Yale University Press, 2000.
Boyer, Paul, and Stephen Nissenbaum, eds. *The Salem Witchcraft Papers.* 3 vols. New York: Da Capo, 1977.
Bozeman, Theodore. *To Live Ancient Lives: The Primitivist Dimension in Puritanism.* Chapel Hill: University of North Carolina Press for the Omohundro Institute of Early America, 1988.
Bradstreet, Anne. *The Works of Anne Bradstreet.* Edited by Adrienne Rich. Cambridge, MA: Belknap Press of Harvard University Press, 1967.
Braithwaite, William C. *The Beginnings of Quakerism.* 1912. Reprint, Cambridge University Press, 1981.
Bray, Alan. "The Curious Case of Michael Wigglesworth." In *A Queer World: The Center for Lesbian and Gay Studies Reader*, edited by Martin Duberman. New York: New York University Press, 1997, 205–15.
Breen, Louise. *Transgressing the Bounds: Subversive Enterprises among the Puritan Elite in Massachusetts, 1630–1692.* New York: Oxford University Press, 2001.
Breitwieser, Mitchell. *American Puritanism and the Defense of Mourning: Religion, Grief, and Ethnology in Mary White Rowlandson's Captivity Narrative.* Madison: University of Wisconsin Press, 1991.
———. *Cotton Mather and Benjamin Franklin: The Price of Representative Personality.* Cambridge: Cambridge University Press, 1984.
Breslaw, Elaine. *Tituba, Reluctant Witch of Salem: Devilish Indians and Puritan Fantasies.* New York: New York University Press, 1996.
Brooks, Joanna. "From Edwards to Baldwin: Heterodoxy, Discontinuity, and New Narratives of American Religious-Literary History." *American Literary History* 22, no. 2 (2010): 439–53.
Brown, Gillian. *The Consent of the Governed: The Lockean Legacy in Early American Culture.* Cambridge, MA: Harvard University Press, 2001.
Brown, Wendy, and Saba Mahmood, eds. *Is Critique Secular? Blasphemy, Injury, and Free Speech.* Berkeley: University of California Press for the Townsend Center for the Humanities, 2009.

Burden, Anne. Letter to George Fox. 1656. Swarthmore Collection. Friends House Library, London.
Burnham, Michelle. "Anne Hutchinson and the Economics of Antinomian Selfhood in Colonial New England." *Criticism* 39, no. 3 (1997): 337–58.
———. *Folded Selves: Colonial New England Writing in the World System*. Hanover, NH: University Press of New England, 2007.
Burrough, Edward. *A Declaration of the Sad and Great Persecution and Martyrdom of the People of God, Called the Quakers, in New-England*. London: Robert Wilson, 1661.
Bynum, Caroline Walker. *Holy Feast and Holy Fast: The Religious Significance of Food to Medieval Women*. Berkeley: University of California Press, 1987.
Cahn, Mark D. "Punishment, Discretion, and the Codification of Prescribed Penalties in Colonial Massachusetts." *American Journal of Legal History* 33, no. 2 (1989): 107–36.
Caldwell, Patricia. "The Antinomian Language Controversy." *Harvard Theological Review* 69, no. 3 (1976): 345–67.
———. *The Puritan Conversion Narrative: The Beginning of American Expression*. Cambridge: Cambridge University Press, 1983.
Caporael, Linnda. "Ergotism: The Satan Loosed in Salem?" *Science* 192, no. 4234 (1976): 21–26.
Carruth, Mary. "Between Abjection and Redemption: Mary Rowlandson's Subversive Corporeality." In *Feminist Interventions in Early American Studies*, edited by Mary Carruth. Tuscaloosa: University of Alabama Press, 2006, 60–79.
Caruth, Cathy. *Unclaimed Experience: Trauma, Narrative, History*. Baltimore: Johns Hopkins University Press, 1996.
Casanova, José. *Public Religions in the Modern World*. Chicago: University of Chicago Press, 1994.
Castiglia, Christopher. *Bound and Determined: Captivity, Culture-Crossing, and White Womanhood from Mary Rowlandson to Patty Hearst*. Chicago: University of Chicago Press, 1996.
Certeau, Michel de. *The Mystic Fable: The Sixteenth and Seventeenth Centuries*. Translated by Michael Smith. Chicago: University of Chicago Press, 1986.
Chauncy, Charles. *Enthusiasm Described and Caution'd Against*. Boston: J. Draper, 1742.
Cohen, Charles Lloyd. *God's Caress: The Psychology of Puritan Religious Experience*. New York: Oxford University Press, 1986.
Cohen, Daniel. *Pillars of Salt, Monuments of Grace: New England Crime Literature and the Origins of American Popular Culture, 1674–1860*. New York: Oxford University Press, 1993.
Cohen, Matt. *The Networked Wilderness: Communicating in Early New England*. Minneapolis, MN: University of Minnesota Press, 2009.
Colacurcio, Michael. "Footsteps of Ann Hutchinson: The Context of *The Scarlet Letter*." *English Literary History* 39, no. 5 (1972): 459–94.
Cooper, James. "Anne Hutchinson and the 'Lay Rebellion' against the Clergy." *The New England Quarterly* 61, no. 3 (1988): 381–97.
Cotton, John. *Christ the Fountaine of Life*. 1651. Facsimile of the first edition. New York: Arno, 1972.
———. *The Way of Congregational Churches Cleared*. 1648. In *John Cotton on the Churches of New England*, edited by Larzer Ziff. Cambridge, MA: Belknap Press of Harvard University Press, 1968, 167–364.

Counihan, Carole, and Penny Van Esterik, eds. *Food and Culture: A Reader.* New York: Routledge, 1997.

D'Antonio, William. "Religion and Political Affiliation." *National Catholic Reporter,* October 24, 2011.

Davidson, Cathy. *Revolution and the Word: The Rise of the Novel in America.* New York: Oxford University Press, 1986.

Davis, J. C. *Fear, Myth and History: The Ranters and the Historians.* Cambridge: Cambridge University Press, 1986.

Delbanco, Andrew. *The Puritan Ordeal.* Cambridge, MA: Harvard University Press, 1989.

Derounian, Kathryn Zabelle. "Puritan Orthodoxy and the 'Survivor Syndrome' in Mary Rowlandson's Indian Captivity Narrative." *Early American Literature* 22, no. 1 (1987): 82–93.

Dillon, Elizabeth Maddock. *The Gender of Freedom: Fictions of Liberalism and the Literary Public Sphere.* Stanford, CA: Stanford University Press, 2004.

———. "Religion and Geo-politics in the New World." *Early American Literature* 45, no. 1 (2010): 193–202.

Douglas, Ann. *The Feminization of American Culture.* New York: Knopf, 1977.

Douglas, Mary. "Deciphering a Meal." In Counihan and Van Esterik, *Food and Culture: A Reader,* 44–53.

———. *Purity and Danger: An Analysis of Concepts of Pollution and Taboo.* London: Routledge, 2002. First published 1966 by Praeger.

Douglass, William. *Summary, Historical and Political, of the British Settlements in North America.* Boston, Rogers and Fowle, 1749. Facsimile of the first edition. New York: Arno, 1972.

Downing, David. "'Streams of Scripture Comfort': Mary Rowlandson's Typological Use of the Bible." *Early American Literature* 15, no. 3 (1980): 252–59.

Drake, Samuel Adams. *A Book of New England Legends and Folklore.* Boston, 1883. Reprint, Boston: Little, Brown, 1901.

Edwards, Jonathan. "A Divine and Supernatural Light." 1734. In *A Jonathan Edwards Reader,* edited by John H. Smith and Harry S. Stout. New Haven, CT: Yale University Press, 2003, 105–23.

———. "A Faithful Narrative of the Surprising Work of God." In *The Great Awakening,* edited by C. C. Goen, vol. 4 of *The Works of Jonathan Edwards.* New Haven, CT: Yale University Press, 2009 144-211.

———. *Letters and Personal Writings,* edited by C. C. Goen, vol. 16 of *The Works of Jonathan Edwards.* New Haven, CT: Yale University Press, 1998.

Eliade, Mircea. *The Sacred and the Profane: The Nature of Religion.* Translated by William R. Trask. New York: Harcourt, 1957.

Elliott, Emory. "The Development of the Puritan Funeral Sermon and Elegy: 1660–1750." *Early American Literature* 15, no. 2 (1980): 151–64.

———. "The Dream of a Christian Utopia." In *The Cambridge History of American Literature,* vol. 1, *1590–1820,* edited by Sacvan Bercovitch and Cyrus R. K. Patell. New York: Cambridge University Press, 1994, 183–204.

———. *Power and the Pulpit in Puritan New England.* Princeton, NJ: Princeton University Press, 1975.

Fairman, Lydia. *A Few Lines and True Testimony.* London: Thomas Simmons, 1659.

Faludi, Susan. *The Terror Dream: Myth and Misogyny in an Insecure America*. New York: Picador, 2007.
Febvre, Lucien. *The Problem of Unbelief in the Sixteenth Century: The Religion of Rabelais*. Translated by Beatrice Gottlieb. Cambridge, MA: Harvard University Press, 1985.
Fell, Henry. Selected Letters. Swarthmore Collection. Friends House Library, London.
Fell, Margaret. Selected Letters. Spence Collection. Friends House Library, London.
———. *Women's Speaking Justified by Scriptures*. London, 1667.
Ferrara, Pasquale. "Globalization and Post-Secularism: Religions and a Universal Common Identity." *Claritas: Journal of Dialogue and Culture* 1, no. 1 (2012): Article 7. http://docs.lib.purdue.edu/claritas/vol1/iss1/7.
Fessenden, Tracy. *Culture and Redemption: Religion, the Secular, and American Literature*. Princeton, NJ: Princeton University Press, 2007.
Field, Jonathan Beecher. "The Antinomian Controversy Did Not Take Place." *Early American Studies* 6, no. 2 (2008): 448–63.
———. *Errands into the Metropolis: New England Dissidents in Revolutionary London*. Hanover, NH: University Press of New England, 2009.
Field, Peter. *Ralph Waldo Emerson: The Making of a Democratic Intellectual*. Lanham, MD: Rowman & Littlefield, 2002.
Fiske, John. *The Beginnings of New England, or the Puritan Theocracy in Its Relations to Civil and Religious Liberty*. Boston: Houghton, 1889. Reprint. Boston: Riverside Press, 1898.
Fitzpatrick, Tara. "The Figure of Captivity: The 'Cultural Work' of the Puritan Captivity Narrative." *American Literary History* 3, no. 1 (1991): 1–26.
Fliegelman, Jay. *Prodigals and Pilgrims: The American Revolution against Patriarchal Authority, 1750–1800*. Cambridge: Cambridge University Press, 1982.
Foster, Stephen. *The Long Argument: English Puritanism and the Shaping of New England Culture, 1570–1700*. Chapel Hill: University of North Carolina Press, 1991.
Foucault, Michel. *Discipline and Punish: The Birth of the Prison*. Translated by Alan Sheridan. New York: Vintage, 1979.
Fowler, Robert. *A True Relation of the Voyage Undertaken by Me, Robert Fowler*. September 1657. Swarthmore Collection. Friends House Library, London.
Fox, George. *The Great Mystery of the Great Whore Unfolded: and AntiChrist's Kingdom Revealed unto Destruction. . . . In Answer to the Many False Doctrines and Principles . . . Sent Forth . . . Against the Despised People of the Lord called QUAKERS, who are of the Seed of that Woman, who have been Long Fled into the Wilderness*. London: Thomas Simmons, 1659.
———. "To All Friends Suffering." 1657. Swarthmore Collection. Friends House Library, London.
Franchot, Jenny. "Invisible Domain: Religion and American Literary Studies." *American Literature* 67, no. 4 (1995): 833–42.
———. *Roads to Rome: The Antebellum Protestant Encounter with Catholicism*. Berkeley: University of California Press, 1994.
———. "Unseemly Commemoration: Religion, Fragment, and the Icon." *American Literary History* 9, no. 3 (1997): 502–21.
General Court of Boston. *Propositions Concerning the Subject of Baptism and Consociation of Churches*. Boston, 1662.

Gildrie, Richard. *The Profane, the Civil, and the Godly: The Reformation of Manners in Orthodox New England*. University Park: Pennsylvania State University Press, 1994.

Gilman, Anne. *Epistle to Friends . . . Letter to Charles, King*. London, 1662.

Goodman, Nan. *Banished: Common Law and the Rhetoric of Social Exclusion in Early New England*. Philadelphia: University of Pennsylvania Press, 2012.

Gordis, Lisa. *Opening Scripture: Bible Reading and Interpretive Authority in Puritan New England*. Chicago: University of Chicago Press, 2003.

Gould, Daniel. *A Brief Narration of the Suffering of the People Called Quakers*. New York: William Bradford (?) 1700.

Greenblatt, Stephen. *Marvelous Possessions: The Wonder of the New World*. Chicago: University of Chicago Press, 1991.

Greven, Philip. *The Protestant Temperament: Patterns of Child-Rearing, Religious Experience, and the Self in Early America*. New York: Knopf, 1977.

Gura, Philip. *A Glimpse of Sion's Glory: Puritan Radicalism in New England, 1620–1660*. Middletown, CT: Wesleyan University Press, 1984.

Gustafson, Sandra. *Eloquence Is Power: Oratory and Performance in Early America*. Chapel Hill: University of North Carolina Press for the Omohundro Institute of Early America, 2000.

Hale, John. *A Modest Enquiry into the Nature of Witchcraft*. 1697. Boston: Kneeland, 1771.

Hall, David. *The Antinomian Controversy, 1636–1638: A Documentary History*. Durham, NC: Duke University Press, 1990. First published 1968 by Wesleyan University Press.

———. "Assurance, Community, and the Puritan Self." In *Puritanism and Its Discontents*, edited by Laura Lunger Knoppers. Wilmington: University of Delaware Press, 2003, 197–209.

———. "New England, 1660–1730." In *The Cambridge Companion to Puritanism*, edited by John Coffey and Paul C. H. Lim. Cambridge: Cambridge University Press, 2008.

———. *Worlds of Wonder, Days of Judgment: Popular Religious Belief in Early New England*. Cambridge, MA: Harvard University Press, 1989.

Hambrick-Stowe, Charles. *The Practice of Piety: Puritan Devotional Discipline in Seventeenth-Century New England*. Chapel Hill: University of North Carolina Press for the Omohundro Institute of Early America, 1982.

Hansen, Chadwick. "The Metamorphosis of Tituba, or Why American Intellectuals Can't Tell an Indian Witch from a Negro." *The New England Quarterly* 47, no. 1 (1974): 3–12.

———. *Witchcraft at Salem*. New York: Braziller, 1969.

Harpham, Geoffrey. *The Ascetic Imperative in Culture and Criticism*. Chicago: University of Chicago Press, 1987.

Harris, Paul. "Passion vs. Puritanism as America Is Gripped by a War Over Sexuality." *Guardian/Observer*, March 20, 2012.

Hartman, Saidiya. "Venus in Two Acts." *Small Axe* 12, no. 2 (2008): 1–14.

Hawthorne, Nathaniel. *The Scarlet Letter*. 1850. Edited and with an introduction by Leland Person. New York: Norton, 2005.

Heimert, Alan. *Religion and the American Mind, from the Great Awakening to the Revolution*. Cambridge: Cambridge University Press, 1966.

Henke, Suzette A. *Shattered Subjects: Trauma and Testimony in Women's Life-Writing.* New York: St. Martin's, 1998.
Henigman, Laura. *Coming into Communion: Pastoral Dialogues in Colonial New England.* Albany: State University of New York Press, 1999.
Henwood, Dawn. "Mary Rowlandson and the Psalms: The Textuality of Survival." *Early American Literature* 32, no. 2 (1997): 169–86.
Hickman, Jared. "Globalization and the Gods, or the Political Theology of 'Race.'" *Early American Literature* 45, no. 1 (2010): 145–82.
Hill, Christopher. *The World Turned Upside Down: Radical Ideas during the English Revolution.* New York: Viking, 1972.
Hill, Frances. *A Delusion of Satan: The Full Story of the Salem Witch Trials.* New York: DaCapo, 1995.
Horle, Craig. *A Listing of the Original Records of Sufferings.* London: Friends House Library, 1973.
———. *The Quakers and the English Legal System, 1660–1688.* Philadelphia: University of Pennsylvania Press, 1988.
Howe, Susan. *The Birth-Mark: Unsettling the Wilderness in American Literary History.* Hanover, NH: Wesleyan University Press, 1993.
Howgill, Francis. "The Cogitations of My Heart . . ." 1662. A. R. B. Collection. Friends House Library, London.
———. *The Heart of New-England Hardened through Wickedness.* London: Thomas Simmons, 1659.
———. *The Popish Inquisition Newly Erected in New England.* London, 1659.
Howgill, Mary. *The Vision of the Lord of Hosts. By a Handmaid of the Lord.* London, 1662.
Hubbard, William. *Chronological History of New England in the Form of Annals to 1680.* Boston: Little, Brown, 1848.
Hutchinson, Thomas. *The History of the Colony and Province of Massachusetts-Bay.* 1936. 3 vols. Reprint, edited by Lawrence Shaw Mayo. Cambridge, MA: Harvard University Press, 1970.
Hutson, Matthew. "Still Puritan After All These Years." *New York Times*, August 3, 2012.
Innes, Stephen. *Creating the Commonwealth: The Economic Culture of Puritan New England.* New York: Norton, 1995.
James, William. *The Varieties of Religious Experience.* 1902. Reprint, New York: Library of America, 1990.
Jantzen, Grace. *Becoming Divine: Towards a Feminist Philosophy of Religion.* Bloomington: Indiana University Press, 1999.
———. *Power, Gender, and Christian Mysticism.* Cambridge: Cambridge University Press, 1995.
Jenner, Thomas. *Quakerism Anatomiz'd and Confuted.* London, 1670.
Johnson, Edward. *The History of New England, or Wonder-Working Providence.* London: Nathan Brooks, 1653.
Jones, Rufus. *The Quakers in the American Colonies.* New York: Norton, 1966.
Joy, George. "Innocency's Complaint against Tyrannical Court Faction in New-england [sic]." Boston, 1677.
Juster, Susan. *Disorderly Women: Sexual Politics and Evangelicalism in Revolutionary New England.* Ithaca, NY: Cornell University Press, 1994.

———. "Mystical Pregnancy and Holy Bleeding: Visionary Experience in Early Modern Britain and America." *William and Mary Quarterly* 57, no. 2 (2000): 249–88.

———. "The Spirit and the Flesh: Gender, Language, and Sexuality in American Protestantism." In *New Directions in American Religious History*, edited by Harry S. Stout and D. G. Hart. New York: Oxford University Press, 1997, 334–61.

Kamensky, Jane. *Governing the Tongue: The Politics of Speech in Early New England*. New York: Oxford University Press, 1997.

Kaplan, Amy, and Donald Pease, eds. *Cultures of United States Imperialism*. Durham, NC: Duke University Press, 1993.

Karlsen, Carol. *The Devil in the Shape of a Woman: Witchcraft in Colonial New England*. New York: Vintage, 1987.

Kaufmann, Michael. *Institutional Individualism: Conversion, Exile, and Nostalgia in Puritan New England*. Hanover, NH: Wesleyan University Press, 1998.

———. "Post-secular Puritans: Recent Retrials of Anne Hutchinson." *Early American Literature* 45, no. 1 (2010): 31–59.

Keith, George. *A Serious Appeal to All the More Sober People*. Philadelphia: William Bradford, 1692.

Kibbey, Ann. *The Interpretation of Material Shapes in Puritanism: A Study of Rhetoric, Prejudice, and Violence*. Cambridge: Cambridge University Press, 1986.

Knight, Janice. *Orthodoxies in Massachusetts: Rereading American Puritanism*. Cambridge, MA: Harvard University Press, 1994.

Knutson, Andrea. *American Spaces of Conversion: The Conductive Imaginaries of Edwards, Emerson, and James*. New York: Oxford University Press, 2010.

Koehler, Lyle. "The Case of the American Jezebels: Anne Hutchinson and Female Agitation During the Years of Antinomian Turmoil, 1636–1640." *William and Mary Quarterly* 31, no. 4 (1974): 55–80.

Lambert, Frank. *Inventing the Great Awakening*. Princeton, NJ: Princeton University Press, 1999.

Lang, Amy Shrager. *Prophetic Woman: Anne Hutchinson and the Problem of Dissent in the Literature of New England*. Berkeley: University of California Press, 1987.

Lawes and Libertyes Concerning the Inhabitants of Massachusetts. Cambridge, 1648.

Lawson, Deodat. "Christ's Fidelity the Only Shield Again Satan's Malignity." 1692. In *Salem-Village Witchcraft*, edited by Paul Boyer and Stephen Nissenbaum. Belmont, CA: Wadsworth, 1972, 124–28.

Lears, T. J. Jackson. *No Place of Grace: Antimodernism and the Transformation of American Culture*. Chicago: University of Chicago Press, 1994.

Lepore, Jill. *The Name of War: King Philip's War and the Origins of American Identity*. New York: Vintage, 1999.

———. "The Prism: Privacy in the Age of Publicity." *New Yorker*, June 24, 2013, n. pag.

Levin, David. *Cotton Mather: The Young Life of the Lord's Remembrancer, 1663–1703*. Cambridge, MA: Harvard University Press, 1978.

Lilla, Mark. *The Stillborn God: Religion, Politics, and the Modern West*. New York: Knopf, 2007.

Lipset, Seymour. *American Exceptionalism: A Double-Edged Sword*. New York: Norton, 1996.

Livingstone, Patrick. *Truth Owned and Deceit Denyed*. London, 1667.

Logan, Lisa. "Mary Rowlandson's Captivity and the 'Place' of the Woman Subject." *Early American Literature* 28, no. 3 (1993): 255–77.

Love, Heather. "Close but Not Deep: Literary Ethics and the Descriptive Turn." *New Literary History* 41, no. 2 (2010): 371–91.

———. *Feeling Backward: Loss and the Politics of Queer History*. Cambridge, MA: Harvard University Press, 2007.

Lynde, Sir Humphrey. *Via Devia, or The By-Way*. London: A. Matthews, 1630.

Mack, Phyllis. *Visionary Women: Ecstatic Prophecy in Seventeenth-Century England*. Berkeley: University of California Press, 1992.

Mather, Cotton. *A Brand Pluck'd Out of the Burning*. 1693. In *Narratives of the Witchcraft Cases, 1648–1706*, edited by George Lincoln Burr. New York: Scribner's, 1914, 253–87.

———. *The Diary of Cotton Mather*. Vol. 1, 1681–1709. New York: Ungar, 1957.

———. *Magnalia Christi Americana*. 1702. 2 vols. New York: Russell and Russell, 1852.

———. *The Selected Letters of Cotton Mather*. Edited by Kenneth Silverman. Baton Rouge: Louisiana State University Press, 1971.

———. *The Wonders of the Invisible World*. 1692. In *Narratives of the Witchcraft Cases, 1648–1706*, edited by George Lincoln Burr. New York: Scribner's, 1914. 89–143.

Mather, Increase. *Cases of Conscience Concerning Evil Spirits*. Boston, 1693.

———. *The Day of Trouble Is Near*. Boston: Marmaduke Johnson, 1674.

———. *The Doctrine of Divine Providence*. Boston, 1684.

———. *An Earnest Exhortation to the Inhabitants of New England*. 1677. In *So Dreadfull a Judgment: Puritan Responses to King Philip's War, 1676–1677*, edited by Richard Slotkin and James Folsom. Middletown, CT: Wesleyan University Press, 1978..167–206.

———. *Renewal of Covenant the Great Duty Incumbent on Decaying or Distressed Churches*. Boston: Henry Phillips, 1677.

May, Henry. *The Enlightenment in America*. Oxford: Oxford University Press, 1976.

McDannell, Colleen. *Material Christianity: Religion and Popular Culture in America*. New Haven, CT: Yale University Press, 1995.

McLoughlin, William G. *New England Dissent, 1630–1833*. Cambridge, MA: Harvard University Press, 1971.

Mead, Margaret. "The Changing Significance of Food." In Counihan and Van Esterik, *Food and Culture: A Reader*, 7–27.

Mencken, H. L. *A Book of Prefaces*. New York: Knopf, 1917.

Miller, Perry. *Errand into the Wilderness*. Cambridge, MA: Harvard University Press, 1956. Reprint, Harvard University Press, 1978.

———. *The New England Mind: From Colony to Province*. Cambridge, MA: Harvard University Press, 1954. Reprint, Boston: Beacon, 1961.

More, Edward Caldwell. "Questions of Religious Freedom." In *Commonwealth History of Massachusetts: Colony, Province, and State*, edited by Albert Hart Bushnell. New York: Russell and Russell, 1927, 382–408.

Morgan, Edmund S. *Visible Saints: The History of a Puritan Idea*. Ithaca, NY: Cornell University Press, 1963.

Morton, Nathaniel. *New-Englands Memoriall*. Boston, 1669.

Murphy, Andrew. *Conscience and Community: Revisiting Toleration and Religious Dissent in Early Modern England*. University Park: Pennsylvania State University Press, 2001.

Myles, Anne. "From Monster to Martyr: Re-presenting Mary Dyer." *Early American Literature* 36, no. 1 (2001): 1–30.

Neuman, Meredith Marie. "Beyond Narrative: The Conversion Plot of John Dane's *A Declaration of Remarkable Providences*." *Early American Literature* 40, no. 2 (2005): 251–77.
———. *Jeremiah's Scribes: Creating Sermon Literature in Puritan New England*. Philadelphia: University of Pennsylvania Press, 2013.
Nevins, W. S. *Salem Observer*, August 30, 1890.
New York Weekly Journal, no. 429, February 15, 1742.
New, Elisa. "Feminist Invisibility: The Examples of Anne Bradstreet and Ann Hutchinson." *Common Knowledge* 2, no. 1 (1993): 99–117.
Nicholson, Joseph. "Letter from a Boston Prison." January 1660. Swarthmore Collection. Friends House Library, London.
———. Letter to Margaret Fell. January 7, 1660. Swarthmore Collection. Friends House Library, London
———. Letter to Margaret Fell. August 10, 1660. Swarthmore Collection. Friends House Library, London.
Norton, Humphrey. "Accursed Are Thy Rulers." 1658(?). Swarthmore Collection. Friends House Library, London.
———. *New England's Ensigne: It Being the Account of Cruelty, the Professors Pride, and the Articles of Their Faith*. London: G. Calvert, 1659.
Norton, John. *The Heart of New England Rent at the Blasphemies of the Present Generation*. Cambridge, MA: Samuel Green, 1659.
Norton, Mary Beth. *In the Devil's Snare: The Salem Witchcraft Crisis of 1692*. New York: Knopf, 2002.
Nuttall, Geoffrey. *The Puritan Spirit: Essays and Addresses*. London: Epworth, 1967.
Oldmixon, John. *The British Empire in America*. 1708. London: Brotherton, 1741.
Palfrey, John. *History of New England*. Vol 1. Boston: Little, Brown, 1859.
Parrington, Vernon. *Main Currents in American Thought: An Interpretation of American Literature from the Beginnings to 1920*. 3 vols. New York: Harcourt Brace, 1927.
Pease, Donald. *The New American Exceptionalism*. Minneapolis: University of Minnesota Press, 2009.
Perkins, Judith. *The Suffering Self: Pain and Narrative Representation in the Early Christian Era*. New York: Routledge, 1995.
Perkins, William. *A Discourse of the Damned Art of Witchcraft*. Cambridge, 1608.
Perry, Dennis. "'Novelties and Stile Which All Out-Do': William Hubbard's Historiography Reconsidered." *Early American Literature* 29, no. 2 (1994): 166–82.
Pestana, Carla. "The City upon a Hill under Siege: The Puritan Perception of the Quaker Threat to Massachusetts Bay, 1651–1661." *The New England Quarterly* 56 (1983): 323–53.
———. "The Quaker Executions as Myth and History." *Journal of American History* 80, no. 2 (1993): 441–69.
———. *Quakers and Baptists in Colonial Massachusetts*. New York: Cambridge University Press, 1991.
Peters, Kate. *Print Culture and the Early Quakers*. New York: Cambridge University Press, 2005.
Petit, Norman. *The Heart Prepared: Grace and Conversion in Spiritual Life*. New Haven, CT: Yale University Press, 1966.
Pew Research Global Attitudes Project. "Among Wealthy Nations: U.S. Stands Alone in Its Embrace of Religion." December 19, 2002.

Pocock, J. G. A. *The Machiavellian Moment: Florentine Political Thought and the Atlantic Republican Tradition*. Princeton, NJ: Princeton University Press, 1975.
Pope, Robert G. *The Half-Way Covenant: Church Membership in Puritan New England*. Princeton, NJ: Princeton University Press, 1969.
Porter, Carolyn. "What We Know We Don't Know: Remapping American Studies." *American Literary History* 6, no. 3 (1994): 467–526.
Porterfield, Amanda. *Female Piety in Puritan New England: The Emergence of Religious Humanism*. New York: Oxford University Press, 1992.
Pratt, Mary Louise. *Imperial Eyes: Travel Writing and Transculturation*. London: Routledge, 1992.
Radway, Janice, and Kevin Gaines, eds. *American Studies: An Anthology*. Oxford: Blackwell, 2009.
Ray, Benjamin C. "Satan's War Against the Covenant in Salem-Village Church, 1692." *The New England Quarterly* 80, no. 1 (2007): 69–95.
Records of the Colony of Rhode Island and Providence Plantations in New England. Vol. 1. Edited by John Russell Bartlett. Providence, 1856.
Records of the Governor and Company of the Massachusetts Bay Colony. Edited by Nathaniel Shurtleff. Vols. 2, 4. Boston, 1853.
Reid, Bethany. "'Unfit for Light': Anne Bradstreet's Monstrous Birth." *The New England Quarterly* 71 (1998): 517–42.
Reising, Russell. *The Unusable Past: Theory and the Study of American Literature*. New York: Methuen, 1986.
Richards, David. *The Memorable Preservation: Narratives of Indian Captivity in the Literature and Politics of Colonial New England, 1675–1725*. Honors thesis, Yale College, 1967.
Rivett, Sarah. "Early American Religion in a Postsecular Age." *PMLA* 128, no. 4 (2013): 989–96.
———. *The Science of the Soul in Colonial New England*. Chapel Hill: University of North Carolina Press for the Omohundro Institute of Early America, 2011.
———. "Tokenography: Narration and the Science of Dying in Puritan Deathbed Testimonies." *Early American Literature* 42, no. 3 (2007): 471–94.
Rivett, Sarah, and Stephanie Kirk. "Religious Transformations in the Early Modern Americas." *Early American Literature* 45, no. 1 (2010): 61–91.
Robinson, William, and William Leddra. *Several Epistles Giv'n Forth by Two of the Lord's Faithful Servants Whom He Sent to New England*. London, 1669.
Rosenberg, John. "Political Correctness Is the New Puritanism." *Minding the Campus*, August 15, 2010. http://www.mindingthecampus.com/2010/10/one_of_the_saddest_effects/.
Rosenthal, Bernard. *Salem Story: Reading the Witch Trials of 1692*. Cambridge: Cambridge University Press, 1993.
Rouse, John. Letter to Margaret Fell. September 1658. Swarthmore Collection. Friends House Library, London.
Rowlandson, Joseph. *The Possibility of God's Forsaking a People That Have Once Been Visibly Near and Dear to Him*. Cambridge, MA: S. Green, 1682.
Rowlandson, Mary. *The Sovereignty and Goodness of God*. 1682. In *So Dreadfull a Judgment: Puritan Responses to King Philip's War*, edited by Richard Slotkin and James Folsom. Middletown, CT: Wesleyan University Press, 1978, 315–69.
Ruttenburg, Nancy. *Democratic Personality: Popular Voice and the Trial of American Authorship*. Stanford, CA: Stanford University Press, 1998.

Ryan, James Emmett. *Imaginary Friends: Representing Quakers in American Culture*. Madison: University of Wisconsin Press, 2009.
Salthouse, Thomas. Letter to Margaret Fell. March 29, 1656. Caton Collection. Friends House Library, London.
Sayre, Gordon. *The Indian Chief as Tragic Hero: Native Resistance and the Literatures of America, from Moctezuma to Tecumseh*. Chapel Hill: University of North Carolina Press, 2005.
———. *"Les Sauvages Americains": Representations of Native Americans in French and English Colonial Literature*. Chapel Hill: University of North Carolina Press, 1997.
Scarry, Elaine. *The Body in Pain: The Making and Unmaking of the World*. New York: Oxford University Press, 1985.
Schmidt, Leigh Eric. *Hearing Things: Religion, Illusion, and the American Enlightenment*. Cambridge, MA: Harvard University Press, 2000.
Schmitt, Carl. *Political Theology: Four Chapters on the Concept of Sovereignty*. Translated by G. Schwab. Chicago: University of Chicago Press, 2005.
Schorb, Jodi. "Hard-Hearted Women: Sentiment and the Scaffold." *Legacy: A Journal of American Women Writers* 28, no. 2 (2011): 290–311.
Schweitzer, Ivy. *The Work of Self-Representation: Lyric Poetry in Colonial New England*. Chapel Hill: University of North Carolina Press, 1991.
Sedgwick, Eve. *Touching Feeling: Affect, Pedagogy, and Performativity*. Durham, NC: Duke University Press, 2003.
Sharf, Robert. "Experience." In *Critical Terms for Religious Studies*, edited by Mark C. Taylor. Chicago: University of Chicago Press, 1998, 94–116.
Shea, Daniel. *Spiritual Autobiography in Early America*. Princeton, NJ: Princeton University Press, 1968.
Shepard, Thomas. *On Ineffectual Hearing of the Word*. 1652. In *The Works of Thomas Shepard*. Vol 3. Boston: Boston Doctrinal Tract and Book Society, 1853, 363–84.
Sievers, Julie. "Refiguring the Song of Songs: John Cotton's 1655 Sermon and the Antinomian Controversy." *The New England Quarterly* 76 no. 1 (2003): 73–107.
Slotkin, Richard. *Regeneration Through Violence: The Mythology of the American Frontier, 1660–1860*. Middletown, CT: Wesleyan University Press, 1973.
Smith, Catherine. "Jane Lead: The Feminist Mind and Art of a Seventeenth-Century Protestant Mystic." In *Women of Spirit: Female Leadership in the Jewish and Christian Traditions*, edited by Rosemary Ruether and Eleanor McLaughlin. New York: Simon and Schuster, 1979.
Stannard, David. *The Puritan Way of Death: A Study in Religion, Culture, and Social Change*. New York: Oxford University Press, 1977.
Starkey, Marion. *The Devil in Massachusetts: A Modern Inquiry into the Salem Witch Trials*. New York: Knopf, 1950.
Stevens, Laura. *The Poor Indians: British Missionaries, Native Americans, and Colonial Sensibility*. Philadelphia: University of Pennsylvania Press, 2004.
Stoever, William. *A Faire and Easie Way to Heaven: Covenant Theology and Antinomianism in Early Massachusetts*. Middletown, CT: Wesleyan University Press, 1978.
Stout, Harry S. *The New England Soul: Preaching and Religious Culture in Colonial New England*. New York: Oxford University Press, 1986.
Summers-Bremner, Eluned. *Insomnia: A Cultural History*. London: Reaktion Books, 2008.

Tarter, Michele Lise. "Nursing the New Wor(l)d: The Writings of Quaker Women in Early America." *Women and Language* 16, no. 1 (1993): 22–35.
———. "Quaking in the Light: The Politics of Quaker Women's Corporeal Prophecy in the Seventeenth-Century Transatlantic World." In *A Centre of Wonders: The Body in Early America*, edited by Janet Moore Lindman and Michele Lise Tarter. Ithaca, NY: Cornell University Press, 2001, 163–76.
Taves, Ann. *Fits, Trances, and Visions: Experiencing Religion and Explaining Experience from Wesley to James*. Princeton, NJ: Princeton University Press, 1999.
Taylor, Charles. *A Secular Age*. Cambridge, MA: Harvard University Press, 2007.
———. "Why We Need a Radical Redefinition of Secularism." In *The Power of Religion in the Public Sphere*, edited by Eduardo Mendieta and Jonathan Vanantwerpen. New York: Columbia University Press, 2011, 34–59.
Tobin, Lad. "A Radically Different Voice: Gender and Language in the Trials of Anne Hutchinson." *Early American Literature* 25 (1990): 253–70.
Tolles, Frederick. *Quakers in the Atlantic Colonies*. New York: Macmillan, 1960.
Tonder, Lars. *Tolerance: A Sensorial Orientation to Politics*. New York: Oxford University Press, 2013.
Toulouse, Teresa. "'My Own Credit': Strategies of (E)valuation in Mary Rowlandson's Captivity Narrative." *American Literature* 64, no. 4 (1992): 655–76.
Ulrich, Laurel Thatcher. *Good Wives: Image and Reality in the Lives of Women in Northern New England, 1659–1750*. New York: Knopf, 2010.
Upham, Charles Wentworth. *Salem Witchcraft*. 2 vols. New York: F. Ungar, 1959.
Vella, Michael. "Theology, Genre, and Gender: The Precarious Place of Hannah Adams in American Literary History." *Early American Literature* 28, no. 1 (1993): 21–41.
Vickery, Amanda. *The Gentleman's Daughter: Women's Lives in Georgian England*. New Haven, CT: Yale University Press, 1998.
Viswanathan, Gauri. "Secularism and Heterodoxy." In *Comparative Secularisms in a Global Age*, edited by Linell Cady and Elizabeth Hurd. London: Palgrave, 2010. 229–46.
Vokins, Joan. *God's Mighty Power Magnified: As Revealed in His Faithful Handmaid Joan Vokins*. London: Thomas Northcott, 1691.
Walker, Williston. *A History of Congregational Churches in the United States*. Boston, 1894.
Ward, Graham. *True Religion*. London: Blackwell, 2003.
Warner, Michael. *The Letters of the Republic: Publication and the Public Sphere in Eighteenth-Century America*. Cambridge, MA: Harvard University Press, 1990.
Warner, Michael, Jonathan VanAntwerpen, and Craig Calhoun, eds. *Varieties of Secularism in a Secular Age*. Cambridge, MA: Harvard University Press, 2010.
Welde, Thomas. *A Brief Narration on the Practice of the Churches in New-England*. Boston, 1651.
Westerkamp, Marilyn. "Anne Hutchinson, Sectarian Mysticism, and the Puritan Order." *Church History* 59, no. 4 (1990): 482–96.
White, Dorothy. *Counsellors Counsel; A Warning from the Lord*. London: Thomas Simmons, 1659.
Whitefield, George. *A Continuation of the Journal of the Reverend Mr. George Whitefield*. Philadelphia, 1740.

Willard, Samuel. *Some Miscellany Observations on Our Present Debates Surrounding Witchcraft*. Philadelphia: William Bradford, 1692.

Winship, Michael. *Godly Republicanism: Puritans, Pilgrims, and a City on the Hill*. Cambridge, MA: Harvard University Press, 2012.

———. *The Times and Trials of Anne Hutchinson: Puritans Divided*. Lawrence: University of Kansas Press, 2005.

———. "Were There Any Puritans in New England?" *The New England Quarterly* 74 (2001): 118–38.

Winthrop, John. *The Journal of John Winthrop, 1630–1649*. 2 Vols. Edited by James Hosmer. New York: Scribners, 1908.

———. "A Model of Christian Charity." In *The Norton Anthology of American Literature*. Vol. A. 7th ed. New York: Norton, 2009, 147–57.

Wokler, Robert. "The Enlightenment, the Nation-State and the Primal Patricide of Modernity." In *The Enlightenment and Modernity*, edited by Norman Geras and Robert Wokler. Basingstoke: Macmillan, 2000, 161–83.

Wood, Timothy. "'Whosoever Will be Great Among You': The Leadership of John Cotton during the Antinomian Crisis." *Christian Scholars Review* 35, no. 1 (2005): 79–95.

Worrall, Arthur J. *Quakers in the Colonial Northeast*. Boston: University Press of New England, 1980.

Ziff, Larzer. *Puritanism in America: New Culture in a New World*. New York: Viking, 1973.

INDEX

Adams, Brooks, 66
Adams, Charles Francis, 64
Adams, Hannah, 63, 63n57
Adams, William, 119, 120n8, 149n39
Affliction, 90; bodily, 102–12, 142; diabolical, 197, 200–201; divine, 109, 120–21, 117, 132, 136, 147, 148, 152, 154, 157–58, 161; exemplary, 122, 129, 130, 131, 138; doctrinal, 111, 122, 130, 153, 157; invisible, 22; psychology of, 158, 161–65; saintly, 111, 150, 157, 162; and agency, 155; and female piety, 129, 131–32; and loss, 122; and narrative, 72, 154; and persecution, 90; and Mary Rowlandson, 136, 161, 162; and Mercy Short, 198; and meaning, 152, 155, 161, 163; and Protestantism, 121, 152, 153, 155; and secularism, 121; and theology, 152; and Tituba, 186; and unbelief, 150, 152. *See also* pain; suffering; torture; trauma
affect, 43, 90, 127, 43n28
Agamben, Georgio, 112n71
agency: confessional, 18, 174–75, 180; diabolical, 83, 109, 188, 200; divine, 56, 125, 148, 200; emotional, 131; female, 29, 31, 54, 60–61, 191, 193; interpretive, 137, 140; involuntary, 194; secular, 10, 92, 95, 111, 114, 121, 143, 155, 202; spiritual, 15, 34–35, 40, 45, 48–49, 51–54, 58, 70, 75–76, 78, 84–85, 97, 99 106, 124, 140, 142; and Protestantism, 193; and Quakers, 78, 84–86; and spirit, 54, 71, 75, 86, 92, 95, 156–57

Ahmed, Sarah, 42, 43n28
America: and Antinomianism, 60–68; and religion, 7, 17, 67, 74, 113, 185, 203–7
American Puritanism, 1–11, 16–20, 24–28, 32–33, 40, 130, 199n47, 203; and Anne Hutchinson, 20, 40, 42–43, 69; and Antinomianism, 69; and declension, 113; and dissent, 32; and exceptionalism, 19–20, 32; and female piety, 1–3, 5, 10–11, 16, 20, 24–28, 32, 43, 90, 117, 119, 122, 126; and Mary Rowlandson, 117, 119, 138, 141, 153n48, 159; and modernity, 20; and New England, 9n21, 13, 18n32, 58, 91, 169, 181–82, 184, 186; and orthodoxy, 127, and pastness, 16–17, 125, 206; and Quakers, 71, 90, 100; and religion, 9, 17; and Salem Witchcraft, 184, 202; and secularism, 4–6, 10–11, 17, 57, 68, 122, 205, 207; and suffering, 93, 161
American Studies, 2, 6, 20, 7n15, 102n60; and religion, 1, 8, 20, 60
Antimodernism, 3
Antinomianism, 32–40, 42, 59; and adultery, 59–61; and America, 63, 68; and American Puritanism, 69, 73; and Anne Hutchinson, 63, 65, 68, 137; and dissent, 34, 55, 65; and female gender 42, 49; and female piety, 73, 164; and female privacy, 18, 22, 26; and feminism, 59–61, 64–65, 68 and historiography, 61, 63, 65–67; and language, 48n37; and male gender, 47, 50; and

mysticism, 47–49, 70; and politics, 45; and secularism 61, 69; 35n12; and theology, 26
Antinomian Controversy or Crisis: 8, 25, 31–32, 37–38, 60–61, 62, 69, 73, 155, 164, 30n2, 50n42, 55n46
Aquinas, Thomas, 83
Armstrong, Nancy, 130, 14n25
Asad, Talal, 5, 61, 106, 121
asceticism, 11, 14, 21–22, 48n38, 81, 86, 106n65, 140n34; and female piety, 126
Audland, Anne, 75, 76n14
Augustine 83, 120, 158
Austin, Anne, 91
authorship, 21, 45n21, 76n15, 137, 181; female, 133, 29–31; and Mary Rowlandson, 132, 135, 138, 146

Balmer, Randal, 203n1
Bancroft, George, 64, 67, 64n58, 67n67
Barbour, Hugh, 73n7, 84n32
Barker, Francis, 70n2
Barker Sr., William, 183, 195
Barker, Mary, 194
Barry, John M., 47n34
Barthes, Roland, 140n34
Battis, Emery, 38–39
Bauer, Ralph, 9n21, 131n25
Baym, Nina, 59–60
Bellah, Robert, 4n7
Bellingham, Richard, 91
Bercovitch, Sacvan: and declension, 4, 8, 35n12; and Halfway Covenant, 168
Berg, Christina, 70
Berkus, Catherine, 24n42
Bernard, Richard, 179
Berry, Philippa, 70
Bill of Rights, 47; and female voice, 67
Bishop, Bridget, 193
Bishop, George, and Quakers 95, 101
Bozeman, Theodore, 52n44
Bradbury, Mary, 183
Bradstreet, Anne, 9, 29–31. See also monstrous birth; authorship, female
Braithwaite, William C., 96n53
Bray, Alan, 159n55

Breen, Louise, 24n42, 46n32
Breitwieser, Mitchell, 127, 153n48, 158n54
Brend, William, 92, 100, 102–3, 111. See also martyrdom; Quakers
Breslaw, Elaine, 185n33, 187n38, 188n39
Brooks, Joanna, 18n32
Brown, Gillian, 19n34, 23n41
Bunyan, John, 120, 121
Burnham, Michelle, 32n5, 169n5
Burrough, Edward, 95, 96n2, 103–5, 111n70. See also Quakers
Burroughs, George, 183–84
Bynum, Caroline Walker, 21n39, 49n40, 140n34

Cahn, Mark, 98n54
Caldwell, Patricia, 48, 168n4, 180n29
Calvinism, 23, 32, 35, 40, 46, 50, 123, 148, 180, 195; and Lot's Wife, 155–57; and Protestantism, 34, 117, 119, 121; and theology, 148–50, 155–57
Candy, 186–87. See also Salem Witchcraft
Caporael, Linnda, 190n42
Carrier, Andrew, 183
Carrier, Martha, 181, 183. See also Salem Witchcraft
Carruth, Mary, 139n32
Caruth, Cathy, 151n45
Casanova, José, 20n35, 164
Castiglia, Christopher, 118n5, 119n7, 131n25, 154n50
Catherine of Siena, 70. See also mysticism
Chauncy, Charles, 15–16
Christine de Pisan, 70. See also mysticism
City on a Hill, 58
Coffey, John, 123n13
Cohen, Charles Lloyd, 9n20
Cohen, Daniel, 27n46, 95n50
Cohen, Matt, 9n20, 78
Colacurcio, Michael, 41n23
confession: 21, 34, 44, 57, 83, 115, 119, 140, 158, 162; and

Congregationalism, 44, 169, 173–77, 182; and Halfway Covenant, 169, 171–78; and Increase Mather, 178–80; and Puritanism, 169. *See also* Salem Witchcraft

conversion: 9, 16n31, 32n6, 51, 57, 72n7, 73n7, 74, 77, 85, 126n17, 142, 145–46, 153, 168n4, 173n14, 175; narrative/relation, 26, 48, 76, 118, 124, 141, 144–45, 168, 174, 177, 180–81, 184, 193, 196; and spirit, 53

Cooper, James, 34n9, 40

Copeland, John, 92–94, 100, 107, 111

Cotton, John, 28, 34n11, 39–42, 46n33, 50, 90, 180; and Anne Hutchinson, 50–55, 58

Counihan, Carole, 140n34, 142n36, 143n37

covenant renewal, 175, 181

D'Antonio, William, 203n2

Davidson, Cathy, 23n41

De Certeau, Michel, 95

declension, 4, 148, 168; and secularization, 5, 113

Delbanco, Andrew, 72n7

Derounian Kathryn Zabelle, 119n7, 132

diabolism, 21, 83, 113, 176, 187–89, 193, 196

Dillon, Elizabeth, 1, 9, 10n22, 18n32, 24, 32n5, 32n6

dissent: religious 8, 17, 23, 26, 34, 47, 63, 67, 74, 89, 171n9; and modernity, 20; and secularism; 20, 24, 32, 47, 63; sexual, 61; and America, 69, 79, 148 and Anne Hutchinson, 18, 32, 47, 59, 65, 68; and Quakers, 76, 80

Donne, John, 86

doubt, 106n25, 158 and modernity, 169; and Mary Rowlandson, 117, 122, 166; and Puritanism, 148. *See also* skepticism; trauma

Douglas, Anne, 4, 8

Douglas, Mary, 35, 36n13, 54, 112n71, 142n36

Douglass, William, 63

Downing, David, 155n51

Drake, Samuel, 65–66

Durkheim, Emile, 4n9

Dyer, Mary, execution 94–95: and Anne Hutchinson, 30, 39, 58, 94; and monstrous birth, 33, 38, 46, 58, 85n34; and Quakers, 36, 37, 38, 111

Easty, Mary, 190

Edwards, Jonathan, 11–16, 18, 26, 42n27, 72n7, 158

Eliade, Mircea, 79n23

Elliott, Emory, 9n20, 27n46, 123n12

Emerson, Ralph Waldo, 72n7, 74

Endicott, John, 108–9, 111

Enlightenment: 26, 79, 81; American, 19, 113; and American Puritanism, 19; and secularization, 11–12, 22, 82, 117, 166, 199, 202

Fairman, Lydia, 77

Febvre, Lucien, 6

Fell, Henry, 77, 85, 93

Fell, Margaret, 77–78, 85, 87–88, 90–91, 93, 94n47, 96, 102, 110–11

female piety, 1, 5, 6, 10, 11, 13–19, 23–27, 31, 37, 48, 60–62, 70–71, 73, 84, 117, 122, 125, 126n17, 128, 158–59, 164, 169–70, 174, 186, 188, 198, 200–202, 205–6; experiential, 40–42, 72n7, 126–27; imitable, 65, 123, 128–29, 132, 196, 201; orthodoxy, 122, 133, 169, 174, 201; radical, 11, 13, 16, 18, 23, 25, 27, 32, 45, 48, 61–62, 69, 86, 95, 121–22, 169, 186, 205–6; and American Puritanism, 10, 11, 21, 71, 117, 166, 186; and Antinomianism, 49–50; and asceticism, 126; and Cotton Mather, 62, 197–202; and funeral sermons, 27, 122–23; and gender, 11, 24, 26–27, 45; and inscrutability, 34, 37, 39n19, 41, 48, 58; and introspection, 23, 31, 35, 49, 73, 178; and Mary Rowlandson, 158, 162, 164, 166; and pain, 162; and publicity, 88, 167, 170, 175, 177; and Quakers, 83–90, 95, 105;

and secularism, 32, 60, 164, 193, 205; and secularization, 6, 10, 26, 48, 50, 58, 60, 68, 93, 118, 162, 164, 169, 170, 202, 206; and suffering, 12, 43, 95, 162;
feminism, 11, 31, 37n16, 37n17, 49n39, 59, 60–61, 64–65, 68, 70n2, 83, 85n34, 139n32; and modernity, 61
Ferrara, Pasquale, 20n35
Fessenden, Tracy, 7n17, 20n38
Field, Jonathan Beecher, 10n22, 32n6
Field, Peter, 74n10
Fisher, Mary, 91
Fiske, John, 66
Fitzpatrick, Tara, 153n49
Flint, Josiah, 149
Food, 12, 21n39, 87, 92, 121; and Mary Rowlandson, 139–48, 158
Foster, Ann, 194
Foster, Stephen, 91n45, 157n53, 174
Foucault, Michel, 23n41, 31, 99
Fowler, Robert, 75
Fox, George, 27, 73, 74n9, 76, 79, 81, 64n32, 93, 96
Foxe, John, 90
Franchot, Jenny, 2, 6, 61n52, 125
Franklin, Benjamin, 41–42, 158n54

Gadney, Bartholomew, 186
gender, 1, 14, 16n31, 22, 24n44, 26, 178, 190, 195; as performance, 26–27; femininity, 1, 10–15, 17, 20, 24–26, 31–32, 34, 42, 45, 47, 49, 57–59, 60–61, 73, 82–83, 86, 93, 95, 97, 113, 118, 126, 131–132, 158, 162, 164, 169, 178, 181, 188, 195, 198, 207; male, 159; and antinomianism, 42, 45–46 49; and authorship, 29, 133; and female piety, 11, 24, 26–27, 45; and Mary Rowlandson, 121, 131, 133; and modernity, 162; and Protestantism, 10, 15n28, 17, 23, 26, 31, 71, 83, 126; and Puritanism, 24n42; and Quakers, 88; and race, 131, 186; and religion, 11, 14, 16, 18, 23, 26, 37, 43, 60–61, 78, 83, 97, 105, 202, 207; and the scaffold, 50n95; and secularism, 5, 18, 43, 50, 114, 158;
and spirit, 14, 37, 40, 42, 45, 70, 83, 85, 93; and theology, 37, 39
Gentleman's Magazine, 14n25, 15
Gilman, Anne, 74
Good, Sarah, 187
Goodman, Nan, 46, 47n34, 50n42, 71n4, 91n45, 94n48
Gordis, Lisa, 9, 34n11, 37n17
Gorton, Samuel, 36
Greven, Philip, 23n42, 86n37, 123n12
Gura, Philip, 35, 73n7, 91n45
Gustafson, Sandra, 9, 15n28, 16n31, 26, 42n27, 177, 188n39

Halfway Covenant, 167–69; and confession, 169, 171–78; and Increase Mather, 172–75; and modernity, 167; and Salem Witchcraft, 170–78
Hambrick-Stowe, Charles, 122, 123n12
Hansen, Chadwick, 185n33, 190n42
Harpham, Geoffrey, 21n39, 48n38, 106n65, 126
Harris, Paul, 3n5
Hart, D. G., 25n44
Hartman, Saidiya, 102n60
Hathorne, John, 186
Hawthorne, Nathaniel, 41n23; *The Scarlet Letter*, 59–61
Henigman, Laura, 24n42, 95n50
Henke, Suzette, 116n3
Henwood, Dawn, 120n9, 133n28, 139n33
hermeneutics, 42, 43, 112, 127, 129, 153, 159
Hickman, Jared, 18n32
Hill, Christopher, 72, 75n12, 178n23
historiography, American: 3, 8, 10–11, 19, 62n54, 63, 82, 172; feminist, 83; and Anne Hutchinson, 30, 32, 38, 45–46, 61, 65; and Salem witch trials, 185n33, 190; and secularism, 64. *See also* pastness
Hoar, Dorcas, 195–96
Hoar, John, 116
Hobbs, Abigail, 195
Holder, Christopher, 92–94, 100, 107, 111
How, Elizabeth, 183

Howe, Susan, 116, 125
Howgill, Francis, 81, 88, 100–101, 110n68
Howgill, Mary, 87
Hubbard, Elizabeth, 186, 190n43, 191
Hubbard, William, 36, 62n53, 62n54
Human Rights, 99, 112–13; and modernity, 112; and religion, 113
Hutchinson, Anne, 7n16, 24n42, 25–28, 30, 32n5, 33–52, 54–55, 57, 58–68; and American Puritanism, 20, 32, 40, 42–43, 69; and dissent, 18, 32, 47, 59, 65, 68; and female piety, 31–32, 34–35, 37, 40–41, 43, 48–50, 58, 60–62, 65, 68–69; and interiority, 41; and historiography, 30, 32, 38, 45–46, 61, 65; and modernity, 35; and John Cotton, 50–55, 58, 90; and Mary Dyer, 30, 39, 58, 94; and monstrous birth, 30–34, 36–40, 57–58, 67, 89, 170; and Quakers, 17, 35–36, 70, 72–73, 89, 105; and revelation (prophecy), 17, 38, 40, 54–55, 58, 70; and spirit, 57. *See also* Antinomianism
Hutson, Matthew, 3n5

Innes, Stephen, 168n5
inner light: and Quakers, 22, 73–74, 77–79, 82, 113
insomnia, 117; and Mary Rowlandson, 119, 151; and modernity, 120
interiority: psychological, 22, 126n17; spiritual, 21, 43; and Anne Hutchinson, 41; and Quakers, 81, 95

James, William, 47, 48n36, 48n38
Jantzen, Grace, 23n42, 37n16, 48n37, 48n38, 83n29
Jehu, 134–37. *See also* typology
Jenner, Thomas, 83, 85, 170–71
Jeremiad, 4, 119, 123, 134, 148–50, 154, 168, 171
Johnson, Edward, 33–34
Johnson, Goody (Elizabeth Sr.), 194
Jones, Rufus, 71n3, 91n45
Julian of Norwich, 70
Juster, Susan, 15n28, 23n42, 25, 39n19

Kamensky, Jane, 24
Kaplan, Amy, 2n2, 8
Karlsen, Carol, 190n42, 201n49
Kaufmann, Michael, 7n16, 16n31, 32n6, 168n4
Kempe, Marjory, 70
Kennedy, John F., 203n1
Kibbey, Ann, 32n5, 126n17
King Philip (Massasoit), 62, 115n1, 146
King Philip's War, 115n1, 119, 124n14, 139n33, 146, 149, 167, 171, 173. *See also The Sovereignty and Goodness of God*
Knight, Janice, 33, 180
Knutson, Andrea, 72n7
Koehler, Lyle, 32n5

Lacey Jr., Mary, 183
Lambert, Frank, 15n29
Lang, Amy Shrager, 24, 32n5, 59
Lears, T. J. Jackson, 117
Leddra, William, 94, 96, 110n69
Lepore, Jill, 22, 124n14, 136n31, 171n9
Leverett, William, 91
Levin, David, 176n21
liberalism, 32n6, 43, 64, 113, 117, 203–4; and Anne Hutchinson, 66; and female piety, 17, 59; and historiography, 63; and Puritanism, 4, 24; and secularism, 1, 206
Lim, Paul C. H., 123n13
Lipset, Seymour, 204n4
Livingstone, Patrick, 88, 89n42
Logan, Lisa, 130n23, 132n26
Lot's Wife, 138, 151, 153, 156–57. *See also* mourning
Love, Heather, 43, 86, 89, 128

Mack, Phyllis, 15n28
Mahmood, Saba, 31, 112n71
Marston, Mary, 194
Martyrdom (martryology), 3, 67, 90, 100, 111–12; and Quakers, 70, 72, 84, 89–90, 95–97, 100–103, 109
Marx, Karl, 4n9
Mather, Cotton, 27, 42n26, 158n54, 162; *A Brand Pluck'd Out of the Burning*, 197–202; and Antinomian

Controversy, 62; and female piety, 62, 197–202; and the Halfway Covenant, 175–76; and monstrous birth, 37–38; and Salem Witch Trials, 179, 182, 184, 197–202

Mather, Increase, 28, 146n38, 164; and confession, 178–180; and Halfway Covenant, 167, 172–75; and King Philip's War, 151–52, 167, 172–73, 175; and Mary Rowlandson, 119, 129, 133–35, 137; and Salem witch trials, 167

May, Henry, 19

McDannell, Colleen, 18

McFague, Sallie, 37

McLoughlin, William G., 91n45, 171

memory: cultural, 123, 202, 206; and Mary Rowlandson, 115–16, 118, 125, 129, 132–33, 138, 146, 153; and narrative 116, 118, 121, 125, 133, 146–47, 153, 160, 161

Mencken, H. L., 3

Miller, Perry, 4, 8, 22, 73n8, 91n45, 148, 155n52, 199n48

Miller, Arthur, 190, 192

modernity, 3–7, 68, 74, 81–82, 95n49, 99, 159, 162, 166–67, 199; and Anne Hutchinson, 35; and dissent, 20, 79; and doubt, 169; and Enlightenment, 81–82; and female piety, 16, 18, 26, 31, 37, 42, 60–61, 71, 118, 162, 164, 207; and feminism, 61; and the Halfway Covenant, 167; and human rights, 112–13; and insomnia, 120–21; and Mary Rowlandson, 157, 162, 164, 166; and nation, 80, 82, 98, 113; and pain, 189; and pastness, 79n23, 122, 133, 157, 202, 207; and personhood 158, 161; and privacy, 22, 26; and Protestantism, 23, 26, 82; and punishment, 99, 126; and Puritanism, 17–18, 25, 202, 157, 205, 207; and Quakers, 78, 80–82, 89; and race, 189; and religion, 13, 35, 45, 79n23, 164; and Salem Witchcraft, 189, 197; and secularization, 11, 19, 22, 43, 48, 60, 78, 150, 164, 202, 204; and skepticism, 45; and spirit, 35, 37, 68, 78, 80, 164; and suffering, 121, 169, 189, 116; and trauma, 122

monstrous birth, 29–33, 36, 39, 46, 109; and Anne Bradstreet 29–30; and Anne Hutchinson, 30–34, 36–40, 57–58, 67, 89, 170; and historiography 38–39, 42, 58; and John Cotton, 40; and John Winthrop, 57–58; and Mary Dyer, 30, 33, 36–39, 46, 58, Quakers, 71, 89, 109; and privacy 58; and Salem Witchcraft, 170

More, Edward, 41n23

Morton, Nathaniel, 182n31

mourning, 120, 127, 129, 132, 138, 153, 160, 162. See also Lot's Wife, Mary Rowlandson

mysticism, 21n39, 22, 23, 41n25, 79n23, 83n29, 125, 137; Christian, 70, 89; female, 39n19, 47–49, 58; and privacy, 47–48; and Protestantism, 34; and Quakers, 76, 79, 93, 105; and religion, 41, 70, 78, 105. See also Antinomianism

narrative: American national, 19, 27, 40, 63–64, 66–67, 90, 204–5, 207; captivity, 126, 129, 139; confessional, 21, 83, 180, 188; conversion, 76, 124, 142–43, 145, 173n15, 180; exemplaristic, 25, 122, 127, 129, 132–33; food, 141, 145, 147–48; historical, 37–38, 42, 137; salvational, 121, 149, 154, 159; secularization, 5–7, 50, 60, 64, 68, 82, 164, 205; spectral, 191–93; survival, 124, 139–40, 142–43; typological, 154, 160; victim, 62, 90, 100–101, 104, 110–11, 116n3, 120, 148, 157, 161, 186, 188, 192–93, 197; and female piety, 164, 184, 186, 202; and Mary Rowlandson, 121, 123, 127, 129, 132, 133n28, 134, 139n32, 157, 161, 164; and memory, 116, 118, 121, 125, 133, 146–47, 153, 160, 161; and mourning, 132, 138; and

suffering, 162. See also *A Brand Pluck'd Out of the Burning*
Natives (Native-Americans), 130–32, 139, 141–43, 147, 156, 159. See also Weetamoo; King Philip; Tituba
Nayler, James, 84n2
Neuman, Meredith Marie, 9, 173n15
Nevins, N. S., 190
New, Elisa, 49n39
Nicholson, Joseph, 87–88, 111
Norton, Humphrey, 26–27, 102–3, 107, 109, 112
Norton, John Eliot, 172
Norton, John, 99–100
Norton, Mary Beth, 170
Nuttal, Geoffrey, 91n45

Oldmixon, John, 36n14
orthodoxy, 8, 17, 23, 27–28, 33n8, 34, 48, 50, 58, 67, 118–19, 126–27, 129, 131n25, 136–37, 142, 145–46, 163–64, 166, 172, 174, 177, 182, 198, 200–201
Oyer and Terminer, Court of, 171, 179, 182–83, 201. See also Salem witch trials

pain, 78n20, 121, 140n34, 189; bodily, 90, 100, 106, 125, 152, 189, 192; and female piety, 162; and modernity, 189. See also affliction; Quakers; suffering; torture
Palfrey, John, 65
paranoia, 43
Parrington, Vernon, 66, 79n23
Parris, Samuel, 168n2, 184, 186–87
pastness: and modernity, 6, 50, 79n23, 122, 125, 133, 157, 202, 207; and religion, 125. See also historiography
Pease, Donald, 2, 8, 205n5
Pequot War, 62
Perkins, Judith, 106n65
Perkins, William, 179
personhood: erasure, 188–189; modern, 19–20, 71; secular, 22 and female piety, 11, 18, 31, 41
Pestana, Carla, 85n34, 91n45
Peters, Kate, 75n12

Petit, Norman, 73n7
Phips, William, 176, 195
piety: male, 27, 158–59; personal, 40–43, 47–48, 70, 73, 75, 88, 122, 131–32, 148, 154, 157, 161–65, 166, 173–174, 203; Protestant, 26; radical, 16, 42, 69, 73, 86, 160. See also female piety
Pocock, J. G. A., 19n34
Pope, Robert G., 167n1, 174n16, 176n21
Porter, Carolyn, 2n2
Porterfield, Amanda, 10n23, 24, 126n17, 170n7
Post, Hannah, 195
postsecularism, 7, 19, 32, 47–48, 89, 113, 206
Pratt, Mary Louise, 80n25
privacy, 1n1, 10, 17, 74, 106n65, 120n10; female, 18, 22, 26, 50, 58, 126n17, 162, 201; spiritual, 13, 30–31, 34–35, 45, 47, 57, 162, 169, 174, 175, 177–178; and Protestantism, 26, 164; and secularism, 164, 168, 198, 201, 206
Proctor, Elizabeth, 192
Proctor, John, 192–93
Protestant selfhood, 31
Protestantism: 20n38, 54, 82, 183, 185; American, 25, 91n45; colonial, 113, 174; exemplaristic, 153; radical, 23, 26, 65, 68, 75n12; spiritist, 23, 26, 35, 52–53, 55, 63, 68, 75, 117, 125–26, 140, and agency, 193; and Calvinism, 34, 117; and gender, 10, 15n28, 17, 23, 26, 31, 71, 83, 126; and mysticism, 34; and New England, 1, 12, 55; and privacy, 26; and Quakers, 74; and religion, 26, 172
punishment, 172; corporal 72, 86, 92; and modernity, 93, 99, 105
Prynne, Hester, 59–60
publicity, 10; and Quakers, 73, 75n12, 76–80, 85, 102n60
Putnam, Ann, 186, 190n43, 191–92
Putnam, John, 186
Putnam, Thomas, 186

Quakers: 15, 18, 21, 28, 37n17, 38, 47, 66, 69–114; experientialism, 70, 72, 82–83; "invasion," 8, 63, 71, 75, 80, 90–91, 93, 97, 99, 102, 112, 170, 173; radicalism, 84, 89, 91n45; suffering, 96, 100, 102n60, 103–6, 109–12; and agency, 78; and American Puritanism, 90, 100, 111; and Anne Hutchinson, 17, 35–36, 70, 72–73, 89, 105; and Antinomianism, 63n57; and female piety, 83–90, 95, 105; and "inner light," 22, 73–74, 77–79, 82, 113; and martyrdom, 70, 72, 84, 89–90, 95–97, 100–103, 109, 112; and mysticism, 76, 79, 93, 105; and publicity, 73, 75n12, 76–80, 85, 102n60; and punishment, 71–72, 92, 94, 98, 105, 112; and secularism, 82, 97–99, 105–8, 112–14; and spirit, 75–77, 79, 81, 86–88, 92, 94–95, 97, 101, 108, 110; and transatlanticism, 78–80, 91–92; and witchcraft, 171. See also Mary Dyer

Radel, Nicholas, 158
Radway, Janice, 2n2,
Ray, Benjamin C., 168n2
Reed, Wilmott, 191
Reid, Bethany, 31n4
Reising, Russel, 8n18
religion, 1, 21, 32n5, 42n26, 59, 71, 97, 99–100, 122–23, 166, 168n5, 171; experiential, 72; and America, 7, 17, 67, 74, 113, 185, 203–7; and American Studies, 1, 8, 20, 60; and gender, 11, 14, 16, 18, 23, 26, 37, 43, 60–61, 78, 83, 97, 105, 202, 207; and modernity, 13, 35, 45, 79n23, 164; and mysticism, 41, 70, 78, 105; and pastness, 125; and privacy, 164; and Protestantism, 26, 172; and Puritanism, 9, 17; and secularization, 4–6, 11, 16, 19, 21n38, 22, 35, 69, 78, 113, 158–59, 189, 199, 206
revelation (prophecy), 22, 31–33, 38, 40, 54–55, 58, 70, 74, 80, 125, 145, 162–63, 171, 194. See also Anne Hutchinson

Richards, David, 133
Richards, John, 176
Rivett, Sarah, 7n15, 18n32, 20n35, 22, 27n46, 35n12, 79n23
Robinson, William, 85–86, 94, 110
Rosenberg, John, 3n5
Rosenthal, Bernard, 185n35, 189, 190n41
Rouse, John, 93–94, 100, 102, 107, 110–11
Rowlandson Mary: and affliction, 136, 161, 162; and American Puritanism, 117, 119, 138, 141, 153n48, 159; and authorship, 132, 135, 138, 146; and female piety, 158, 162, 164, 166; and food, 139–48, 158; and insomnia, 115–17, 119–20, 151; and Lot's Wife, 138, 151, 153, 156–57; and memory, 115–16, 118, 125, 129, 132–33, 138, 146, 153; and mourning, 120, 127, 129, 132, 138, 153, 160, 162; and Natives, 130–32, 139, 141–43, 147, 156, 159; and secularism, 115, 117, 121–22, 150, 152, 158–59, 162, 164; and spirit, 156, 160, 162–63; the *Sovereignty and Goodness of God*, 115–65; and suffering, 115, 117, 131, 138, 143, 146, 151, 162–63, 169; and Weetamoo, 130–32, 159
Rowlandson, Joseph, 150n42n43
Ruether, Rosemary, 70n2
Ruttenburg, Nancy, 76, 177
Ryan, James Emmett, 71n3

Salem witch trials (Salem Witchcraft): accused, 18, 166, 179, 181, 186–87, 191, 194, 201; accusers, 18, 21, 170, 171–78, 181, 183–85, 187, 189–92, 197; confessing witches, 21, 170–71, 177, 183–84, 189, 193–96; confessional culture, 18, 83, 168, 169, 178–84, 193–94, 197; Oyer and Terminer, 171, 179, 182–83, 201; witch, 83, 91; witchcraft, 8; and civil space, 201; and coercion, 193–96; and consent, 193–95; and confession-denial, 187; and Cotton

Mather, 179, 182, 184, 197–202; and Halfway Covenant, 170–78; and historiography, 185n33, 190; and monstrous birth, 170; and race, 186–89; and Puritanism, 169; and Quakers, 171; and religious speech 183, 193; and secularism, 169, 189–90, 193, 196, 198–99, 201–2, 202–7
Salthouse, Thomas, 90
Sayre, Gordon, 9n21
Scarry, Elaine, 106n65, 152
Schmidt, Leigh, 19n34
Schmitt, Carl, 5n11
Schweitzer, Ivy, 24, 49n40, 126n17
scaffold, 8, 10, 27n46, 94–95
secularism, 2, 5–7, 11, 16, 35, 41–42, 60, 61, 71–72, 77, 78n20, 150, 199, 204, 206; and American Puritanism, 4–6, 10–11, 17–18, 57, 63, 68, 122, 205, 207; and dissent, 20, 24, 32, 47, 63; and female piety, 60, 164, 193, 205; and gender, 5, 18, 43, 50, 114, 158; and historiography, 64; and Human Rights, 113; and Mary Rowlandson, 115, 117, 121–22, 150, 152, 158–59, 162, 164; and privacy, 164; and Quakers, 82, 95, 97–99, 105–8, 112–14; and religion, 19–20; and Salem Witch Trials, 169, 189–90, 193, 196, 198–99, 201–2, 202–7; and spirit, 42, 71, 113
secularization: thesis, 4–7, 10, 18–19, 204, 206–7; and declension, 5, 113; and Enlightenment, 11–12, 22, 82, 117, 166, 199, 202; and female piety, 6, 10, 26, 48, 50, 58, 60, 68, 93, 118, 162, 164, 169, 170, 202, 206; and privacy, 35; and religion, 4–6, 11, 16, 19, 21n38, 22, 35, 69, 78, 113, 158–59, 189, 199, 206
Sedgwick, Eve, 42–43
sermon: funeral, 8; and female piety, 27, 122–23
sexuality 3; difference, 23, 26, 40, 60–61, 158–59
Sharf, Robert, 72
Shea, Daniel, 116n3

Shepard, Thomas, 45
Short, Mercy, 176n21, 197–202. See also Cotton Mather
Sibley, Mary, 186, 188, 192
Sievers, Julie, 55n46
skepticism, 13, 42, 120, 133, 163, 168, 197
Smith, Catherine, 70
Society of Friends. See Quakers
sovereignty, 5n11, 19, 25; divine, 44, 49, 74, 118, 156; personal, 61, 68, 95, 97–98, 117, 154
Sovereignty and Goodness of God. See Mary Rowlandson
spirit, 13, 21, 25n44, 31–32, 33, 37, 39, 45, 51–54, 56, 70n2, 82–83, 91n45, 118, 120n8, 128, 139, 142, 149, 187, 189; diseased, 14; divine, 73, 177; embodied, 71, 82, 86–88, 97, 105–6, 151; experiential, 70, 126; female/feminine 2, 14, 16, 37, 39, 42, 49, 83; 105; inward, 21, 58, 73n8, 77, 81, 130, 169; radical, 13, 16, 39, 42. 68, 95, 113; and agency, 54, 71, 75, 86, 92, 95, 156–57; and Anne Hutchinson, 57; and conversion, 53; and inviolability, 35, 68; and Mary Rowlandson, 156, 160, 162–63; and modernity, 35, 37, 68, 78, 80, 164; and personhood, 41; and Quakers, 75–77, 79, 81, 86–88, 92, 94–95, 97, 101, 108, 110; and secularism, 42, 71, 113
spirituality: female, 58, 85, 140n34. See also female piety
Sprague, Martha, 194
Stannard, David, 123n13
Starkley, Marion, 185n33
Stephanie Kirk, 18n32
Stephenson, Marmaduke, 94
Stout, Harry S., 25n44
suffering, 12–13, 62, 70, 72, 89–90, 96, 160; divine, 152, 154; redemptive, 157; and Mary Rowlandson, 115, 117, 131, 138, 143, 146, 151, 162–63, 169; and Mercy Short, 202; and modernity, 121, 189; and Puritanism, 161; and Quakers, 96,

100, 102n60, 103–6, 109–12. See also affliction; trauma
Summers-Bremner, Eluned, 120

Tarter, Michele, 37n17, 83n29, 85n34
Taves, Ann, 21n39
Taylor, Charles, 5, 61, 78n20, 82n28
Tennenhouse, Lennard, 130
theology, 12, 26, 32, 35, 50–55, 57–58, 60, 62, 63n57, 66, 69, 73, 80, 89, 95, 97, 119, 148, 162, 199–201; covenant, 182; mystical, 47, 49; personal, 40–43, 70–71, 73, 75n12, 129, 132, 178; political, 5n11, 18n12, 71, 78n20; preparationist, 34–35, 52–53, 140; vernacular, 21, 27, 34, 55, 70, 76, 109, 119, 142, 157, 194, 198, 200, 201; and affliction, 152; and Calvinism, 148–50, 155–57; and gender, 37, 39
Tituba, 185–89. See also Salem Witch Trials
tolerance, 20, 25, 63, 66, 78–79
Tolles, Frederick, 71n3, 79, 80n24, 91n45
torture, 93, 98, 103, 106n65, 107, 113, 192, 20. See also affliction
Toulouse, Teresa, 131n25, 133n28
transatlanticism, 178; and Quakers, 73, 78–80, 83n29, 89, 91–92
trauma, 62, 116, 120–22, 127, 129, 142–44, 148, 151, 157, 166, 170, 189; and doubt 122; and modernity, 121. See also affliction, suffering
Truslow, James, 67
Tyler, Hannah, 196
Tyler, Mary, 196
typology, 90, 100, 106–7, 109, 121, 134–37, 146, 151–55, 157, 172, 195

Ulrich, Laurel Thatcher, 14n25
unbelief, 6n13, 136, 150, 152, 154, 156,
Upham, Charles, 190, 197n45

Van Engen, Abram, 24
Van Esterik, Penny, 140n34
Vane, Henry, 45, 50, 58, 64, 97
Vella, Michael, 63n57
Vickery, Amanda, 14n25
Viswanathan, Gauri, 5n11
Vokins, Jane, 76, 88, 89n42

Walcott, Mary, 190n43
Walker, Williston, 66
Ward, Graham, 6
Wardwell, Samuel, 196–197
Warner, Michael, 5n11, 10n22, 19n34, 23n41, 42n26
Warren, Mary, 183, 190n43, 192
Waugh, Dorothy, 90, 92
Weetamoo, 130–32, 159–60. See also Mary Rowlandson
Welde, Thomas, 33, 44n30, 58, 62
Westerkamp, Marilyn, 41
Wheelwright, John, 34n9, 45, 47, 50, 58. See also Antinomianism
White, Dorothy, 75, 76n14
Whitefield, George, 14–15
Wigglesworth, Michael, 158
Willard, John, 191–92
Willard, Samuel, 179n27
Williams, Abigail, 186, 190n43
Williams, Roger, 25–26, 31, 46–47, 58, 63, 65, 97, 99
Winship, Michael, 20n37, 31n5, 39n20, 40n22, 50n41
Winthrop, John, 24, 30, 33, 34n9, 36–39, 44–46, 51, 54–58, 60, 62, 64, 66, 69, 89, 138, 157n53, 170
Wokler, Robert, 19n34
Wood, Timothy, 41
Worall, Arthur J., 71n3

Ziff, Larzer, 180n29, 199n47

LITERATURE, RELIGION, and POSTSECULAR STUDIES
Lori Branch, Series Editor

Literature, Religion, and Postsecular Studies publishes scholarship on the influence of religion on literature and of literature on religion from the sixteenth century onward. Books in the series include studies of religious rhetoric or allegory; of the secularization of religion, ritual, and religious life; and of the emerging identity of postsecular studies and literary criticism.

Female Piety and the Invention of American Puritanism
  Bryce Traister

Secular Scriptures: Modern Theological Poetics in the Wake of Dante
  William Franke

Imagined Spiritual Communities in Britain's Age of Print
  Joshua King

Puritanism and Modernist Novels: From Moral Character to the Ethical Self
  Lynne W. Hinojosa

Conspicuous Bodies: Provincial Belief and the Making of Joyce and Rushdie
  Jean Kane

Victorian Sacrifice: Ethics and Economics in Mid-Century Novels
  Ilana M. Blumberg

Lake Methodism: Polite Literature and Popular Religion in England, 1780–1830
  Jasper Cragwall

Hard Sayings: The Rhetoric of Christian Orthodoxy in Late Modern Fiction
  Thomas F. Haddox

Preaching and the Rise of the American Novel
  Dawn Coleman

Victorian Women Writers, Radical Grandmothers, and the Gendering of God
  Gail Turley Houston

Apocalypse South: Judgment, Cataclysm, and Resistance in the Regional Imaginary
  Anthony Dyer Hoefer

www.ingramcontent.com/pod-product-compliance
Lightning Source LLC
Chambersburg PA
CBHW030135240426
43672CB00005B/132